COOPERATION AND COMMUNITY

COOPERATION
AND COMMUNITY

Economy and Society in Oaxaca

JEFFREY H. COHEN

University of Texas Press, Austin

Requests for permission to reproduce material from this work
should be sent to Permissions, University of Texas Press,
P.O. Box 7819, Austin, TX 78713-7819.

⊗ The paper used in this book meets the minimum requirements
of ANSI/NISO Z39.48-1992 (R1997) (Permanence of Paper).

Library of Congress
Cataloging-in-Publication Data

Cohen, Jeffrey H. (Jeffrey Harris)
Cooperation and community : economy and society in Oaxaca /
by Jeffrey H. Cohen.
p.   cm.
Includes bibliographical references and index.

0-292-71221-9 (pbk. : alk.paper)

1. Zapotec Indians—Social conditions. 2. Zapotec Indians—
Economic conditions. 3. Zapotec Indians—Kinship.
4. Cooperative societies—Mexico—Santa Ana del Valle.
5. Community organization—Mexico—Santa Ana del Valle.
6. Ceremonial exchange—Mexico—Santa Ana del Valle. 7.
Social change—Mexico—Santa Ana del Valle. 8. Santa Ana del
Valle (Mexico)—Social life and customs. 9. Santa Ana del Valle
(Mexico)—Economic conditions. I. Title. F1221.Z3C54 1999
306'.0972'74—dc21   99-24836

For Maria

Contents

List of Illustrations

List of Abbreviations

AGEO	*Archivo General del Estado de Oaxaca* (General Archive of the State of Oaxaca)
BANFOCO	*Banco de Fomento de Cooperativas* (Bank for Cooperative Development)
CMSD	*Comité del Museo Shan-Dany* (Shan-Dany Museum Committee)
CONASUPO	*Compañía Nacional de Subsistencias Populares* (National Commodity Program)
CTV	*Curato de Teotitlán de el Valle Su Patrona Titular* (Parish Records of Teotitlán)
DIF	*Desarrollo Integral Familiar* (Family Development Programs)
FONART	*Fondo Nacional para el Fomento de las Artesanías* (National Foundation for the Development of Crafts)
INAH	*Instituto Nacional de Antropología e Historia* (National Institute for Anthropology and History)
INEGI	*Instituto Nacional de Estadísticas, Geografía, y Informatica* (National Institute for Statistics, Geography, and Information)
INI	*Instituto Nacional Indigenista* (National Indigenist Institute)
OTSF	*Oficina Tipográfica de la Secretaría de Fomento* (Secretary of Development)
SEN	*Secretaría de la Economía Nacional* (Secretary of the National Economy)
SIC	*Secretaría de Industria y Comercio* (Secretary of Industry and Commerce)

Preface

THE ISSUES discussed in this book—cooperation, economy, and culture change—have been on my mind for quite some time. However, I had not originally planned to write on the economy. As I first went to Oaxaca in the mid-1980s, I was primarily interested in craft production and aesthetics. The roots of this project are founded in the time spent during my second summer in the field (1987) and in conversations with informants, friends, and colleagues concerning the issues of economy and society. A second influence on my ideas comes from my father's work on the ways in which we perceive the world—and the mistakes that often take place when we assume others understand us. This book is a continuation of these and other conversations (particularly the ones that now take place in the classroom as I explain anthropology to students at Texas A&M University). At its most basic, the book is concerned with why people choose to enter reciprocal and cooperative relationships. There is often the belief that as a society develops (particularly when it develops toward a more capitalistic system), cooperation, reciprocity, and social solidarity will decline. This ethnography of a rural, indigenous community in central Oaxaca suggests this is not always the case. As I demonstrate, villagers reinvent and reinterpret cooperation and reciprocity to fit new economic realities, respond to new situations, and support their community in its reproduction (in other words, its creation, re-creation, and maintenance) and success.

As with any research project there are many individuals and institutes to thank for support, assistance, and patience. For introducing me to the world of the Zapotec and Oaxaca, my thanks to Anya Peterson Royce and her husband, Ronald R. Royce, who opened the doors to a journey of discovery that continues to both exhilarate and amaze.

My first opportunity to visit the state of Oaxaca was in 1986 when, as a graduate student from the University of New Mexico, I attended the Instituto Cultural Oaxaca. I had three goals that summer: to improve my skills in Spanish, start learning the Zapotec spoken in the valley, and begin (I hoped) to map out a possible research project. Everything worked out better than expected, and the people at the Institute—María de la Luz Topete (former director of INAH, the National Institute for Anthropology and History for the state of Oaxaca), and Rex and Lolly Marcum— were more than helpful, introducing me to Mexican and American anthropologists, sociologists, and archaeologists working in the region. The Institute arranged for me to live with the Martínez-Hipolito family and they welcomed me into their home. The family was from Teotitlán del Valle, a Zapotec-speaking, craft-producing village documented by Lynn Stephen, among others. I spent many weekends with the Martínez family, learning to weave, trying new foods, and getting to know the community in an introductory fashion. Guadalupe Martínez (an agronomy student in the local university) and I spent many evenings talking about the culture and history of the Zapotec, the environment of the region, and the kinds of hopes and dreams she had for the future. In 1992, Lupe passed away quite unexpectedly, and I am sorry that I cannot share this work with her.

I returned to Oaxaca with a grant to do preliminary research over the summer of 1987. I want to thank Philip Bock and Mari Lynn Salvador, who were important teachers and mentors during the training for my master's degree at the University of New Mexico, and helped me prepare for this first taste of ethnographic fieldwork. This trip to Oaxaca involved an exploration of the aesthetics of weaving in Teotitlán del Valle. As I learned to weave alongside Teotitecos, and visited Santa Ana for the first time, I began to realize that there was much more to production than aesthetics. The weavers were often shrewd entrepreneurs, playing to their audience (the tourists) and vying with one another for shares of the local market and export economy. So began my journey into the world of economic anthropology and my growing concern with the interaction of local communities, international capital, and tourism.

I returned to Bloomington in 1988, and was once again attending Indiana University, working on my doctorate. In the fall I met Richard Wilk who has since become my teacher, mentor, and friend. Rick, more than anyone outside of my family, has supported me throughout my work, and I hope he knows how much his time, patience, and support have meant. Other folks at Indiana who have been a great help are Raymond DeMallie in anthropology, Roger Janelli and Henry Glassie in folklore, and Dennis Conway in geography. I also want to thank the Indiana Center on Global Change and World Peace, as well as the Harold K.

Schneider Fund, for their support of my project. Besides my professors, many friends have given of their time, and I would like to mention a few in particular: Robert Dover, Stephen Miller, Jayne Howell, Loren Demerath, and the members of my dissertation support group—Frank Hall, Cathy Jones, and Julianne Short.

I joined the faculty in the anthropology department at Texas A&M University in 1995 and returned to Santa Ana to make a brief follow-up visit and to begin outlining a new project focused on migration in 1996. Texas A&M University's Program to Enhance Scholarly and Creative Activities and the International Research Travel Grant generously supported this work. I also continue to learn from new colleagues and friends including David Kyle, Norbert Dannhaeuser, and Lee Cronk.

During our time in Oaxaca, many people have been helpful and friendly. In the city, María Topete remains as supportive as she was when I first arrived, allowing us to use the Institute as a post office and refuge. Pedro Lewin and Gudrun Dohrmann opened their home for us, and I want to thank them for the hot showers, good meals, and friendship. I extend thanks to Cuauhtémoc Camerena and Teresa Morales, both of INAH and involved in the management of Santa Ana's museum, for their support and input. While we were in the field, William Wood (who was doing research of his own) and Lori Foulke became our close friends.

My greatest debt is to the many Santañeros who helped us throughout the year. Specifically I want to thank Mauricio García Morales and his family for their generosity; Librado Bautista Aquino, the president of the community when we arrived; Cristoforo Cruz, the president during the last half of our stay; Félix Morales García, who was an early friend; Alberto Sánchez García; Domingo Hipolito García; Aaron Hipolito Morales; and finally, Porfirio Bautista Matias, my assistant who was more help than he will probably ever know.

The staff at the University of Texas Press has been wonderful to work with. My gratitude to Theresa May for first looking over my manuscript and carefully choosing helpful reviewers. My appreciation also goes to the readers who commented on the text and in particular, the constructive reviews by John Watanabe and Arthur Murphy. Finally, thanks to Sheryl Englund for her time and efforts on my behalf.

Throughout my study and my life, my family has always been of great support. To my parents, who went above and beyond what they needed to do, I offer my love and thanks. Thanks also to Rhoda and Herb Rosenthal for their support and editorial assistance, and for giving Maria and me a much-needed vacation in February 1993. Finally, to Maria, who makes all of this possible, who put up with no running water, no toilet or shower, and not much of a kitchen for nearly a year, and who suffered through all the bad days and doubts right next to me, I dedicate this work, and promise next time to undertake a project where the water runs more freely.

November 1998

COOPERATION AND COMMUNITY

Introduction

Cooperation in Context

A Framework for Analysis

SANTAÑERO: Do you like our village?

VISITOR: Why yes, it seems very nice.

SANTAÑERO: You know we work very hard here, we help each other out, we support each other.

VISITOR: Uh-huh, nice.

SANTAÑERO: Yes, but you see that village across the valley? San Juan. . . . In that village they will steal your money. Over here, near us in Díaz Ordaz. . . . There they are all involved in illegal drugs. And Teotitlán. . . . Oh my, don't go there, they will rob you. But not here. Here it is peaceful and everyone helps out.

VISITOR: You don't say. . . .

SANTAÑERO: Yes, but make sure to be careful as you go about. And if you spend the night, hide your valuables from the thieves.

WHEN STRANGERS enter Santa Ana del Valle, Oaxaca, Mexico, whether tourists on a day trip or anthropologists planning a year's fieldwork, they are greeted by this odd and often repeated dialogue concerning the village, its peaceful qualities, and the cooperative goodwill of the inhabitants. The exchange is one that I engaged in regularly, especially during the early months of fieldwork. It is the incongruous punch line of the dialogue that captures my attention, and I remain intrigued by the juxtaposition of village peace with the suggestion of local thievery and mistrust.

The contradictions of the scene might suggest that Santañeros are hiding something. Perhaps in some instances, they really do *not* cooperate, and this story of village harmony is nothing more than a narrative used in conversation with the occasional visitor to deny a less congenial reality. However, among Santañeros the evidence of cooperation is abundant. Family, friends, and households regularly participate in formal as well as informal relationships that include *guelaguetza* (reciprocal exchanges of gifts and services) and *compadrazgo* (godparenthood). Parents and children work together at looms, weaving woolen textiles and pooling resources for shared futures. Friends lend assistance to one another when the time comes to plant and harvest. Households come together around celebrations, during fiestas, and for important rites of passage. Beyond ties of kin and friendship, Santañeros invest their time, effort, and wealth in *tequio* (community-based labor projects), *cooperación* (money given to support village projects and programs), *servicio* (voluntary service in one of the community's many *cargos* or committees), two *mayordomías* (family-sponsored saint's day celebrations), and many village fiestas following local custom and tradition (see Acevedo and Restrepo 1991; Monaghan 1990; Nader 1969). Román Sánchez, a middle-aged former village leader, described the situation honestly when he said, "Why do we do these things? Because we must . . . they make us Santañero."

In this world of mutual aid, reciprocity, and support, contradictions abound and mistrust is often manifest among villagers. Individuals complain when the time arrives to repay a guelaguetza debt. Tequio crews are typically hard to organize. Finding willing participants to staff even small-scale work projects can be daunting. Cargos and committees are often difficult to fill, and village leaders sometimes find it necessary to push Santañeros forcefully into *nombramientos* (positions of service in village committees). Cooperation itself can become a coercive force. Heads of households (male and female) use the histories of their familial investments (both real and fictitious), reciprocal relationships, and authority in order to control (some might say through inducing guilt) the labor and earnings of their children (see Cook and Binford 1990). Textile workshops that employ entire families in production typically put children to work at looms, preparing threads and finishing projects, with little or no remuneration. Fathers expect the support of their sons and daughters who live and work outside natal homes, and mothers demand assistance from their children in the care and maintenance of their households.

The commitments and contradictions inherent in cooperative and reciprocal relationships extend beyond the physical confines of Santa Ana.

Migrants living in Los Angeles participate in their home village society through the continuous support of family, household, and community. Most Santañeros cite the commitment to family and the need to support children as a primary motivating factor in their decision to migrate, and many officers in the local political hierarchy rely on migrant remittances or savings to cover their commitments and expenses of office. The point is not to determine whether all Santañeros remit to support their families and households, or even if those Santañeros who talk of familial support always practice what they preach. Rather, in the examples of cooperation that fill the remainder of this text, we are interested in understanding the ways in which cooperation and reciprocity become structures for rationalizing social action (see Chapter Three).

Similar patterns of cooperation and reciprocity, though in very different social settings, are found among Santañeros who have chosen to convert and follow evangelical faiths in place of traditional Catholicism (see Chapter Four). For these families new relationships have replaced cooperative ties traditionally created within the village. *Evangélicos* (converts to evangelical Protestant sects) pitted their practices against the Catholic majority in 1991 and again in 1996. For many Santañeros the problem that strained community morality and caused tensions to flare was not whether evangelicals shared core religious doctrines, but the converts' failing belief in the central place of traditional cooperative and reciprocal ties (Cohen n.d.).

Finally, real divisions of class and status continue to grow among households and families within the community, even as cooperative ties link the various social strata of the village. Nearly all families cooperate, or talk of cooperation. However, the actions and expectations of the wealthy and high-status members of the community are different from the needs and actions of poor or low-status members of the village. Wealthy Santañeros have the luxury of participating in the relationships they choose, although they can never forget that their social status is determined largely by that participation (Scott 1989). On the other hand, a poor family may have a much more realistic need for cooperation in its struggle to survive and prosper in a rapidly changing economy. Thus, while wealthy, high-status Santañeros explain cooperation using the same terms as low-status relatives, the reasons for entering reciprocal relationships and the expectations placed on the resulting alliances are quite different from those of the poor, low-status individual or family.

Approaching Cooperation

Given the contradictions in Santañero reciprocity, how are we to explain cooperation's role in social life? Contemporary theories typically explain cooperative and reciprocal relationships by framing them as structures through which prosperity is gained and community built (see, for example, Fukuyama 1995: 186, 205–207; Putnam 1993). On the other hand, cooperative relationships are also defined as exploitative structures that obscure the exercise of power (see Bourdieu 1977: 192). The first approach fails to recognize the place of coercion in the construction of social order (Portes and Landolt 1996: 20). The second forgets that cooperation does in fact work for those involved in reciprocal relationships (Axelrod 1984). It plays a role in the reproduction of a group's social universe and in its construction of identity. Simultaneously, it limits and places constraints on what is proper, normal, and expected by defining codes of conduct and action (Brandes 1988: 160; Eriksen 1991; Jenkins 1992; Watanabe 1992).

This ethnography of Santa Ana del Valle, Oaxaca, Mexico, offers a new approach to the study of cooperation, and a new framework for understanding the contradictions inherent in social life. Rather than defining cooperative relationships as determinative structures based upon social custom (Durkheim 1964; Mauss 1990) or, fundamentally, the division of labor (see McLellan 1977: 170), I approach cooperation and reciprocity as the outcomes of individual social actions and choices, made within the confines of households and communities. I concentrate on the ways in which cooperative practices create and/or reproduce identity and become frameworks for negotiating and coping with ongoing social, economic, and political change (Giddens 1984: 25; Ortner 1973: 154; Robben 1989: 7).[1]

Custom and division of labor certainly constrain and limit the actions of individual actors, as does history, education, practical cultural knowledge, and political or economic realities. However, working within the above limits of competence and situation, people create their own social realities—constantly manipulating, interpreting, subverting, and re-creating the world in which they live (Moore 1975; Watanabe 1992; Wilson 1993).[2] In other words, people are not automatons serving out socially predetermined roles; neither are they fully free and independent actors, willfully creating the world as they see fit (Jenkins 1992: 71). Rather, they are social actors, free in varying degrees to create personal realities. The convergence of experience, ability, history, and situation defines the constraints of social action.

Cooperation in Practice

To understand the limits that exist and define Santañero social reality (which social practices reproduce and even at times transcend), Chapters One and Two explore the historical development and current economy of Santa Ana.[3] Rather than setting forth a detailed history of Santa Ana, which is beyond the scope of this work, Chapter One outlines four important periods of social development and transformation in the community: first, the pre-Columbian origins of the village; second, the reorganization of the community as a *congregación* (ecclesiastical settlement) in the early years of New Spain; third, the *Porfiriato* (the period during which Mexico was under the control of Porfirio Díaz) and the establishment by foreign investors of a mining settlement on community lands; and fourth, the devastating impact of the Mexican Revolution on the local population.

The discussion of local history notes the connections between Santañeros and the state, the nation, and the world through time, to show that the cooperative and reciprocal relationships that typify the community are neither isolated inventions of a recently formed closed corporate system, the outcomes of a mythic and timeless pre-Hispanic past, nor a reflection of the shared psychological attitude of a population (see, for example, Redfield 1928, 1950). Structures of cooperation have evolved within the village and its population through time (Wolf 1986). As the needs of villagers have changed, so have their cooperative relationships and the meaning of reciprocity and communal action.

Chapter Two defines changes in the current economy. In particular, I discuss the growing importance of the production of handwoven, woolen textiles for export, the increase in transnational migration, and the decline of subsistence agriculture among villagers.

There has been a marked shift in economic activity among Santañeros. Only twenty years ago, villagers were concerned primarily with the reproduction and provisioning of the household and with meeting basic family needs. Much of a household's efforts focused on subsistence agriculture. Santañeros produced textiles and migrated for employment, but did not follow current patterns of production or levels of movement. Two decades ago, the migrant who left the community typically returned quickly and likely ventured no farther than Mexico City or Chiapas to fill seasonal jobs in the city or on coastal plantations. The weaver was likely to rely on his or her work as a minor supplement to farming, and lacked an export market for finished work.

Access to new markets, a growing demand for consumer goods, a rapidly increasing population, and Mexico's continued economic crisis brought Santañeros more directly into the global economy in the late 1980s and early 1990s. Nearly all families produce woolen textiles for export and sale in the local tourist market. Subsistence farming is on the decline and there is a growing number of villagers with little or no land for cultivation. Transnational migration is increasing as well. Santañeros may leave the village for years, returning infrequently, if at all, to visit family and friends (Cohen 1998; Conway and Cohen 1998).

Given these changes in local economic patterns and practices, cooperation remains a "key symbol" of Santañero life and an important element in the construction of modern Santañero society. As a key symbol, cooperation elaborates experience, orders knowledge, summarizes and grounds meaning, and orients social action (Ortner 1973). When older Santañeros recall a past where people supported and protected each other in trust and good faith, they are not simply telling us that cooperation is part of a bygone era and no longer important. Rather, they are using cooperation to evaluate and organize a world that is rapidly changing. Cooperation is more than an empty tradition. Members of the community invent new ways of cooperating and reorient traditional relationships to meet new needs, even as they participate in traditional forms of association and, in the process, rebuild the community as a social entity (Wilson 1993).

Chapters Three through Six define the structure of cooperation in Santa Ana, and explore the role of reciprocity in the construction, reproduction, and negotiation of social life. Used in the negotiation and evaluation of social life, cooperation has a complex nexus of meanings. It is rooted in the past and in traditional practices, but gains renewed importance through its application and purpose in the present. We can think of cooperation as a form of *habitus*. It is "history turned into nature." Cooperation and reciprocity are motivating structures, or "durable, transposable disposition[s]" that frame action and through which a group can formally measure behavior (Bourdieu 1977: 78, 73).

The Nature of Reciprocity and Cooperation

Cooperation is not restricted to a particular social context. It functions among household members, and between households in their associations with one another. Beyond the household, cooperation and reciprocity establish long-term relationships between friends and neighbors and within the community as a whole. Cooperation also organizes relationships at a distance, such as those that exist between Santañero migrants and their friends and relatives at home (see Hirabayashi 1993).[4] Cooperation is the basis for the most intimate, profound, and long-lasting relationships any individual will hold. The ideologies of mutual support and harmony create strong bonds among family members (Nader 1990). Of course, these relationships are not the same for every individual, in every family or household. Furthermore, the structure of cooperation does not remain constant through the life course of a particular family, household, or network. Thus, after defining basic patterns of association, I examine how cooperation becomes a setting for the negotiation of status and prestige through time.

Restricted to the household, cooperation would not be the powerful social force it is in Santa Ana. Chapters Four and Five consider the place of cooperative relationships in community life. Attention is paid to the ways in which systems of guelaguetza, compadrazgo, and tequio reproduce the cooperative goals found within the family. Again, in this respect, cooperation is a key symbol through which villagers can talk about the social world, objectify and enact conventions of morality and community, and critique the world beyond the village (Ortner 1973; Watanabe 1992). Thus, cooperation and reciprocity create bonds between the various strata of Santañero society, and bring a sense of *harmonía* (harmony) to a system that might otherwise be marked by a great degree of conflict and contest (Nader 1990).

Santañero society is marked by both commitment and contest. Cooperative relationships are one way in which local hierarchy is constructed and power exercised. Reciprocity and cooperation can be structures for contest, and at the same time, platforms through which state hegemony is mediated. The mediation of state power happens in at least three ways: through the structure of local authority, the organization of local politics, and the limits that local systems for dispute resolution place on the state's legal bureaucracy.

First, the structure of authority in the community is not based on blatant coercion and open physical domination; rather, authority and power are exercised through reciprocity, patronage, and the careful movement of individuals through ever more prestigious (and burdensome) positions in local government (see López-Cortés 1991). The staged development of authority in the community parallels and reproduces the very hierarchical structure of local society, and the abuse of power is, to a degree, mediated by the public nature of local power (see Hardin 1993; Mousse 1988). In this familiar setting, individual politicians are easier to approach than they would be if installed through the exercise of state power or terror. Furthermore, political control—while unequally distributed and often favoring the wealthy at the expense of the poor—remains embedded in local systems of morality and service (see Coleman 1988).

Following Bourdieu (1977), it can be argued the situation is a classic example of symbolic violence. The rhetoric of cooperation is manipulated in the service to and construction of hierarchy. But it is a local hierarchy measured by local ideas of morality and commitment. As such, power and prestige within the community cannot be amassed like economic capital or used in the brute exercise of political domination. Scott makes the point quite clearly when he states "one can amass wealth whether or not others believe one to be wealthy. But prestige is something that others confer, not something that can be unilaterally acquired" (1989: 249).

A second set of contests occurs around the negotiation of political power and prestige in Santa Ana. Santañeros may be cynical when it comes to national presidential elections; however, where local politics are concerned, the ballot box and an ability to build a consensus remain influential correctives to the outright abuse of power within the village. In fact, one villager went so far as to suggest that the president of the Republic needed to visit Santa Ana to understand the meaning of the term democracy. Putting his fate in the hands of villagers rather than the hands of big business would teach the president how to govern with the support of his constituency.

Nombramientos and cargos (like guelaguetza and compadrazgo) bring Santañeros together and establish "cross-linkages" (Nader 1990), or structures that work to unite local society into a cohesive unit (El-Guindi and Selby 1976). All Santañeros, rich and poor, of high and low status, serve in local government from time to time as representatives of their families. Thus, a second way in which hierarchy is reproduced (and yet mediated) in local government is through the dynamic mix of wealthy and poor that marks the individuals who fill village committees.

Third and finally, the importance of local dispute resolution by village leaders limits the involvement of the state in community life. Local officials (typically *alcaldes*) adjudicate many of the disputes that arise among villagers in order to avoid the involvement of Mexico's formal judicial system (Nader 1990; Parnell 1988). Large disputes, such as the 1991 struggle between Catholic and evangelical factions, ended with outside mediation. However, the majority of decisions continue to be made within the village by the community's alcaldes (Cohen n.d.).

Cooperation is a powerful symbol used in the definition and social construction of community. Santañeros describe themselves as members of their community by fate of birth. However, community is more than a birthplace or birthright, and to remain an active participant in the social life of the community demands participation in locally sanctioned and defined relationships (see Watanabe 1992).

Thus, cooperation is not simply a story told about village life. Rather, it is a set of practices through which Santa Ana as a social entity is created. Cooperation and reciprocity are the arenas through which socially significant actions take place and through which the practices and commitments of Santañeros are measured (Barth 1992; Bender 1978). Geography comes to be less important than commitment. The migrant living far from home can be an active participant in the creation of community (Conway and Cohen 1998; Hirabayashi 1993). Alternatively, the local who declines to take part in cooperative relationships and the social life of the community will hold little meaning or importance in the construction, reproduction, and development of society.

Furthermore, cooperation is an evaluative structure that creates local identity through which Santañeros separate themselves from other communities and populations (see Eriksen 1991; Watanabe 1992). It matters very little that cooperative structures are found in most rural, indigenous communities in Mexico and Mesoamerica. For Santañeros, cooperation defines their community as a unique and uncommon entity. In this respect, cooperation becomes a framework for the mediation of ongoing social and economic change. Reciprocal ties and their historical development (whether real or simply perceived) become structures through which the community is defended against the impact of global capitalism (see Chapter Six and Conclusions). Santañeros may be part of a global economy, but cooperative networks locate the individual in a set of relationships that transcend the oppressive force of capitalism and the sometimes overpowering reach of the market. Santañero migrants who work in low-paying, low-prestige jobs know that they are not defined solely by their positions. They are also important members of families, households, and community as established through their social networks. In other words, cooperative and reciprocal networks divide the world into friendly and unfriendly realms, rendering it safe, knowable, and "according to the standards prevailing in society" (Marshall 1973: 72; Tester 1992: 10).

As a structure for the critique and comprehension of social, economic, and political forces, traditional social relationships are a measure against which Santañeros can judge themselves as well as their changing world. To be a Santañero is to choose a particular path, one defined by the reciprocal relationships shared with others. The pursuits of personal fortune (typically identified as antithetical to the structure of the Mexican peasant community, in Beltran 1967; Crumrine 1969; Redfield 1960) are not as problematic as the ways in which the resulting wealth is framed and, to some extent, used (see Greenberg 1995: 78). Thus, the wealthy Santañero who shares in the support and management of the community is looked upon with high regard. On the other hand, the merchant who severs social ties to the community but continues to live in its center is ridiculed (see Chapter Five). Furthermore, outsiders who enter the village (and here I am thinking of individuals hailing from as far away as Mexico City who have married into the village) and embrace the local framework of meaning and action as active participants are more likely to become successful members of the community than native-born Santañeros who choose to reject their role in village life.

Cooperation in a Changing World

Why does cooperation continue as a framework for action when research suggests it should decline in response to the growing involvement of the community in capitalism (see Hart 1982; Heyman 1990: 355; Marx 1906: 370; Mauss 1990: 46; Weber 1946: 215–216)? One key is the continued viability of cooperation and its local worth and status vis-à-vis the realities of Mexican politics and global market economics (see Granovetter 1995; Greenberg 1995; Stark 1992: 9; Wellman 1979).[5]

Santañeros rely on, but are not necessarily limited by, the cooperative relationships in which they choose to participate. Associations that no longer serve to meet local needs are modified or abandoned. For example, the use of tequio to complete community projects is decreasing as work requirements change and the number of men available to participate declines in response to the rapid increase in migration. Alternatively, cooperación is increasing as Santañeros become embedded in global capital markets and comfortable with cash-based transactions.

Santañeros have established new ways of cooperating in response to changing situations and the demands (as well as possibilities) of a changing economy. Migrants develop social networks once they are settled in their new households (see Hirabayashi 1983; Kearney 1994, 1995). At home, basketball teams organized among friends and relatives create new frameworks for cooperation and contest within the village. Cooperation in these settings is based not on the need for mutual aid to guarantee survival but upon shared morality.

New opportunities and new markets lead to an improving local economy (although many families continue to struggle). Furthermore, market transactions have developed to replace subsistence agriculture and barter. However, cooperation remains important and develops as a social goal in and of itself. It is also a symbol of local identity and a tool in the constant evaluation and manipulation of local social relationships (Cohen n.d.).

The example of Santa Ana and the continued importance of cooperative relationships present an interesting contrast to Cancian's restudy of Zinacantán (1990; 1992). He found the village cargo system in sharp decline upon his return to the community. The decrease in participation was a dramatic change from his earlier research. At that time Zinacantecos competed for prestigious cargo offices, and the waiting lists that accompanied many posts were long (Cancian 1965). Participation in the cargos is waning as Zinacantecos grow involved in cash-based, extra-local economic relationships and business investment.[6] As a result, Cancian found Zinacanteco society becoming more "atomistic" (Gilmore 1975), or focused on the individual, and less concerned with the well-being of the village (Cancian 1990).[7]

Given parallel macroeconomic changes in Santa Ana and Zinacantán, how are we to explain the maintenance of cooperation in the former and its decline, signified by the collapse in the cargo waiting lists, in the latter? First, while changes in each community are similar, Santa Ana is smaller and lacks a set of satellite settlements around which conflicts arise. In fact, Santa Ana can be categorized as an economic satellite of Teotitlán. Not surprisingly, Santañeros are united in their dislike and mistrust of Teoti-tecos (people from Teotitlán, the dominant weaving village in the area). Santañeros describe their relationship with Teotitecos as "us against them." The ambivalence Santañeros feel toward Teotiteco merchants and intermediaries creates common ground in the village, and local conflict is, to a degree, less pronounced as tensions are eased by shared attitudes.

Second, Zinacantán is a site of political infighting. Mexico's various parties are associated with particular individuals, towns, and hamlets in the area (Cancian 1992: 150). In contrast, the PRI remains powerful in Santa Ana and there are few if any struggles over political parties and control.

Third, while Santañeros participate in a global market economy, much like Zinacantecos, the market is not a localized site for competition. In Zinacantán, economic development is manifest in the growth of the lo-cal trucking industry. In contrast, there are few opportunities for eco-nomic investment in Santa Ana. Apart from a handful of stores and busi-nesses, the outward signs of growing class differences are few. Santañeros become part of the global economy through migration and the produc-tion of woven textiles for export, not through localized economic de-velopment. And while Santañeros weave for tourism and export out of their homes, the industry remains a mix of traditional technology, family workshops, and modern market relationships (Cook 1984). Weaving re-lies on the unpaid or underpaid participation of many family members, and is itself a framework for cooperative actions.

Fourth and finally, Santañeros working in the United States have not abandoned their reciprocal ties to family and community. Rather, mi-grants are instrumental in the maintenance of community and the contin-ued development of the village (Smith 1992). Thus, in Santa Ana coop-eration remains a viable framework for the organization and development of social solidarity.

In understanding the viability of cooperative associations in Santañero daily life, we do not necessarily need to deny the presence of tension, contradiction, and contest. If cooperation were a perfect system, we would not expect to hear words of mistrust such as those at the end of the "greeting dialogue" described in the opening of this introduction. Why the caution if the community is as peaceful as villagers maintain? Santañeros do cooperate, but they also use their relationships, symbols, and ideals to vie with one another for power and status within the com-munity. We should not mistake the presence of cooperative relationships as evidence that local harmony always works, and that conflict is non-existent among villagers (see Portes and Landolt 1996). Thus, understanding the meaning and place of cooperation among Santañeros demands that we determine how cooperative relationships are represented and manipulated in the service of local hierarchy, authority, and prestige.

The issues of contest in cooperation that are discussed throughout the text are highlighted in Chapter Six, where the tensions surrounding local politics are explored in detail. In 1992, a new generation of community leaders clashed with Santa Ana's "old guard." The village's new *presidente municipal* came into office with a set of projects and programs that he hoped would jump-start Santa Ana's economic development and lead to the improvement of the village's infrastructure and educational system (Cohen 1994).[8] While most Santañeros supported the plans of the new administration, the president and his officers struggled throughout the early months of their tenure. The problems faced by the administration were not due to a lack of goals or a divergence of ideas between community and president. Rather, the difficulty lay in the misjudgments the president made, when it came time to promote a new set of developmental goals, concerning the importance of traditional practices (such as ritual drinking). The analysis of the president's controversial actions in Chapter Six, allows the opportunity to explore how cooperation, as a set of ideals as well as real relationships, becomes a setting for (and a force in) the negotiation of prestige, social identity, and community development.

Conclusions

The practice of cooperation and reciprocity in Santa Ana is not simple; rather, it identifies a set of complex relationships and attitudes used in the negotiation and evaluation of everyday life. It is rooted in household relationships and repeated in an ever widening circle of associations that can reach well beyond the physical boundaries of the village. This ethnography describes the meanings and uses of cooperation in contemporary Santañero social life.

Santañeros do not live in a vacuum, removed from external influence and interaction. The community is part of a rapidly globalizing market society. Therefore, an additional goal of this ethnography describes how cooperative relationships are built on local knowledge and traditional practices and remain viable in an increasingly cash-based economy (Wilson 1993). Finally, anthropologists have long been interested in the nature and meaning of community. However, in our analyses we are often tempted to overemphasize the importance of geography and misinterpret the centrality of social practice. Through the analysis of cooperative networks among Santañeros, we are able instead to define community as a "context of actions and result of actions but not as a thing" (Barth 1992: 31; Eriksen 1991). An emphasis on the use of social networks in the negotiation of social life, locally and beyond the physical village, allows us to understand how community becomes a powerful symbol even for migrants living far from their natal home. In effect, cooperation is a social filter mediating external forces of change and, in the process, defending cultural beliefs (Greenberg 1995; Mallon 1983; Smith 1989).

Is cooperation relevant and meaningful in a society that is growing ever more involved in international economics, politics, and culture? The example of Santa Ana suggests that structures of mutual support and reciprocity remain vital, and can increase in importance as tools to help a population make sense of change. In addition, cooperative relationships play an important role in self-defense and self-definition as a community makes and remakes itself as a social entity over time. I return to the odd juxtaposition of harmony and mistrust that opened this introduction and finish unraveling its meaning in the conclusions to this work. Cooperative relationships are the setting for consensus and contest, for resistance and hierarchy. They are the central symbols of what it means to be Santañero, and it is through the enactment of the various relationships that villagers create themselves and their community, and interpret their world.

Chapter One

Four Eras, One Village

Geography and History in
Santa Ana del Valle

In all the general impression given by the village is that of a poor, quiet and peaceful place which has seen better days, in which people work hard and punctuate their labor with short spasms of insensate drunkenness.

—Stuart Plattner on Santa Ana del Valle, 1965

MY FIRST IMPRESSIONS of Santa Ana mirrored Stuart Plattner's comment written thirty years ago. Tucked along the foothills of the Sierra Madre del Sur and off the Pan-American highway's bus and tourist routes, Santa Ana seems the typical peasant village. It is a little dusty and dilapidated, a little noisy, and there are plenty of children running about. For tourists in search of handmade woolen textiles, the village seems a timeless and idyllic oasis of indigenous harmony. The promises of travel guides spring to life as Santañeros welcome visitors to their homes (see Freundheim 1988). The sounds of weavers working at their looms echoes from most homes and creates a syncopated rhythm to local life. The community plaza is bright with the colors of finished textiles (collectively called *tapetes*) available for sale from the Artisans' Society shop. The village church, repainted in 1992–1993, adds a splash of color to the browns and greys that dominate the landscape.

The vision of a peaceful and timeless tranquility found in tourist brochures and the brief visit to the community belies social and economic realities in Santa Ana. Santañeros continue to farm the surrounding countryside as they have for generations and weave on looms that are little changed from those introduced by the Dominicans hundreds of

Plaza and church, Santa Ana del Valle

years ago. Nevertheless, Santañeros are a population firmly engaged in the global economy through commercial textile production, migration, education, and communication. Santañeros hold an ambiguous place in this web of changing material and ideological influences. Largely powerless to alter the situation, Santañeros nevertheless build and rebuild a sense of themselves and their community. They blend indigenous social formations and transnational forces in this process of self-creation and afford a dynamic setting in which to study the ways people cope with economic change.[1]

Change in Santa Ana is a process that has continued throughout the community's history. It is nothing as uniform as the slow-paced crawl or plodding steps forward that have come to characterize many development models (see, for example, Rostow 1960). Cultural change, technological advancement, and social transformations have come intermittently, waxing and waning through various eras and with various positive and negative outcomes. At times, as during the seventeenth century, colonization involved Santañeros in a process that fundamentally changed the structure of the village. Dominican missionaries introduced new technologies, redefined the division of labor, and established the village as a religious settlement. Treadle looms replaced back-strap looms, wool replaced cotton, and men replaced women as primary weavers. At times, the village and its population turned in upon itself, severing many links to the state. For example, following the Mexican Revolution, Santañero interaction with external forces and institutions declined considerably.

I explore the context and process of change in the community in this chapter. I begin with a brief discussion of geography and ethnicity to contextualize the place and people for the reader. Following this outline I describe four moments in village history: first, the community's pre-Columbian roots; second, the conquest and late colonial period; third, the years of the Porfiriato; and fourth, the Mexican Revolution. This is not meant as an exhaustive history of Santañero life, which lies beyond the scope of this text. My goal is to illustrate Santa Ana's shifting relationship to the world over time. Defining the trajectory of change over these four periods will show that the current rise of "transnational" life (whether we are discussing migration or communication) is only the most recent manifestation of this historical process. It is within this framework of constantly shifting political, economic, and social patterns that cooperative and reciprocal relationships are constructed and recast.

Geography

Hidden within the jumble of southern Mexico's mountains is the central valley of Oaxaca. Separated from the Mexican plateau by one chain of peaks, and the Pacific coast by another, the central valley is a welcome pause in a difficult landscape. The valley covers more than 1,700 square kilometers, and includes three distinct arms (north, south, and east) that radiate from the central valley floor. At the valley's center is Oaxaca City, the state capital, and the archaeological site Monte Alban.

The central valley has four distinct ecological zones: mountain, piedmont, and high and low alluvium (Kirby 1973). The Etla arm of the valley reaches north toward Puebla and the region known as the Mixteca Alta (or Mixtec highlands).[2] The Ocotlán-Zaachila branch of the valley (named for two important market centers) runs to the south toward the Pacific coast. The eastern arm of the valley is named for Tlacolula, a political center and market site.[3]

The Pan-American highway is the primary artery for local and inter-

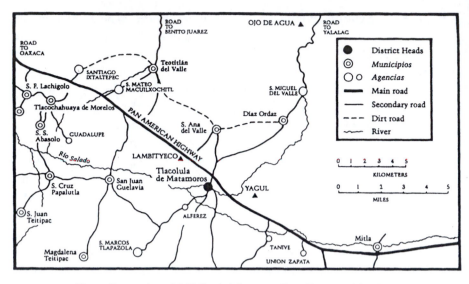

Map 1 Santa Ana del Valle and Surrounding Communities. From
Zapotec Women, *by Lynn Stephen.*
University of Texas Press: Austin, 1991, p. 5 (adapted from Welte, 1965).

state traffic. The highway comes out of the northwestern highlands
through the central valley (a day's drive from Mexico City), and follows
the eastern valley on its way to the Isthmus of Tehuantepec and Guatemala. An elaborate market system that dates at least to the early colonial
period integrates villages throughout the valley (Cook and Diskin 1976:
29).[4] Each day a different community is host to the market. Each market
also has a specific specialty, although most goods are available at every
market.[5]

Santa Ana del Valle is one of four villages, including Teotitlán del Valle,
San Miguel, and Díaz Ordaz, associated with treadle-loom weaving. The
four communities are found in the valley's eastern branch near one another and Tlacolula. Santa Ana is 42 kilometers east of the state capital,
Oaxaca City, and 4 kilometers north of Tlacolula (see Map 1). A road,
paved in the mid-1970s, connects Santa Ana to Tlacolula and provides
access to the Pan-American highway.

The village sits along the southern piedmont of the Sierra Madres that
rise dramatically to the north of the valley. The center of the community
is 1,780 meters (5,874 feet) above sea level. New *colonias* (neighborhoods

or settlements) have formed above the main village and higher on the mountainside.

Santa Ana is a small *municipio* (county equivalent) and covers 2,844 hectares (7,028 acres). Of this total, 1,195 hectares make up the "ranch." The ranch includes municipal lands that are in the mountains directly to the north and above the village. Some families own private plots of ranch lands; however, most Santañeros use the ranch as a source for firewood and animal pasture, and only farm valley plots. By the 1970s, the ranch and a small settlement named Las Carritas were essentially abandoned.

Las Carritas and the ranch hold special significance for Santañeros. During the Mexican Revolution villagers sought refuge in the mountain site for three years (see discussion in "The Mexican Revolution"). Families visit the ranch to collect *flores de los muertos* (flowers of the dead) to display on their altars and to place in the cemetery during the celebration of *el Día de los Muertos* (Day of the Dead).

Collecting Flores de los Muertos, 1992

Santa Ana is linked to Tlacolula and Díaz Ordaz by paved roads. The main two-lane road to Santa Ana also provides access to the Pan-American highway (4 kilometers south of the village). In addition, paths and dirt roads connect Santa Ana to other area villages, including Teotitlán del Valle. The trail to Teotitlán follows the *camino real* (royal road) established by the Spanish following the conquest, and continues on toward the center of the valley. The village borders Tlacolula to the south, Díaz Ordaz to the west, San Miguel to the north, and Teotitlán to the east.

The central valley is a region with a diversity of ecological zones conducive to intensive farming (Lees 1973). Nevertheless, the variability in rainfall throughout the valley (from a low of 490 millimeters of rain around Tlacolula and Mitla to 740 millimeters in Ocotlán) limits fertility (Kowalewski 1982; Whitecotton 1977: 20). The rains are unpredictable. Some years there is almost no precipitation (as in 1992, when most crops around Santa Ana failed), while other years are wet and can bring localized flooding (as in 1996). Most villagers complain of increasing droughts over the last decade, although there is no conclusive evidence. In any case, farming is a tenuous proposition and crops can be lost for myriad reasons.

Life follows a regular cycle in Santa Ana. During the rainy season families concentrate on farming and the care of crops. Textile production increases during cooler months and around high points in the tourist calendar (particularly, Christmas and the late summer, when the state-sponsored *Guelaguetza* takes place). Migrants time their sojourns around ritual and production calendars. For example, full-time farmers, who are less likely than independent weavers to migrate, plan their trips to coincide with the season's demands (Conway and Cohen 1998).

The rainy season begins in May and continues through September. As the weather cools from the dry heat of late spring and rains arrive, Santañeros begin planting. A guessing game goes on as villagers try to anticipate the start of steady precipitation and the optimal time to begin work in their fields. The rest of the year is parched and dry. At times, believing anything grows in Oaxaca is difficult.

Cold generally sets in through December and January. Nighttime temperatures can drop to the low forties.[6] The weather warms considerably as the calendar creeps toward the months of March and April. Hot winds blow relentlessly from the east and bring heavy dust. We would often sit on our porch and watch the dust devils dance along the valley floor. Rains usually return by June and overnight the brown dusts of the valley give way to a thick, lush green.

Land quality is quite varied in the valley, and represents a problem separate from weather for most Santañeros (Kirby 1973). Soils range from rich and loamy to dry, clay pack (Kowalewski 1982). Land in the valley is ranked along a three-tier scale, first-, second-, and third-class. First-class land with rich soil is irrigated and usually supports two crops a year, even when rains are scarce (Kowalewski 1982: 150). First-class lands are found on the valley floor and around the communities of Macuilxóchitl and Tla-cochahuaya (located to the west of Santa Ana). Traveling with Santañeros past Macuilxóchitl's green fields often brought a wistful sigh and comments concerning the poor quality of Santa Ana's lands. Second-class land is not irrigated, but "combines 'marginal water table' land and 'good flood water farming' land" to support intensive agriculture during the wet months of the year (Kowalewski 1982: 150). Teotitlán has some second-class land and a small amount of first-class land (Stephen 1987a).[7] Third-class land has no irrigation and floodwaters are not regularly available (Kowalewski 1982: 150).

Santa Ana's lands are predominantly third class or *temporal* (1,694 hect-ares—or 4,186 acres), and gently rise toward the mountains above the village. The slope and uneven qualities of third-class lands, and the vagaries of rainfall, make production difficult. In drought years the weather can effectively destroy production. A few Santañeros are digging wells to begin irrigation projects.[8]

Ethnicity

Scholars and politicians identify Santañeros as Zapotecs and therefore members of one of Mexico's indigenous groups. The label sticks for many reasons, the most important being the presence and use of a native language by a majority of the local population (although language patterns are changing). The politics of identity in Mexico are a dynamic arena with a rich history (see, for example, Knight 1990). However, being ethnically indigenous (i.e., as Zapotec) has little bearing on the structure of local identity and social organization (Cook and Joo 1995).

Nader describes the Zapotec as a diverse population adapted to various ecological and socioeconomic niches: " . . . valley Zapotec may have more in common with valley Mestizo towns than either have with the Tehuan-tepec Zapotec" (Cook and Joo 1995; Nader 1969: 331). Santañeros do not talk about themselves as Zapotec, nor do they self-identify as Indian; instead, they call themselves Santañero. They reserve the term "Zapotec" to describe the ancient peoples of the region and the term "Indio" (Indian) to talk about other ethnic minority populations.[9] This does not mean the category Indio is insignificant in local affairs; in fact, one reason a community like Santa Ana is politically and economically marginal has to do with the perceptions and assumptions by outsiders concerning identity and ethnic difference (see Watanabe 1995). In this discussion I will refrain from using the term Zapotec as a putative identifier of Santañero ethnicity (that is, one based upon a list of attributes—language, dress, foods, and so forth). Instead, I will explore the politics of identity, the importance of *indigenismo,* and the ways in which Santañeros manipulate external perceptions of ethnicity and are, in turn, manipulated by these perceptions. With this brief introduction to Oaxacan geography and ethnicity, we turn to the history of the village and community.

Origin Story

Long before, itinerant salesmen from Macuilxóchitl [a town west of the village and the site of Dainzu, a classic period site] would pass through this area on their way to the Sierra. They would stop at a spring—where the main well is today. They began to dig at the spring, opening it wider to reach the water more easily. And so, where they were digging, they uncovered a figure of Señora Santa Ana—she appeared there in the spring. They didn't know she was a saint; they thought she was an idol. Yes, they thought she was an idol, because they found her hidden in a bundle and set upon a stone in the spring.

The travelers took the figure to a place away from here, and began to put up their shelters for the night. But the saint didn't stay with the travelers; she went back to the spring where they had found her. The next day, the travelers returned to the spring and brought the saint out again, but again she returned. It went on like this; they would take the image from the spring to bring her with them, but she would always go back.

They thought this must be a sign of something, and they decided to stay at the spring. More people came and they got together to put up a building like a church. Later a priest came to take away the figure, but the people knew it wasn't possible to move the saint. So they convinced the priest to build another structure—a church, the church we have today. So there she has stayed, she never left again, and she is only a few meters from the well. It is very miraculous to stand under her altar. There have been miracles. The adoration that the people feel for her and her miracles have brought more people to the community. It started with two or three travelers, and then grew more and more to around the two thousand people who live here now.

—Alejandro, New Year's Eve 1993

I first heard this story during the celebration of New Year's Eve 1993. My wife Maria and I joined in with community members in a parade that began with rockets and music at the chapel near the eastern border of the village. En masse we marched through the village, stopping at homes and shrines to sing and drink. One of the more important stops was in front of Santa Ana's main well (located just to the south of the central plaza). At the well we offered prayers to the village *patrona* (patron saint, in this case, Saint Ann) and the story of Santa Ana's founding was recounted. I collected three additional versions of the story, each following the series of events mentioned above quite carefully. Each storyteller, two men (one in his late 60s, the other in his 30s) and one woman (in her early 30s), dwelt on the conversion of the idol to the saint in great detail.

Months later, I was reading in the Welte Institute (a private anthropological library in Oaxaca City) and discovered that Santa Ana was the site of a congregación, an ecclesiastical settlement founded by Dominicans to concentrate the indigenous population that survived the pandemics of the conquest (Taylor 1972: 26). What struck me was the way in which the story of the village's origins paralleled its historical development. The conversion of the idol to saint captures the transformation of Santa Ana from an indigenous settlement to Catholic community. Whether the story is old and timeless, or a recent invention, it is an indication of the ways in which Santañeros assimilate and reorganize cultural knowledge in the creation and reproduction of local meaning and identity.

Pre-Columbian History

Santa Ana was founded as little more than a way station along trade routes that carried goods and information between the central valley and

Sierra villages. Originally a small settlement, it was probably dependent on nearby population centers like Macuilxóchitl and Teotitlán del Valle. Ceramics from the area indicate a settlement in the vicinity of Santa Ana as early as 600 B.C., but the extent and size of the population are difficult to determine. This early settlement corresponds with the middle to late formative, or Guadalupe, period. It is associated with the development of a sedentary, nonmigratory lifestyle based upon maize production (Kirby 1973; Kowalewski 1982; Nicholas et al. 1986; Whitecotton 1977: 26). There is no indication of weaving during the early stages of the community's history. There is evidence of ceramic production and at least one kiln has been found in the village (see CMSD 1992; Feinman 1982).

By the fourteenth and fifteenth centuries the community was under the domination of Teotitlán. It appears as an *estancia* (small ranch or settlement) in early colonial records (see, for example, AGEO 1580; Redmond 1983). As a small settlement under Teotitlán's authority, Santa Ana sent cotton textiles, precious metals, fowl, chilies, and slaves as tribute to Tenochtitlán (the Aztec capital in the central valley of Mexico) and Zaachila (the center of Zapotec political and cultural power) (Chance 1978: 23; Whitecotton 1977: 123). A typical tribute payment in the late fifteenth century included four hundred small and eight hundred large cotton cloths every six months (Vásquez and Vásquez Dávila 1992: 1). Women likely wove on back-strap looms using cotton threads during the pre-Columbian era. It was only with the introduction of larger looms, and more important, a new division of labor and morality by Spanish missionaries, that men moved into this occupation (Vásquez Dávila et al. 1992: 207).

From this brief sketch we note the presence of craft specialization existing hand in hand with the practice of subsistence agriculture on the surrounding valley floor (Brandomín 1978: 185; Bustamante 1963: 7). Mountain holdings were likely used to produce crops as well, and today there remains evidence of orchards on ranch lands. Additionally, strict social hierarchies within each village paralleled the political hierarchy that organized valley communities into tribute payers and receivers (Redmond 1983). Zapotec society was divided into four classes or castes— nobles, commoners (including merchants), serfs, and slaves. Nobles were further divided between *caciques* (ruling families who were hereditary landholders by right of descent) and lesser nobles who served as administrators and priests (Chance 1978: 25). Thus, the community was in no way isolated. It was part of an indigenous "transnationalism" that bridged a diversity of cultural systems and traditions. Trade, communication, and social practice organized the powerful (those who demanded tribute) and the powerless (those who paid tribute, including the ancestors of modern-day Santañeros) into a dynamic social universe.

Conquest and Colonial History

The Spanish entered the central valley in 1521 and had assumed control of Oaxacan social life, political organization, and economy by the middle of the sixteenth century (see Chance 1978; Gay 1986). The isolation of Oaxaca, bounded by mountains in every direction, meant that it played a minor role in the overall economic and political development of New Spain (Taylor 1976: 66). However, Oaxaca City, called Antequerra, was an important center for the region, controlling commerce and trade, and organizing the political, religious, and social life of the central valley (Gay 1986).

The members of small villages and hamlets around the valley traded one form of domination for another as Spaniards replaced indigenous rulers and introduced the systems of *encomienda* (granting themselves the right to extract goods and tribute from a population) and *repartamiento* (a labor draft that demanded a set amount of service from most adult males). The stress of the social and cultural changes brought by the Spanish, the added burden of the repartamiento, and the impact of new diseases dramatically reduced the indigenous population of the central valley. The population of the valley dropped from approximately 150,000 people in 1568 to a low of between 40,000 and 50,000 in 1630 (Taylor 1976: 64). Through the next two centuries epidemics continued to take a high toll on the population. Taylor (1979: 137) notes that a smallpox epidemic led to the quarantine of Teotitlán's population in 1793 and likely included villagers from Santa Ana. The quarantine was later overturned in a colonial court.

Santa Ana was reestablished as a congregación, perhaps as early as 1580 according to a synopsis of the state published in 1883 (Cuadros Sinópticos 1986: 667), although the Dominicans founded most of the settlements between 1595 and 1605. Congregación settlements fulfilled many goals for colonial administrators. Centralizing indigenous populations eased political administration and management, expedited tribute collection, enhanced security, and simplified religious training (MacLeod 1973). Congregaciones also redefined social organization since diverse ethnic populations with contradictory ideas of status and government were forced to live together and local elites lost hereditary status (Chance 1978: 27). Finally, congregaciones, by their very nature, ended, or at least put a great deal of stress on, the rules of local endogamy (Hill 1992: 43).

The Spanish introduced new technologies, animals, and materials to the central valley (plows, presses, livestock, and so forth) in the name of "civilization," and to increase tribute (and see Foster 1979). The Spanish brought upright looms to replace the indigenous back-strap loom. Dominican missionaries trained men as artisans to replace women as weavers in Teotitlán and Santa Ana (Chance 1978: 110). Sheep were introduced to highland towns to promote local wool production and to foster trade links between valley and mountain communities. Additionally, the Spanish also introduced new techniques for spinning yarns and new dyes to the area (Vásquez Dávila et al. 1992: 226). Records show that the textiles from Teotitlán were popular with the Spanish, and the weavers were respected as competent craftsmen.

Brandomín (1978: 185) quotes the following colonial report on Teotitlán's weavers and textiles, " . . . *tejían las mantas muy galanas de mil colores y figuras las que ellas querían, y tan finas como las Castilla, y tejían las mantas de muchas maneras . . .* " (They wove very fine cloths [textiles] of as many colors and designs as they desired and as fine as Castellans, and they wove in many manners.) Similarly, Chance (1978: 110) cites a report by Francisco de Burgoa that singles out Teotitlán and the pottery-producing village of Coyotepec as two of the more commercially oriented towns in the region, with strong craft-producing traditions.

The Spanish brought many technological and structural developments to Oaxaca, yet they did little to change the political and economic inequalities that marked indigenous life. Spanish elites were not unlike their Zapotec or Aztec predecessors who controlled the region before the conquest. Thus, communities like Santa Ana continued to pay tribute, but rather than sending payments to Tenochtitlán and Zaachila, their tribute now went to the Dominicans stationed in the nearby monastery in Tlacochahuaya. Each family head sent eight *reales* of gold and one-half a *fanega* of maize annually (Vásquez Dávila et al. 1992: 226). The crown encouraged craft and crop specialization to enhance the earning power of rural communities and thereby increase tribute (and see Hill 1992).

Little was written about Santa Ana through the remainder of the colonial era. A church was completed in 1632 to serve the village. In 1723 the community became an independent settlement, ending its status as an estancia of Teotitlán. Santa Ana's sixty-two families remained under the political purview of Teotitlán as an independent pueblo (CTV 1748: 167).

Small-scale enterprises were begun in the community during the colonial era. In 1815, records show that Don Pedro Jose Buiton solicited and was granted a license to produce mescal in the village (AGEO 1815). The business was short-lived, and there is no record of a second attempt at alcohol production in Santa Ana. There is also little evidence of textile production in the community at the time. The only facts we can be sure of are the continued centrality of subsistence farming, limited wage labor on large farms in and around Tlacolula, and hauling of goods from the valley into the surrounding mountains.

Intermittent territorial disputes between Santa Ana and Tlacolula erupted throughout the late eighteenth and early nineteenth centuries due to population pressures and the political divisions of the valley lands between competing villages (see Lees 1973). The final disagreement was settled in a colonial court in 1893, and the frontier of both communities was delineated (noted in Taylor 1972: 210).[10] In the late nineteenth century Santa Ana became an independent *municipio,* the equivalent of a county in the United States. Around the same time, a second land dispute erupted between Santa Ana and Teotitlán over their shared border. At issue was not only the borderlands of each community, but land that was rich in precious metals. The court in Tlacolula later adjudicated the dispute in favor of Santa Ana. Throughout the colonial era we find that Santa Ana was a small community, but in no way an isolated one. It may have been unimportant economically, yet it held strategic importance because of its location on a primary trade route into the Sierra. Furthermore, as I note below, the linkages between Santa Ana and the global market were about to increase quite rapidly.

The Porfiriato

Toward the end of the nineteenth century, economic development in Mexico gained momentum under the rule of Porfirio Díaz. Foreign business interests came to the country in search of good investments and high returns. Santa Ana and its population of 892 people (Cuadros Sinópticos 1986) were drawn into this new set of socioeconomic relationships when silver was discovered on community lands near the village's border with

Table 1.1 Santa Ana's Population, 1880–1990

Year	1880	1900	1920	1930	1940	1950	1960	1970	1980	1990
MALE	461	537	341	371	480	550	679	792	1,065	1,015
FEMALE	431	490	375	382	498	618	687	852	1,082	1,205
TOTAL	892	1,027	716	753	978	1,168	1,366	1,644	2,147	2,220

Sources: Cuadros Sinópticos 1986; OTSF 1904; SEN 1934, 1943, 1953; SIC 1963, 1971; INEGI 1983, 1992a

Teotitlán (see Table 1.1). A British investor leased land and opened three mine shafts, called the Trinidad, the Guadalupe, and the Soledad, following the discovery of precious metals.

The owner established a small settlement around the mines for his workers. According to María Gutiérrez, the daughter of a miner, men from around the world arrived to work the mines. They hired Santañeros to do heavy and unskilled labor. Doña María describes the wealth such work brought to the village:

> My father and uncle worked at the mines for a long time. They carried stones and helped break up the rocks. They were paid a peso a day for their work. Oh, that was a lot of money then . . . In the 1930s a day's work as a field hand paid twenty centavos. There were people from all over then; they took gold and silver from the mines. But now, well now, it is closed. My brother mined a little after the war, after we came back from the ranch, but really, the mines are closed.

Many of the mines' records and those of the community in general were destroyed when the village was burned during the Mexican Revolution. However, limited information concerning the mines can be found. According to older villagers, the mines were forced to close in response to the growing revolt against the policies of the Porfiriato and rising levels of local violence. Local leaders brought state engineers in to inspect the mines and evaluate the potential to reopen one—if not all three—shafts in the mid-1980s. The engineers found high levels of gas in the shafts and restricted any further access to the shafts. It may be that the presence of gas in the mines contributed to the abandonment and closing of the site; today little remains of the site. Access to the shafts is nearly impossible because the entrances to each were sealed. The foundations of a few homes and processing buildings are the only obvious evidence of the site's presence and size.

Santa Ana's population grew to 1,027 by 1900. Many Santañeros worked as laborers *(mozos* and *peones)* at the mines or for larger land-holders in and around Tlacolula. In particular, the Chagoya family (who today produce mescal and market it in a nearby shop) employed many Santañero workers. Another source of income was to sell firewood collected in the mountains at the market in Tlacolula. Textile production remained near a self-consumption level (Bailón Corres 1979: 92). In Santa Ana one dry-goods store was available to families as a supplement to trips to Tlacolula's market.

During the early part of the twentieth century, the central plaza was completed. The church bordered the plaza to the east. Communal, multipurpose buildings were constructed along the north and south sides of the plaza and a room designated as a school was on the west side. An area near the community's main well was dedicated to washing (today it is the location of a small covered market area), and one pipe transferred water to a fountain on the central plaza. Paths and the camino real linked the village with Tlacolula to the south, Teotitlán to the west, and the Sierra to the north.

The Porfiriato administration planned for the forcible assimilation of indigenous peasant communities (Knight 1990). In Santa Ana, state-sponsored teachers arrived to educate children in the society of the nation (see Kowalewski and Saindon 1992). Stories told by older citizens suggest two brothers dispatched to teach in Santa Ana introduced the *danza de la pluma* (feather dance) around the turn of the century. The danza has become a symbol of local traditions and figures prominently in communal celebrations in both Santa Ana and Teotitlán (J. Cohen 1993; Harris 1996). As with earlier periods, we can note intense connections between the community, state society, and international economics. It is only following the devastation of the Mexican Revolution that Santa Ana begins to look like the isolated, independent peasant settlement conjured by the most romantic images of Mexico.

The Mexican Revolution

The Mexican Revolution, which began in 1910, disrupted Santañero society and nearly destroyed the village. Three large battles and many smaller skirmishes took place over the next ten years as federal troops and *Serranos* (rebel forces loyal to a state sovereignty movement) fought for the control of a strategic pass through the Sierra Madres that ran through Santa Ana's lands. Federal troops (called *Carrancistas* for Venustiano Carranza, president of the Republic from 1917–1920) were stationed in Oaxaca City, with a smaller garrison housed in Tlacolula. To the north in the mountains, were the Serranos, or the *Batallón de Sierra Juárez* (the battalion of the Juárez Mountains). This guerilla army was under the direction of a breakaway political group headed by Benito Juárez Masa, the son of Benito Juárez, and dedicated to Oaxacan independence (CMSD 1992; Garner 1990).

Fighting during the Revolution was intense in and around Santa Ana and most villagers fled the community in 1916. For the next three years the village's population lived in a small makeshift settlement called Las Carritas (site of the ranch), in the nearby mountains. A community project recorded stories of the survivors of the Revolution. Francisco García García stated:

> In 1914 we were hungry, we were tired, tired of the constant state of war, and that we could not plant our crops. The Carrancistas burned all of our land. Beans, corn, garbanzos, and everything else they encountered was destroyed. They ate our animals too. Suffering, we Santañeros went up to the mountains, and there we could plant, but only in small plots. Unfortunately we could not wait for the harvest. Driven by hunger we ate very young corn, saplings, squash and grasses. For sweets we ate honey. We didn't have sugar or salt since we could not leave the mountains. We cooked cactus fruits, and chewed maguey leaves (CMSD 1992: 11).

Terror and warfare were a part of daily life for the displaced Santañeros. Kearney (1986: 31), quoting Iturribarría, suggests that the lack of work and the destruction of farmlands, as well as the charisma of political strongmen and the rhetoric of state sovereignty, created an environment in which there were few alternatives to fleeing or fighting (and see Taylor 1979: 167; Womack 1969: 42–43). Santañeros were caught in just such a position in relation to both federal and guerilla forces. Pressured by opposing armies and at the mercy of either, they chose to flee and sought refuge in the mountains. Younger men from the community sided with the Serranos and fought with them for state sovereignty.

Large-scale battles roared through the area on three occasions as Carrancistas attacked Serrano strongholds and tried to break guerilla control of the mountain pass bisecting village lands. Federal troops and Serranos fought the final battle for control of the pass to the Sierra in 1920 and involved men from Santa Ana. Santañeros worked with Serrano soldiers to cut trenches that impeded the movement of the federal troops (the trenches can still be seen today). According to the Shan-Dany's oral history project, "the excellent work of Santa Ana and the Sierra forces caused many problems for the Carrancistas, stopping their third and last attack" (CMSD 1992: 13).

By the early 1920s fighting had ended, but it was some time before life returned to normal in Santa Ana. Some families remained around Las Carritas, living in the ranch rather than moving back to the village. Others returned to the village, which the Carrancistas had burned.

Post-Revolutionary History

Those Santañeros who returned from Las Carritas found their home community destroyed. The village's population fell from 1,027 in 1900 to 716 in 1920, a drop of approximately 30 percent in twenty years (Peñafiel 1904; SEN 1934). Homes had been burned, community land was fallow, and animals were starved and slaughtered for food or stolen by soldiers and looters. One of the few buildings outwardly unscathed by fighting was the church, which had suffered only minor damage during the conflict. Inside, soldiers had ransacked the building. A handful of objects survived the fighting and older Santañeros told of two particular church icons that weathered the fighting with no damage. Locals believe these figures hold miraculous, curative, and predictive powers.

There were few economic opportunities available to villagers following the Revolution. The mines were abandoned, land needed to be reopened for farming, and village homes had to be rebuilt. Informants who remembered this period focused on the terror and devastation of the Revolution as motivation for a self-imposed isolation. Village leaders passed up potential development projects offered by the state. When the state proposed a road to link the village to Tlacolula and Sierra towns in the late 1960s, the village authority declined the project, stating that they feared strangers would threaten the population.

A few families did not return to the village and chose to remain in the ranch at Las Carritas. Señora Minerva Matias Cruz, a sixty-year-old woman born and raised in the ranch remembers:

It was nice up in the ranch. The land was good, and the air was fresh. My father died when I was young, so I learned from my uncle how to herd animals and grow corn. We grew everything there, corn, beans, squash, even wheat. I worked just like a boy, going to the fields early. I didn't come to the village to study or go to school; we stayed up there in the ranch, me and my mother and uncle.

Señora Cruz spent the 1950s and 1960s moving back and forth between homes in the ranch and the village proper. Women like Señora Cruz and her mother earned limited incomes by hauling goods between Tlacolula and Las Carritas, a trip that could take a few hours, and then selling those goods to ranch families and travelers moving into the Sierra.

Beyond the geographic separation of village and ranch, there was a social boundary between the populations. There were few marriages between individuals from the ranch and village, and ranch families did not often serve in village cargos. If they did serve, their posts fell into minor cargos holding little status and low rank. The one exception was the cargo dedicated to the care of a small chapel and cemetery in the ranch.[11]

The boundaries between ranch and town created somewhat separate population centers. Families moved from ranch to town as responsibilities, desires, and opportunities arose. While there were differences in class, status, and political power between the two populations, the separation of ranch and village was primarily one of convenience. Las Carritas assumed a subordinate political position in relation to Santa Ana; however, the ranch never became an official settlement tied to Santa Ana in the way Santa Ana had existed as an estancia of Teotitlán.[12]

Families did leave Las Carritas to return to the village to fill minor positions in the political or religious hierarchy of the community, to care for a family member, or for wage labor. Involvement in wage labor was perhaps the most important factor influencing the gradual abandonment of the ranch. Many Santañeros left the village in the 1940s to work on the Pan-American highway. Others went to jobs as field hands in Tlacolula.

No single women or men remained on the ranch. Living in the ranch added a difficult and time-consuming commute for men who worked in local wage positions, and this was long before there was bus service between Santa Ana and Tlacolula. Textile production also brought ranch families to the village. Weaving full-time, or even part-time, required Santañeros be near both the markets for supplies and the market for finished products. Time given to textile production also meant a household had

Altar decorated for Día de los Muertos, 1992

less time for farm work. By the beginning of the 1970s, most families had left the ranch and returned to living full-time in the village. Today the ranch remains empty and is used primarily as pastureland for livestock.

Contemporary economic activity slowly began to appear in Santa Ana from the 1940s on. The production of woven art did not become an important venture until the tourism boom of the 1970s. In fact, there was a drop in production through the 1940s and 1950s as imported and ready-made goods flooded the market and the price of wool rose (Bailón Corres 1979: 93). The importance of labor migration, which today ranks as one of the most profitable economic strategies available to a family, began in the late 1950s, when locals left for the United States to work in the Bracero Program.[13] While the program had its problems (see Cockcroft 1983: 172), Mauricio García Mateo fondly recalled his time as a bracero. He worked in Texas and California, and went as far north as Michigan to pick apples. An elderly informant recalled watching the first migrants leave the community:

> We thought they would never come home. I was sure they would die. There was just no reason to leave and nobody did. Why leave? What did we need? But they came back. Now everyone is leaving. When I was just a child, we never even went to Oaxaca. It was a day away. Now everyone goes there and farther. Who even knows how far away they go.

Many Santañeros chose to stay closer to home, going only as far as the Isthmus of Tehuantepec to work on the Pan-American highway. Domingo Hipolito García watched one Santañero die during construction of the highway through the mountains of Oaxaca. Other villagers headed for the coffee plantations of Chiapas, the tobacco and cotton fields of Vera Cruz, or the dreamed-of wealth of Mexico City. As we will see in the next chapter, it was not until the crisis of the 1980s that migration grew to be a core economic strategy.

Conclusions

The current economic and political organization of Santa Ana and its relationship to external markets and social forces is not altogether new. Rural Oaxacans were involved in broadly based sociocultural, economic, political, and religious articulations that occurred first during the pre-

Columbian history of the region. While the structure of association has shifted since Santañeros paid tribute to Zapotec elite in Zaachila, the overall relationship of powerful and powerless remains quite constant.

Santa Ana is a poor community linked to an ever-changing world (whether one of tribute and empire or of transnational process). The community is politically and economically dependent upon many external markets and institutions. What we can learn from the Santañero example is how a local population copes with the changes caused by these linkages. After outlining the contemporary political economy of the region and community in the next chapter, I return to these issues and explore in detail how Santañeros have adapted traditional patterns of cooperation to the exigencies of daily life.

Chapter Two

Economy and the Structure of Production
in Santa Ana del Valle

People are always asking us, "Why do you Mexicans leave for the United States?" Because we can find *mano de obra* [contract work]. So the answer is easy: in the United States we can earn the minimum wage. For example, if we work for the Chinese, they'll pay twenty-one dollars a day. And we guard that money. Those of us already married, we have responsibilities to our families. We have families, we have houses, we have children, everything! So we guard our wages and send them back to Mexico. When this money arrives in Santa Ana, that is when it comes together because the dollars are worth so much more than pesos. For example, when the dollar is worth three thousand pesos [circa 1992], it is a lot of money. If you can get together two hundred dollars, you have a lot of money to work with. I was able to build my house. It is of simple construction, but I could do it, working and working and I made all of this in six years [motioning to the three room brick house, walls of the *solar* (homesite), well, and large gate]. All with the money I earned in the United States.

—Mario Bautista

FORGETTING THE CONNECTIONS that Santañeros share with both the national and global economy is easy as one works to harvest corn in a field on a hot and dusty afternoon. The monotony and strain of the harvest are only broken by the jokes we tell each other and the food brought out by our wives and families. We walk down row after row of dried corn stalks, bending to cut them with a hand sickle, bundling the stalks into manageable bunches, and hauling them in an ox cart to storage. It does not feel or seem like twentieth-century work. Yet the young man who directs us has use of the field in exchange for a loan he made to its owner. He also plans to leave the village for a job in the United States once the harvest is completed. The bulls that pull the cart were purchased with money earned when he worked as a busboy in a Chinese restaurant in Santa Monica, California.

Weaving on a loom that is older than its owner and working in the shade of a solar also carries a timeless quality. Weavers talk about learning their designs in their dreams. They tell visitors of the way the mosaics of Mitla inspire their choice of motifs. Master-dyers blend cochineal and plants to produce a range of natural colors that does not seem quite possible without chemicals. The traditions that surround weaving mask changes in the meaning and the structure of textile production. Textiles are made for an international market and tailored to meet international tastes (Cohen 1998; Cook 1993; Stephen 1991a). The local uses of *tapetes* and *cobijas* (a generic term for textiles) have disappeared. Weavers no longer make the heavy, dark red skirts (called a *biug*) that women typically wore, and few people can afford to keep textiles for home use.

Mario's experiences, leaving the village in search of higher wages, are typical of many young Santañero men. These experiences are one indication of the growing importance to household survival of wage labor and transnational migration. As Maria and I adjusted to life in the village, we heard men and women tell of experiences that paralleled Mario's. We watched international buyers and tourists come to the village to visit the small local museum or look for a textile bargain. We also regularly accompanied men, women, and families to the bus station and airport in Oaxaca City and watched as they left to chance a border crossing into the United States in anticipation of steady work and higher wages.

Santa Ana was not the place we expected. It was not a community of peasant farm families tangentially dependent on external markets that had little interest in their progress (Thorner et al. 1966). Nor were Santañero families part of a homogeneous, indigenous society where a shared psychological outlook mediated conflict and contest (Redfield 1950). Santañeros were (and are) part of the global economy through dependency, desire, and need (Cohen 1998; Conway and Cohen 1998; Cook and Binford 1990; Kearney 1996). This chapter outlines contemporary economic strategies in the community and sets the scene for the analysis of cooperative relationships that follows.

The Santañero Economy

Santañero economic life remains organized around three primary strategies in the 1990s: agricultural production (primarily subsistence farming with limited sales locally and in Tlacolula), commercial textile production (for sale to tourists locally and for export), and national or international migration. The current socioeconomic structure of the community differs from that of twenty years ago in five specific ways detailed below.

First, the population of the community continues to increase (from 1,634 in 1970 to 2,220 in 1990). This increase places production pressures on local land holdings that must generate food for more individuals, and income pressures on local workers as they must cover the costs of larger families. Second, the number of Santañeros involved in agricultural production dropped from 17 percent to only 5 percent of the working population between 1970 and 1990 (INEGI 1992b; SIC 1971). Third, tourism, important for decades and central to Santa Ana, is one of the top income generators for the country, accounting for 7 percent of Mexico's GNP in 1990 (FONATUR 1992). Fourth, economic growth through the early 1980s began to unravel as the peso collapsed (falling by 60 percent in value in 1976), and the economy entered the first of many difficult periods during Luis Echeverría's presidency (see Barkin 1990; Dominguez 1982). Fifth, cyclical migration to the United States has replaced short-term internal migration in response to the ongoing economic crisis within Mexico (Cornelius and Bustamante 1989; Jones 1995; Verduzco Igartúa 1995).

Demography

The national census counted 1,634 people in Santa Ana in 1970. Of this total, more than half the community's working population (279 of 432 individuals) was involved in agriculture and 111 listed weaving as their primary occupation (SIC 1971).[1] The population of the village increased to 2,147 people by 1980. However, the number of full-time agriculturalists decreased to 211 individuals out of a total of 876 working adults, or 24 percent of the working population.[2] In contrast, 462 Santañeros chose weaving as their primary occupation, more than tripling the number of weavers in ten years and constituting just over 50 percent of the total work force (INEGI 1983).

Between the 1980 and 1990 census there was another shift in the structure of Santañero economic activity (see Table 2.1). The overall number

Table 2.1 Working Population in Santa Ana

Year	Total Population	Female Population	Male Population	Farmers	Weavers	Other
1970	1,634	842	792	279	111	42
1980	2,147	1,082	1,065	211	462	203
1990	2,220	1,205	1,015	126	379	72

Sources: SIC 1971; INEGI 1983; INEGI 1992b

of working Santañeros decreased from 876 in 1980 to 577 in 1990. This decline occurred even as the population remained almost constant, increasing by only 73 people in the decade. The number of Santañeros who identified themselves as farmers decreased to 126 individuals, and the number of weavers in the community declined by almost 100 individuals to only 379 in 1990 (INEGI 1992b).

An option for a growing portion of the village's workforce is wage labor. Many younger villagers work on local construction projects; others go to Tlacolula and seek employment as skilled and unskilled laborers, as mozos or *jornaleros* (day laborers). One of the most important local projects was the construction of a retaining dam for a planned reservoir on community land, begun in the late winter of 1996 and employing a dozen villagers.

A minority of people in the community work as professionals, teachers, nurses, or governmental appointees. People also run small businesses in the village. There was one *tortillería,* one barbershop, two metal door/window makers, one car repair shop, twelve dry-goods stores (an increase of five from the seven identified in 1992), one restaurant, two grinding mills, and one glass cutter in 1996. Two village residents also worked as large-scale textile buyers, and many Santañeros will purchase textiles from time to time to round off orders for their own work. In all, workers employed outside of textile production and agriculture constituted only 12.4 percent of the population in the 1990 census, or 72 individuals (INEGI 1992b).

The slow growth in population and the declining number of Santañeros involved in agriculture and textile production are not necessarily indicative of a decrease in the birth rate for the village, an increase in village deaths, or an overall drop in village employment. The decline in population growth and local employment between 1980 and 1990 are outcomes of the rapid increase in out-migration from the community (Embriz 1993).[3] In other words, economically active Santañeros were choosing new forms of employment that removed them from consideration when the census was counted.

The influence of migration on the structure of the community was manifest by 1990 in the total number of males and females counted in the census. Throughout the 1960s, 1970s, and 1980s, the percentage of males and females in the village remained constant over time. But, the census counted nearly two hundred more women than men in 1990. The difference cannot be attributed to an increase in the birth rate of females, nor to the untimely death of Santañero men. The missing men are largely adults between the ages of fifteen and thirty-nine. In 1980, there were 104 men and 99 women between the ages of fifteen and nineteen living in the village. In 1990, the total for this same cohort shifted to 39 men and 79 women in the village, a decline of 65 men and 20 women. A relatively low death rate of 5/1,000 cannot account for the discrepancy, particularly when the village grew by over 3 percent for the decade (INEGI 1992a). Most of the Santañeros are not dead; rather, they are no longer physically in the village. Most likely they are migrants working and living in the United States (see discussion in "Migration").[4]

The structure of Santa Ana's economy and the choices made by Santañeros are more fluid and more complex than the national census reveals. Santañeros respond first to shifts in the structure of the village and the local economy. A decline in demand for textiles and rising production costs (see Cohen 1998; Cook and Binford 1990) combine with new opportunities for income outside the community to drive migration. The continued crisis in the national economy transforms migration from an internally based process to one that takes villagers across the border and into cities like Los Angeles and Santa Monica, California. The growth in family demand for goods, services, and education at home places increasing pressure on migrants to earn the funds needed to cover the costs— and places additional pressures on agricultural production.

It is also difficult to identify workers when the choices they make concerning their jobs are influenced by the calendar. Textile production is at a minimum or it takes a back seat to farm work during the summer. Following the harvest, weaving increases. In January, Umberto Martínez told me, "All I do is weave all day long, pure weaving." Yet he would not hesitate to call himself a *campesino* (depending on how it is read, a peasant or, in this case, a farmer). By June he was preparing his fields. Now when I asked about weaving, he responded: "Oh, you know it is hard to find the time to weave, I have so many things I have to do. I am getting ready to plant, I need to train my oxen, and my brother needs help too. I would like to weave, but frankly, where will I find the time?" In sum, involvement in the economy is difficult to track. Individuals selling tortillas and eggs door-to-door do not report their earnings, nor does the census recognize migrant remittance levels among households. Because of the combined pressures of a changing economy, local demand, the combination of various economic strategies, and the vagaries of what is and is not "work" in a system where everyone "pitches in" for the good of the unit, it is difficult to classify workers (see Acheson 1996; Wilk 1989).

Agricultural Production

While agricultural production continues to decline in the village, land ownership remains a goal for many Santañeros. It is an important symbol of wealth and status, whether one chooses to farm, to rent, or leave it fallow. Santañeros who farm are, like all agriculturalists, at the mercy of the environment. The situation is compounded by the quality of local land holdings. With little irrigation available to third-class lands, Santañeros are always hoping for regular rains. In a good year most men felt they could produce enough corn to meet daily needs for eight to twelve months, even with as little as one hectare of land. And the crops produced, while labor-intensive, are not capital-intensive. Once seeds are purchased, there is little actual money invested into fieldwork: farmers do not think about the hourly costs of their efforts and most use a limited amount of fertilizers or pesticides. The trade-off is lower output per hectare of land for less overall investment.

The continued connection of Santañeros to their land is one indication of the way in which farming serves more than an economic function in the village. Sheridan (1988) points out that land is not only important in financial terms, it is also a manifestation of independence, and a symbol of local identity (see Watanabe 1992: 62), the ever elusive "rootedness" anthropologists seek. Working with Sonoran peasants and cattle ranchers, Sheridan states, "peasant households may not be able to own their own ranches or drill their own wells, but they are capable of working a few hectares of milpa or temporal" (1988: 191). Similarly, Santañeros may have little control over their lives. They do not command the market for textiles; they have little control over the sales of finished tapetes, and they can bring few additional jobs to their town. However, a hectare of land (or a half-hectare, or whatever) lends a degree of independence no matter the land's quality, no matter the presence or absence of irrigation. Land is a sign of a family's strength, wealth, and tie to the community.

Santañeros with little or no land can rent empty communal property through a petition to the central authority and *Buenas Comunales* (the village resource management committee). They also rent one another's holdings. In one example collected in 1992, a young man took land as collateral and partial payment for a loan. Mario Sánchez held a nine-year title to a fellow villager's land as a loan guarantee. He also held use-rights to the land instead of interest. If the family fails to repay the loan, Mario can request the land.

Sipping beer in the afternoon shade of the plaza in 1993, two young men mentioned their hopes of buying land in nearby Tlacolula. Other villagers spoke about reopening the ranch for farming. At the time, these options did not appear to be more than dreams brought on by the difficulties of a long day's work and the effects of a bit of alcohol. However, when I was in the village in 1996, I discovered that a handful of families had in fact purchased land in Tlacolula. One family hoped to open a small artisan shop; a second was farming a small plot. A third family purchased a one-room house on the outskirts of Tlacolula with money earned in the United States. They set up a small textile workshop with a loom, wool, and a few amenities (a hot plate, television, etc.). The shop was a place to escape the demands of the family and to weave in peace and quiet.

A minority of Santañeros hold enough land to produce surplus crops that can be sold locally or in Tlacolula. On irrigated plots of land near the village's southwestern border with Teotitlán, the Santañeros grow alfalfa and garbanzos (chickpeas), corn, squash, and the maguey used in the production of mescal. However, production for sale is risky. Regular and sufficient rains helped produce a large crop of garbanzos for a few Santañeros in 1991—yet a drop in prices, owing to an oversupply and low demand, meant most Santañeros made little profit. Therefore, farming is not a common moneymaking strategy. For most Santañeros farming is a means of reducing the pressure that results from limited wage labor alternatives. Producing corn to support a family, even for half a year, means there is more money left to cover educational and health expenses and the expenses associated with rituals and celebrations (Wilk 1991).

Families also keep livestock (goats, sheep, burros, and pigs) as walking "banks." Most animals are described as *oro* (here not gold, but a savings account). Families also own chickens and turkeys but do not classify the birds as oro; they are simply a food source (see Gudeman and Rivera 1990). Men aspire to own a *yunta* (team of oxen). A yunta is more than a savings account with legs; it is also an income producer (see Cook and Binford 1990: 44). Throughout the year the team is rented out to haul goods and plow fields.

Stephen points out that animals demand a steady supply of food and care (1987a). However, Santañeros invest little money or effort in an animal's welfare. In fact, free pasture is one of the few uses that Santañeros make of the community's ranch lands. Our home in the *colonia nueva* was en route to the ranch. We regularly saw young people marching livestock back and forth to the mountains.

The shifts in agricultural production among Santañeros are tied to many changes in the community. First, there is the increase in the village's population, and limits on land to meet that increase. Second, there is a shift in how individuals and families hope to use their land. More families are building more homes, shifting land-use patterns. Don Mauricio, our landlord, looked around at the dozen homes built in the last four or five years on what was formerly a cornfield, saying, "Look at all of these; this was pure corn before, just trees and such. But look at it . . . it is all houses . . . Soon every bit of fields, even this [pointing to the ground], will be gone."

Third, as noted above, there are new demands by the population for goods and services, a slow shift toward wage labor, and a rapid rise in migration. Changes in labor patterns are a limited challenge to the primacy of textile production and agriculture. However, over time, the cumulative effect of these shifts—what Alarcón (1992) describes as the process of *norteñización,* or the "North Americanizing" of Mexico—will take place (and see Frye 1996). The question remains: What does this process mean for the production and reproduction of local social patterns of cooperation?

Textile Production

For centuries in Teotitlán and throughout the region, lessons in weaving and spinning have been part of childhood.
—Betty Freundheim (1988)

Dyeing yarns

Two- and four-harness looms and home-based wool textile production were introduced in the sixteenth century by Dominican friars. The technology used by Oaxaca's treadle-loom weavers remains essentially unchanged at the present. Looms are made of hardwood, and the heddles are driven by the weaver who stands on two large foot peddles. Modern innovations, such as a flying shuttle, are not present. One shift noted by Santañero weavers is the disappearance of four-harness looms used to weave the biug, a jacquard wool skirt worn by local women. The decline in the production of goods for local use, and the rise in weaving for tourism and export, signify the fundamental changes that have influenced the textile industry even as technology remained constant (García Canclini 1993). The rising costs of production, the availability of cheap, ready-made goods, and the importance of cash incomes (generated largely through weaving and little else in the local economy) mean most textiles go directly to the market. Few weavers remember or know how to produce *rebozos, plias* (water-repellent wraps), or the biug.

Textile production occupies most Santañero households throughout the year, and is an important moneymaking activity. Production is particularly strong during the fall and winter months in response to increased export and tourist demand around the Christmas and New Year holidays. Like craft production elsewhere in Mexico, weaving exists in tandem with agricultural production. Textile production is based on undercapitalized labor and antiquated technology, and its products are consumed in a global market (see, for example, Clements 1987; Cohen 1998; Cook 1984; Littlefield 1978; Nash 1994; Stephen 1991b; Tice 1995).[5]

Weaving occupies all members of a household and in Santa Ana, men, women, and children weave. Men outnumber women behind looms by more than two to one (273 to 106); however, this figure does not include the prepping work done by women in support of their husbands (INEGI 1992b). That women weave is a change from trends noted as recently as the 1960s. Plattner reports "women may know how to weave, but they never do so" (1965: 23). Currently, women weave alongside men and pro-

Spinning bobbins

Weaving

duce textiles in just as wide a variety in quality and design. The shift is due in part to the increasing use of factory-spun and factory-dyed yarns. In the past, preparation included carding and cleaning raw wool, spinning yarns, preparing dyes, dyeing finished yarns, and preparing skeins for weaving (CMSD 1992; Vásquez Dávila et al. 1992; Vásquez and Vásquez Dávila 1992). Few weavers spin their own wool into yarn. Most weavers buy their yarn by the kilo locally or at a small plant in Teotitlán, in bulk from the local cooperative (see Chapter Six), or directly from manufacturers (Cohen 1998). Yarn is pre-dyed at the factory for use, although there is an increasing demand for natural dyes (particularly cochineal) among consumers (Wood 1995). The arrival of factory-made yarns

Table 2.2 Employment Patterns among Santañero Weavers, 1990

	Total Weavers	Mano de obra	Employees	Indepen-dent Weavers	Patrons	Unpaid Laborers	No Response
FEMALE	106	4	1	89	0	10	2
MALE	273	9	2	239	1	18	4
TOTALS	379	13	3	328	1	28	6

Source: INEGI 1992b

means less time and effort is invested in preparation, which now includes wrapping warp threads and readying them for the loom, stringing looms, cleaning and dyeing yarns when necessary, and winding bobbins. Young children usually support older siblings and parents by winding bobbins and cleaning the finished textiles once they are cut from the loom.

Textile producers in Santa Ana are in direct competition with weavers in Teotitlán del Valle (the village that dominates production), and to a lesser degree, the communities of San Miguel del Valle and Díaz Ordaz (see Stephen 1991b). Weavers organize production following one of three strategies: independent production, mano de obra, and wage labor (see Table 2.2). Each has its advantages and drawbacks, and each incorporates various sets of local and external social and economic relationships.

Most Santañero weavers identify themselves as independent producers selling their tapetes on the open market. The 1990 census noted 328 of the 379 weavers in the community were independent producers (INEGI 1992b). Survey data from 1992–1993 shows a more complex situation indicating that what Santañeros mean by independent weaving is quite different from what is meant by researchers. In 1992 and 1993, fifty households were randomly selected for a survey. Out of this total, only two households were not involved in textile production. Of those that remained, twenty were involved in independent production (selling on the open market). Twelve weavers who identified themselves as independent producers were involved in mano de obra relationships. Often an informant would describe his or her approach to textile production, saying: "Of course, I am an independent producer." The informant would then go on to tell me that he or she worked on a contract with a particular patron in Teotitlán for many years. Weavers were also asked where they purchased their yarns. An independent weaver who answered that he or she received yarn from an *acaparador* (buyer) or a patron often indicated involvement in contract work as well. Thus, according to our survey only eight households employed purely independent production strategies. Sixteen weavers identified their households as maintaining mano de obra contracts with buyers in the village, Teotitlán, Oaxaca City, or the United States (a total of twenty-eight households in our survey).[6]

The 1990 census also identified one Santañero as a patron or buyer (INEGI 1992b). This number was underreported. There were two more buyers in the village, an older man and a widow who continues to buy textiles through the business begun by her husband (although she is slowly moving out of the business). There were also households that bought in small quantities to round off their contracts or to hoard tapetes when prices were low in anticipation of future markets. Well underreported in the census are the many Santañeros who work as unpaid laborers and apprentices in family workshops.[7]

The situation had changed, but not by a great deal, in 1996. Of fifty-four families surveyed, ten were identified as independent producers. Eight were involved in strict mano de obra. Of the remainder, eleven combined independent production with farming; eleven combined mano de obra with farming; and three households combined farming with weaving and one additional form of work (two homes were involved in small businesses, and the third ran a bakery).

As the census and survey responses indicate, most Santañeros identify themselves as independent producers. Most weavers tie the idea of independence to owning a loom, and the majority of weaving households own at least one loom. Obviously, how we define independent production is, in this instance, quite different from our informants' definition. The difference involves space and the lack of direct control by a working superior (here a patron). Working at home with the support of family and limited direction creates a sense of independence among weavers. Furthermore, the distance from contractors and patrons (typically individuals living in Teotitlán, a twenty-minute drive from Santa Ana) adds to the sense of independence. In other words, Santañeros do not leave home for work, they do not punch a clock, and they are not supervised throughout their workday.

Most Santañeros choose mano de obra as a stable way to make a living. In an interview one weaver stated, "My patron gives me the design, and I give him whatever he wants." Another weaver added, "It is safe this way

Cleaning finished tapetes

[mano de obra],” when asked to describe the difference between his approach and that of the independent weaver. He added, “This way I get paid; if I was an independent weaver I might not . . .” A weaver working full-time, mano de obra (eight to ten hours a day), could expect to earn from sixty to one hundred dollars a week in 1993. The amount dropped by nearly half, ranging from thirty to seventy dollars by 1996. Nevertheless, a family that combines textile production with migration, agriculture, and limited wage labor can often more than cover its expenses. Thus, parallel to Acheson’s (1972) work among Tarascan businesspeople, it is not surprising to find many Santañeros were more concerned with money they made in the moment (described as *ganancia* by Acheson), rather than with the generation of capital for long-term investment.[8]

Mano de obra in Santa Ana follows a weekly production cycle that starts and finishes on Sundays. Santañeros travel to Teotitlán or are visited by patrons who will pick up orders and leave supplies for the coming week. Many Santañeros walk or bike along the camino real that links the villages and follows the base of the Sierra Madre heading west toward Oaxaca City. Once in Teotitlán, the Santañero goes to the home of a patron to turn over his or her textiles for a contracted price.[9] Weavers also receive yarns and design requirements for the next week's contracts. Payment is on a per piece basis and disregards the time required for work. Prices for finished goods range from a low of 5,000 pesos (or $1.60) for a small *servilleta* (placemat-sized rug), to 60,000–90,000 ($20.00 to $30.00) for a standard "tourist" design (typically 80 cm wide × 150 cm long) based on the geometric patterns (called Grecas) found on the walls of the archaeological site of Mitla (about one-half hour west of the village). Money earned is typically spent in Tlacolula's Sunday market, where a family buys food and supplies for the next week. One way to gauge the importance of this weekly cycle, and the number of Santañeros it involves, is to walk around the village Monday morning and count the number of people preparing warp threads for the next week's contract. In fact, Mondays were a particularly bad day for interviews due to the time Santañeros needed to prepare their looms and yarns.

The relationship of a weaver to a patron follows the pattern of a dyadic contract. As such, informal social guarantees are placed on what would otherwise be a formal economic transaction (see Foster 1961; Foster 1963). The dyadic contract builds on familiar patterns of association, reproducing relationships based on the logic of kinship and friendship in a situation that would typically be defined by market economics (see Holmes 1989: 92). Dyadic contracts grant a degree of security to Santañeros dependent on the weekly sale of textiles by creating a social link between the weaver and the patron. The weaver is essentially secure in the knowledge that he or she can make a sale, even if the market is tight. Weavers build on these contracts, asking patrons to serve as *compadres* (godparents) for their children to further the social guarantee.

An exploitative effect of the dyadic contract is to guarantee a patron a steady supply of textiles at a price lower than the open market. Thus, in establishing a dyadic contract and practicing mano de obra, the weaver gains security but earns less. The patron profits from a steady supply of textiles at reduced prices; however, he or she is obliged to buy from contract weavers even in a depressed market.

Some weavers choose independent production to avoid contracts and patronage. When necessary, a member of the household will take a trip to Tlacolula, Teotitlán, or Oaxaca City in search of buyers. Independent weavers like to receive buyers in their homes, although it is not necessary. Independent work requires weavers or households to invest their time and money in preparation, production, and sale of their textiles. Yarns are bought on the open market and time is invested in dyeing, planning, and design. Time must also be devoted to the sale of completed products. Finding a buyer can be difficult, particularly during slow months when few may be in the region (Wood 1996). On the other hand, independent producers earn higher incomes from their work. "I can sell to whomever I would like, whenever I like," said one young man. A second added, "I can work more, and make more to sell this way. I don't have to wait for anyone." While their freedom may increase, a weaver involved in independent production has to watch the market carefully, gauging changes in design and color tastes. During July 1996, the textile market hit a lull. In response, one weaver stockpiled tapetes in anticipation of a better market, rather than sell at a loss. The family used money earned from migration to cover its expenses, and hoped their funds would last until they made a large sale.

Some weavers who choose to work independently specialize in a particular type of weaving that is different from the average work and is therefore in greater demand and easier to sell. Such artisans are often identified with their specialty and will be sought out for special orders. For example, Aron Sánchez and his son weave *pasajes,* representations of country scenes that include wild animals, rivers, and farmers, as wall hangings. Umberto Mendoza and his daughters specialize in smaller weavings that are intricate reproductions of European paintings and fanciful childhood scenes. The finished pieces are made into pillows that are then sold. Households that specialize typically have one member involved in mano de obra production. In the Sánchez home, for example, the female head of the household weaves tourist designs of lower overall quality that she sells on contract in Teotitlán.

A few weavers in Santa Ana produce large, high-quality weavings on a small scale. This form of production does not necessarily bring more in-

A finished Greca de Mitla design

dependence than mano de obra. A talented weaver in the village produces textiles, often measuring two to three meters in width, on contract for a patron in Teotitlán. Like typical mano de obra, he is given a design and a deadline for the project. Yet another Santañero frees his time for indepen-dent, high-quality weaving by engaging in small-scale buying. He keeps a stock of textiles on hand that he can quickly sell if necessary, using his time to weave larger works himself.

Three families maintain stalls in the *Mercado de Artesanías* (Artisans' Market) in Oaxaca City in addition to weaving in their homes.[10] These families often buy the work of their extended family, and when there is demand, contract with other individuals to fill orders. However, two of the three stall owners reported their sales have been poor in the market for well over a year; therefore, one owner no longer maintains his space regularly.

A few Santañeros are nearly full-time buyers. In his work, Plattner (1965: 25) noted five buyers living in Santa Ana in the 1960s (and see Cook and Binford 1990). However, I was aware of only three households involved in large-scale buying, who are called patrons or acaparadores by the population. One of the families was in the midst of withdrawing from business, due to the death of the household head who had been the chief buyer. His wife continued to buy textiles on a part-time basis, but she was of waning importance in the local economy. Of the two remaining buyers in the village, one, Señor Marciano, has a reputation for paying very little for finished work and then inflating his selling price.[11] Most Santañeros sold to him only if necessary, when they were desperate for money. Informants noted they might sell to Marciano if they had been invited to a *compromiso* (family party) or celebration and needed cash to cover a gift or contribution to the family. The last buyer, a widow, continued to buy locally and ran a small store at the entrance to the village.

Tourism in the valley is not a dependable market for most weavers. Bailón Corres (1979: 100) notes that only 10 percent of textile sales are made directly to tourists. The majority of tapetes are exported or sold nationally. While the market remains centered in Teotitlán and Oaxaca City, demand is determined in the United States, Europe, and Japan. Currently, there are a few Santañeros trying to gain more direct access to the market. Three households worked with exporters on special orders in the spring of 1993. Village women are independently involved in a state-run cooperative through DIF (*Desarrollo Integral Familiar*—a national family support program) and fifteen weavers are involved in a village cooperative. However, the power and control of Teotiteco businesspeople make it difficult for Santañeros to break into the direct export market (see Cohen 1998, 1999).

Teotitlán's ascendancy is due as much to geography as anything else. It is the closest weaving community to Oaxaca City, and therefore the first, and often the only, stop on a tour. Many exporters who work in the treadle-loom market make their first connections with local weavers as tourists (see Wood 1995). Teotiteco businesspeople manage these connections and will contract with tour guides to build a clientele (Cohen 1998).

Teotitlán is also of historical importance as a dominant population center in the valley, one that vied for prestige and power with Tlacolula (Stephen 1991b). Regular bus service between Teotitlán and Oaxaca City also benefits Teotiteco weavers and merchants. Santa Ana, on the other hand, began as a small settlement dependent on Teotitlán. It remains a smaller community, removed from the tourist path. A visitor must transfer first in Tlacolula to a local bus to get to Santa Ana, and it was only in 1984 that bus service began between Tlacolula and Santa Ana.

The decline in local buyers is a response to the control Teotitecos exercise over the textile industry as a whole. Teotitlán's buyers and exporters control at least 40 percent of the weavings produced in Santa Ana (Cook and Binford 1990: 89). Surveys in 1992 indicate that the number of tapetes going to Teotitlán was over 60 percent of the total number of tapetes produced. Shop owners, buyers, and patrons also exert control over the textile industry through their definition of style and design. Patrons are particular about what they will and will not buy. Working with exporters, they promote specific styles and motifs. In 1992, 1993, and 1996, designs and colors taken from the art of the Navajo Indians of the United States were in vogue.

The rhetoric and history of weaving in the region also influence and enhance Teotitlán's advantage. Most popular writing on the area, and especially reportage intended for tourists, focuses on the woven art of Teotitlán (for example, see Freundheim 1988; Oglesby 1940). There may be no mention of the existence of Santa Ana as an additional weaving community. Where Santa Ana's textiles are mentioned, they are usually described as poor comparisons to the high-quality Teotiteco work. Professional writing on the region focuses on Teotitlán, setting it apart from Santa Ana, Díaz Ordaz, and San Miguel. Anthropological studies also suggest that Teotitecos produce the highest quality textiles available (Cohen 1990; Cook and Binford 1990: 89; Stephen 1991b: 136).

Experience and skill are important considerations in any discussion of the quality of goods produced by a population. There are more "tourist-influenced" designs and commercial textiles coming out of Santa Ana, and the rate of innovation in color schemes, designs, and sizes is higher in Teotitlán. However, the differences between the communities owe more to the control of Teotitlán's merchants than any measure of skill. It is also likely that Santañero textiles, when well produced, are sold in Teotitlán as local goods, and when Teotitecos weave poorly, their wares are sold as products of Santa Ana.[12]

Migration

Many Santañeros are turning to migration, given the uncertainty of farming, the low return on weaving, the lack of wage labor, and the growing demand by villagers for goods and services. According to the 1990 census, 78.7 percent of the working population in the state of Oaxaca made no more than twice the minimum wage of 9,920 pesos per day (or approximately $3.30).[13] During our stay (1992–1993), the minimum wage rose to 15,000 pesos (converted to 15 nuevos pesos in January 1993 and worth about $5.00). Nearly 25 percent of working Oaxacans above the age of twelve earned no direct return for their employment and were instead engaged in unpaid labor in family businesses (INEGI 1992a).[14]

A difficult situation has been made even more complicated by the ongoing crisis in Mexico's economy. In response, many Mexicans choose to migrate, and the percentage of rural Oaxacan workers leaving has rapidly increased over time (CONAPO 1987).[15] With few alternatives open to Santañeros who want to "advance themselves," many villagers are migrating to the United States (see Embriz 1993; Rouse 1991; Smith 1992). Nearly every Santañero family has at least one member in the United States, Mexico City, or another part of Mexico, working to earn cash.

Migrants from Santa Ana follow a circular pattern in their movements (Hulshof 1991). Throughout a family's life cycle, members leave at regular intervals to meet particular goals (see Tables 2.3 and 2.4). Typically, men migrate in greater numbers than women; however, there are a growing number of women either leaving Santa Ana alone or with their families.

Santañero men migrate first to finance their formal wedding ceremonies. Women usually remain in the village, caring for children.[16] Newlyweds hope to build their own home as soon after their wedding as possible. Thus, a second period of migration follows as the individual migrates again, this time to earn enough cash to build a home. Throughout the expansion of the family, further episodes of migration take place. These occur around life-cycle rituals, and as a man moves up the political and social hierarchy of the community. During periods of residence in the village, he fulfills his commitment to community service, taking a role in one of the many village committees (see Chapter Six). Between periods of service he migrates again, in part to replenish savings that may have gone to community programs and fiestas (Conway and Cohen 1998; Smith 1992).

The process of migration has changed dramatically since the 1950s,

Table 2.3 Number of Trips and Lengths of Stay for 36 Migrants

Length of Stay	One Trip	Two Trips	Three Trips	Three Trips or More
Less Than 6 Months	1	1	1	2
Less Than 1 Year			5	1
1–1.9 years	3	4	7	
2–2.9 years	2	1		
3–3.9 years		3	2	
4–4.9 years				
5–5.9 years	2			
6–6.9 years		1		
7–7.9 years	2			
8–8.9 years	1			
9–9.9 years				
10 or more years			1	

when Santañeros migrated in small numbers as braceros or to work on coastal plantations. One informant recalled carrying candies into highland Chiapas villages for a commission of a few pesos a day. Contemporary Santañero migrants leave for the United States, and typically live in or around Santa Monica, although some have traveled as far as Michigan, Kentucky, and Hawaii. A few men have green cards and fondly recall the Reagan administration's amnesty program. Others have entered marriages of convenience to get their "papers."

Once in the receiving community, the migrant enters a social web which reproduces and parallels networks in Santa Ana (see next chapters). The experience of Santañeros in the United States is unlike the media's image of the Mexican migrants as frightened and solitary individuals dashing across the Rio Grande, or paying *coyotes* (professional smugglers) to be smuggled across the border. Santañero migration is well established, and most migrants leave for the United States with a goal in mind. Often a Santañero is met by a relative at the border, lending the process the quality of a long-distance commute.

There are a variety of jobs that attract the migrant; among them are agricultural fieldwork, gardening, and construction. Through the early to

Table 2.4 Employment and Migration in 1996

Work Description	Workers	Migrations
Campesino	6	9
Independent weaver	10	35
Contract weaver	5	8
Professional	1	2
Curandera	1	0
Housewife/Contract weaver	1	2
Baker/Campesino	1	2
Campesino/Independent weaver	11	27
Campesino/Contract weaver	11	14
Campesano/Textile merchant/Independent weaver	1	27
Independent weaver/Business owner	1	2
Campesino/Independent weaver/Business owner	1	2
Contract weaver/Campesino/Carpenter	1	3
Campesino/Textile merchant	2	0
Contract weaver/Professional	1	0

mid-1990s, most Santañero migrants were working in family restaurants. Jobs often became the property of a family or set of individuals who regularly replaced one another in a position. Just as social networks tie individuals and families together in Santa Ana, the same relationships are at work in the United States (see Hirabayashi 1993). Santañeros in the United States celebrate fiestas and organize themselves to aid others who may need help.

Growing trends in migration are for an entire family to move, to follow the movement of the family head, and to establish a new family by marriage in the United States (Massey et al. 1994). Currently there are a few Santañeros who have married American women. It is still too early to know what the long-term outcomes of migration mean for the community and its definition as a social place. However, there are first-generation North Americans who are the children of Santañero migrants and are only now visiting their parents' home community for the first time. For these children, being Santañero will likely be a quite different experience from that of their parents and grandparents.

Other Alternatives

Santañeros are also small-business owners. Bakers supply village needs and take their breads to market in Tlacolula. A few of the local teachers are from the village, and a handful of Santañeros commute to Oaxaca daily to teach in arts and music programs through the *Casa de la Cultura* (a Oaxacan Arts program), or to work in state government. The village boasts two brass bands and a *conjunto* (a quartet that uses electronic instruments and plays private fiestas around the area).

There are landless Santañeros who do not weave and have little to fall back on when it comes to making a living. Generally these men and women work as jornaleros and mozos, finding work wherever they can. Their efforts earn from three to five dollars a day. One neighbor who owned no land, and did not weave, tended the goats of a Oaxacan businessman. In addition to a small stipend, he was allowed to keep one of every two kids born to the herd.

Conclusions: Santañeros in the World Economy

Santañeros do not live in isolation, nor are they naive about the world or their place in the global economy. In fact, their primary means of economic advancement is to place themselves directly in international and transnational markets through commercial textile production and migration. Santañero textiles hang in homes as far away as Japan, and Santañeros themselves are working in restaurants that are at one end of distant, long-term migrations from their village.

Nevertheless, Santañeros have little control over the economic future of their town. They are a population that must respond to international shifts in labor market demands as well as trends in consumer styles and tastes (Cohen 1998). Demand for textiles develops far from Santa Ana in places like Santa Fe, New York City, and the major cities of Europe. That Santañeros remain in control of their means of production, but not their finished products, is a sign of the marginal economic return on weaving and the lack of control they exercise over marketing (see Smith 1984).

Migration is a growing alternative and carries with it higher wages and good job prospects, since there is no shortage of low-status work in the

United States. However, migration is not without its personal and social costs, which include separation from family and friends. A change in the economy of the United States or Mexico can affect migration. The economic boom ongoing in the United States offers many opportunities for the Santañero migrant. On the other hand, there are Santañeros who have returned to the village and have decided not to pursue migrant work further. These returnees describe their experience as quite stressful. Much of their concern comes from the tensions that surround migration and rising anti-migrant sentiment among North Americans (particularly in California).

Eric Wolf (1986: 216–217) argues for a bridge between the analysis of social structures and individual decision making in his reconsideration of peasant studies:

> Recently, anthropologists have increasingly been tempted to divorce social behavior from culturally encoded symbolic forms, rather than to inquire into the ongoing dialectical interpenetration of these two realms.

One goal of my examination of cooperation in Santa Ana is to meet Wolf's challenge (and see Roseberry 1989). With these two preliminary chapters, I have outlined Santa Ana's history and economy, and established a framework for the consideration of cooperation. I begin the examination of cooperative relationships with a discussion of its place in the Santañero family. My intention is to define the way in which cooperation becomes the idiom through which Santañeros not only deal with one another, but also the structure through which villagers interact and interpret the world.

Chapter Three

Patterns of Cooperation
in the Santañero Household

I can go like this [walks up to the altar in the church] to the saint
and ask for a car or a yunta or whatever I want to have. I take an
offering and tell the image that I want to buy this. I might get a
figure of what I want and put it in the church. There is a place in the
church that is full of *milagros*. We call them milagros—they are small
figures. If one has a desire, you bring the figure to the altar and leave
it there to be guarded and then wait to get it. You've asked and so
you have to wait. In the United States you work, you don't need to
ask, you don't need to wait. Here too we work, but it isn't the
same—you make very little. You have to work hard here, and the
saints, they help us.

—Aron Sánchez explaining why Santañeros make *promesas*
(pledges or promises) to saints

ARON'S STATEMENT summarizes the realities of village life. Santañeros are part of an economy that reaches well beyond the community. In the previous chapter, I pointed out some ways all of us (here
I mean Santañeros and North Americans) are bound by the global market
system. Aron has hopes and dreams, and wants and desires, for himself
and his family with which we can easily identify. Yet, even with a shared
economy and desires, there are many differences between Aron Sánchez's
life (as representative of all Santañeros) and the life of the average North
American.

Our situations are informed by related but different histories, similar
but divergent cultural practices, and parallel social relationships that remain organized around different values and ideas about self and society.

Central to this difference is the taken-for-granted attitude most North Americans have toward such complex needs as clean water, electricity, education, and transportation. Furthermore, the social identities of most North Americans are arguably more malleable and open to various possibilities to a degree not found in rural Mexico. And while we admit the presence of inequality and injustice in North American society, the extent of that inequality does not typically create the kinds of marginalities that are found throughout the Third World.

The legacies of marginality and dependency are painted across the landscape of most indigenous and peasant communities in rural Mexico. The history of neglect that marks these communities can add a sense of desperation to the struggle to improve standards of living and foster a future that is better than the past. Thus, while Aron Sánchez shares our dreams and hopes, he starts at an economic place well below the average American mark. The first two chapters outlined how local patterns of history, society, and economy combine to create and re-create Santa Ana as a social setting in which Aron and his compatriots must act. Of particular importance in the discussion was the rapid growth of the village's population over the last thirty years, the rise of weaving for export, the decline of subsistence-based agriculture, and the rapid arrival of large-scale emigration of the community's youth that occurred within Mexico (primarily to Tapachula, Chiapas) and transnationally (to enclaves in Santa Monica, California, for example).

By following these patterns of change and development in Santa Ana, one can localize the impact of macro-level global processes (Kearney 1996). We can begin to define what these changes mean to the average Santañero and describe how Santañeros respond to external pressures. These are difficult issues that have occupied the field of anthropology over the years. Nevertheless, it is possible to use the example of Santa Ana to advance anthropology's quest to understand the consequences of socio-economic change.

The next three chapters describe Santañero responses to global capitalism. In doing so, the investigation shifts from the definition of the macro-level forces that influence local cultural patterns to an analysis of the ways in which people cope with their changing world. The point is not to become bogged down in what Arizpe (1981: 628) refers to as "personal idiosyncrasies." Rather, it is to concentrate on the ways in which the stories we hear reveal social patterns.

First, let us look at Aron's quote in more detail and move beyond macro-structural explanations of social change (although never losing sight of their importance). He tells us, "In the United States you work, you don't need to ask [a saint for support and aid], you don't need to wait. Here too we work, but it isn't the same, you [Santañeros in general] make very little. You have to work hard here, and the saints, they help us." His statement highlights the importance of reciprocal aid and its central role in Santañero society. People are not fatalistic. They do not place their future in the hands of supernatural forces. Rather, they are involved in socially constructed relationships that demand their time and effort, and in response, create networks of support and aid (Axelrod 1984; Kropotkin 1989). It is the structure of cooperation within the household that interests us in this chapter.[1]

Cooperation (often framed as the reciprocal exchange of goods and services or shared support) is the foundation upon which Santañero society is organized and through which it is produced, reproduced, and enacted. Cooperation and reciprocity carry a sense of tradition and a quality of mutual trust and respect in their performance. Cooperative relationships can be lovingly developed, but they can also be exploitative, abusive, and costly (in social and economic terms). It is no surprise, then, that cooperation is often described as a burden. It is a weight that can and does overwhelm some villagers (and not only the poor). Reciprocal contracts are established for altruistic as well as selfish reasons, to honor as well as contest status and place in local society.

For most Santañeros, cooperation is a strong organizing principle. But it is doubtful that individuals are driven by some innate force to cooperate. Their psychic well-being is not at risk of loss with the arrival of capitalism (see Redfield 1950). Nor are cooperative relationships simply the "glue" that drives the Santañero social order (see, for example, Durkheim 1964). Yes, relationships of mutual aid are readily entered into, and cooperation is an important resource, depended upon and cherished. Nevertheless, cooperation is also an arena for contest and conflict and for the negotiation and renegotiation of meaning (see Portes and Landolt 1996; Roseberry 1996; Smith 1989). The reality of cooperation, then, is as present in the affectionate support a parent gives his or her children as it is in the grudging payment of guelaguetza or the arm-twisting that often accompanies the organization of tequio.

Cooperation is rooted in shared history and daily practice, and it remains the most ambivalent of forces (El-Guindi and Selby 1976). The repetitive, historical expectedness of these relationships (perhaps also the

Preparing tamales

fear of not knowing what might occur if they were not there) leaves little that is uncertain (Axelrod 1997). Nevertheless, as pointed out above, cooperation is an individual response, not one motivated by communal force. Cooperation as a structurally powerful social measure develops from the "consequences of emulative performances" (Turner 1994). In other words, cooperation works and in its success is repeated, becoming a patterned behavior that seems rooted in the very fabric of Santañero society. To understand how cooperation and reciprocity become powerful frames of reference demands a focus on the various levels at which these relationships are found: in the family/household, between households, and within the community at large. In this chapter, we begin in the household, the most fundamental level of social interaction for Santañeros.

The Santañero Household

The opening of this chapter comes from an interview with Aron Sánchez, a man whom I dealt with on a nearly daily basis.[2] His statement high-

A meal during harvest time

lights the importance of cooperation in his description of the promesas in Santañero spiritual life. Part of the message is that life in Santa Ana is difficult and uncertain. A second element, and the one we are most interested in for the moment, is the reciprocal relationship that the promesa creates between saint and individual (and see Brandes 1988). When a Santañero asks for assistance, he or she is not asking for a handout, nor does he or she expect support (or good fortune) to come freely. The key to the promesa, and the central feature of the reciprocal relationships, is the importance of correctly exercising cooperation and meeting the social expectation of reciprocity.

A cooperative relationship demands that nothing be given for free, and nothing is received without anticipating a debt. Put bluntly, social transfers are almost never fully altruistic acts. Thus, it should come as no surprise that an agreement of mutual support (whether corporeal or spiritual) is not a relationship entered into lightly. Rules are followed and roles managed to meet the situation at hand. The Santañero known for lying does not find it easy to secure support. The wealthy villager who declines to cooperate may find his social position vis-à-vis others in doubt. On the other hand, the poor household that invests wisely will discover its status and prestige enhanced in relation to other households. The same pattern is at work in the promesa. The agreement between a saint and an individual (no matter the subject, from good luck in a basketball game to the healing of an infirmity) is no guarantee of success. It is up to the individual to "act well." To perform a role correctly is to prove, and in the process, enhance social place and status. The outcome, however, is not guaranteed. No relationship works without the investment of time and energy. Cooperation comes at a cost. And while losses can mount, a balance among Santañeros is usually established through these relationships (see Monaghan 1995; Nader 1990).

Learning social rules takes place primarily in the home and through constant participation in the cooperative relationships that follow Santañeros throughout their lives. It must be emphasized that the role of cooperation in the daily life of the individual is not deterministic. It does not "mold" action. Not all Santañeros choose to cooperate. Those that do, do not always cite similar reasons or explanations for their actions. As will become clear, cooperative relationships are used in the successful construction and reproduction of self, and in the process, the reproduction of society, but never because it is the only way to act (see also Monaghan 1995; Watanabe 1992).[3]

Cooperative relationships in the Santañero household are organized and allocated along formal and informal lines and are dependent upon numerous local and exogenous factors. There is the tendency to assume that social processes of the sorts Santañeros are involved in (a growing economy, transnational migration, and export markets), change the very structure of the household and family (and typically these changes are for the worse; see Le Play, cited in Zimmerman and Frampton 1935: 362). Wellman (1979: 104) defines the perceived decline in sociability in response to change as "community lost" in his critique of communal studies in sociology. The "community lost" model is built upon the assumption that expanding capitalist markets and increasing divisions of labor must lead to weakened communal solidarities. On the other hand, there is evidence that a growth or revival of community can take place with the arrival of capitalism (Campbell 1994; Durand et al. 1996a; Smith 1992). The continued viability of the Santañero household and the importance of cooperation in Santañero society, given the rise of migration, new markets, and the expanded presence of the state in local affairs, is an opportunity to explore models of the community and assumptions concerning sociability (and see Wilson 1993).

Señor Valeriano cleaning his wife's grave, Día de los Muertos, 1992

Defining the Household as a Unit of Study

Wilk approaches the household not as a static social structure, distinguished by common residency, but as a dynamic focus for social action (1991). He defines a model of the household that takes account of social process and social dynamics, life courses, changes in cultural beliefs, demography, economy, and so forth (and see Wilk 1989). "Households are depicted as social units that organize production and consumption activities" through time and in response to or anticipation of natural and constructed environments and economies (Wilk 1991: 39–40). Using such a definition moves well beyond putative generalization and the assumptions such generalizations contain. In effect, we capture the dynamic nature of the household and its changing role through time.

This dynamic approach to the household also moves the analysis away from the deterministic approaches to native peoples that typically homogenize descriptions. A cursory review of Santa Ana reveals the differences that exist among Santañero households (although morphologically the village appears uniformly organized into nuclear units that follow a neo-local residency pattern). The wealthy and successful members of the community live a life removed from the struggles of neighbors who may to this day live in cane structures and eat little more than beans, salsa, and tortillas. Furthermore, as with many Mesoamerican communities, families of varying status are spread in an organized pattern across the landscape (Royce 1981). High-status households are concentrated around the central plaza, even as the village expands into new *colonias* (neighborhoods) that climb the piedmont. Households compete and come together in a variety of ways to organize for change and to challenge the state and the economic control of Teotitecos. Holding the system together are dynamic ties of reciprocity and cooperation.

Anthropologists have noted the importance of cooperation in Zapotec society since Parsons first worked in the central valley in the 1930s (see Leslie 1960; Nader 1969; Parsons 1936; Stephen 1991b). In the family, the reality and rhetoric of cooperation are powerful. They tie children in service to their parents, especially their mother, and to one another. The services rendered by children and expected by their parents are reinforced through didactic, discursive, imitative, and practical experiences (see Mathews 1992: 141). Put simply, Santañeros cooperate. They talk about cooperation. They use their actions and the actions of others to measure and mark social norms. Parsons described the situation in *Mitla* (1936: 68):

> The daily life between related families is intimate, even when a cactus hedge is planted between their yards. The children play together; the women visit, they borrow things from each other, they exchange little services. There is an attitude of reciprocal helpfulness in all the little affairs of the day, as well as in major concerns.

Actions and words come together to educate children and remind adults what is considered appropriate and expected. In Santa Ana, cooperative behavior within the household includes sharing in housework, assisting in the preparation of materials for weaving, herding animals, working in the fields, working without pay in family businesses, and contributing money made in wage labor or migration to the family's common fund. Cook (1984: 192) notes this pattern of unpaid familial labor, and the surrender of funds to the head of the household is typical of most simple commodity-producing communities throughout Oaxaca, as well as Mexico and the Third World. At a practical level, these funds secure the capital needed to meet the reproductive costs (food and other expenses incurred in the maintenance of the home and family) of the household. However, these activities also serve to produce meaning, identity, and ideology, or what Watanabe describes as the conventions of morality and responsibility (1992). Such constructions highlight a "shared" way of being and action, and as cooperative relationships reach beyond the immediate family (in both words and practice), they become a central feature in the creation and maintenance of the community as a social place.

Parents frame their behaviors and actions in terms of altruism and industriousness, whether real or imagined (Leslie 1960: 72).[4] Señor Mendoza, like most heads of households, described his life as "one of burdens and expenses, of hard work and suffering," all done in the name of his children and family. Similarly, children follow the lead of their parents, creating simpler forms of cooperation in relationships with relatives, friends, and peers. They are expected to participate in the maintenance of the household. Quickly they learn how to organize their actions in and out of the house.

A young boy's first responsibilities to his household often are herding animals and lending a hand at household projects (whether the help is useful or not). A boy's role increases in importance with age and ability. Martín (now thirty-nine) recalled his excitement at the prospect of working in the fields:

> When I was growing up, I couldn't wait to work with my dad. He would go to his land and I would ask over and over, "Can I come and help?" He would hold up his basket and tell me, "No, not until you are big enough to carry this [motioning to a large basket] on your back . . . and full!" So I would stay home. Finally, he began to take me to the fields, I would carry his machete, oh, it was almost as big as I was, but I carried it, and I would try and help, but it is difficult work, and I really wasn't big enough. Now look at my kids, they bother me to come to the fields. Sometimes I bring them, but frankly they are too small.

Young girls help around the house and may herd a family's animals as well. This is especially true among families with no sons. Minerva Aquino described her childhood one afternoon as we collected firewood:

> My poor departed father taught me how to plant, to cut *linea* [firewood], how to drive a yunta, because he didn't have a son. When I was young I worked just like a boy, and look at me at sixty-three years, I am still working hard.

A daughter's role in the household and family also grows in importance with age. Most teenage girls learn to weave and work alongside parents in support of the family. Children also learn to cooperate as they play together and mimic their parents and elders. Sitting in the plaza, I watched young boys form groups that mirrored the actions of older men. The boys played basketball and other games and served one another soft drinks with the solemnity men maintain when drinking mescal at fiestas. As children gain skills, they will assist the family in its textile production. First they may be asked to prepare bobbins of yarn, clean finished tapetes, and tie off the loose threads on a completed project. Only later will the children begin to weave alongside other family members. Pedro, a sixty-eight-year-old Santañero, told this story:

> My poor father taught me. But he taught me what they made before; it was a tapete called *tapete café* [tan weaving]. You don't know it, that is what I first learned when I was eighteen years old. I began to weave *rayados;* we called another *tapetes de las cintas* [various designs based on horizontal bands of different colored yarns] that were only lines. That was the second kind I wove. After that my father taught me to weave with eagles, that are called *aguila en el aire* [eagle in the air], that is what I did, I remember I was twenty years old. Then I began to weave *aguila en banda* [a design based on the Mexican national flag].

Many children learn to weave as apprentices, exchanging labor for instruction. Such relationships are mutually beneficial. The children learn to weave and the instructor is aided by additional sets of hands that he or she does not pay. These relationships also follow a reciprocal model; the knowledge of the instructor is exchanged for the services of the students. The exchange can reach beyond the apprenticeship, and the bond between artisan and students is often the basis for future associations. Often a mentor in such a setting is a relative and/or *compadre/comadre* (godfather or godmother), and the relationship creates a long-term and enduring social bond that extends beyond the workplace.

There are many reasons why young weavers seek apprenticeship with accomplished weavers. First, many need training and instruction that can only come from an excellent weaver. Second, a good weaver is not always a good teacher. Third, a minority of informants stated that their fathers did not encourage their specialization. They explained their fathers' fear of losing mano de obra contracts and workers easily controlled (i.e., their children) to the market for upscale products.

Typical, Crisis, and Successful Households

Acheson's (1996) recent analysis of artisan production in northern Mexico offers an approach that takes account of household-based social practices, demography, and family-based decision making. He categorizes Purepecha households into three types—typical, disaster (what I call "crisis"), and successful—following local definitions and in response to patterns of investment and resource pooling. The typical household is marked by well-organized pooling, but little investment or entrepreneurism. Crisis households are limited poolers and tend to spend funds haphazardly as they move from one disaster to another. The successful household, on the other hand, pools and invests for planned economic growth. Using the examples of typical, crisis, and successful households to illustrate the dynamic nature of cooperation in the Santañero household offers us the opportunity to understand patterns of cooperation better.

Typical Household I, Flor and Vera Sánchez

Two sisters with whom Maria became especially close during our stay supported their household of five through contract weaving. Flor (thirty-one) and Vera (twenty-one) Sánchez learned to weave from their father when they were in their teens. Flor told us, "It only took a day to learn, and it is work I like to do." Vera has a young daughter with her common-law husband, Jorge Aquino.[5] Vera and her sister spend on average six to eight hours daily weaving *servilletas* (small napkin and placemat-sized textiles) for their patron in Teotitlán. Their father also weaves; however, his loom is currently disassembled. Two standard looms fill a one-room *carrizo* (cane) structure lit by a naked bulb. Their compound includes two additional cane rooms and a one-room adobe structure completed in the spring of 1993. The compound is in the westernmost colonia, balanced against the mountainside, and open to the constant blowing of the winds.

Each Sunday we watched their Teotiteco patron drive up the dirt road to their compound in his late-model Ford truck. Flor and Vera earned approximately two dollars for a completed tapete. They also received a new supply of yarns and design specifications for the coming week's order. Flor makes three or four complete weavings in a day. Vera could weave more; however, she divides her time between work and the care of her daughter. The sisters together earn approximately seventy dollars in an average week. This is enough money to cover food and the cost of hauling two hundred gallons of water a week to their home, but little else.[6]

Don Francisco (their father) had not used his loom in more than two years. He split his time between work on the new room, farming, and community service he took on in the name of Tomas, a son who migrated to the United States. Once the rains return, Don Francisco will plant a crop of corn on a one-half hectare plot of third-class land. As he told me one day, "Even if it rains I don't get much corn; it is very tired. It's all third-class land." However, working his land and helping his children, and in return receiving their support, allows him to supplement the household budget. Don Francisco's wife, Consuela, maintains the household and prepares yarns for weaving. She does not weave herself and says she was never taught. A bad week in their household was always apparent. Instead of a truck hauling water to the household, Don Francisco would carry two large water tins tied to a yoke down into town to fill with water at a municipal well.

To supplement the household's income, Doña Consuela sells tortillas and eggs. We often watched her walking down to the center of town to purchase a few kilograms of corn from the community's CONASUPO store.[7] She took the corn home, soaked it in a lime mixture—then if the family had the money—she or one daughter went to the grinder. Otherwise, the first grinding was done at home by kneeling at a *metate* (grinding stone) for hours, working the corn into a coarse meal. After a second grinding that was always done at home, Consuela pressed fresh tortillas, cooking them on a *comal* (an earthenware griddle) set over an open fire in the corner of her kitchen (a cane room with a dirt floor). She earned a few thousand pesos (two to five dollars) every few days to contribute to the household from the sale of tortillas door-to-door.[8]

Vera is in a unión libre with Jorge, a young man who is working as a migrant in the United States. A house site was ready for them below

Francisco and Consuela's main homesite. At the site were the supplies that Vera bought with funds remitted by Jorge. In 1993, he visited for the first time in three years and met his daughter (she was born after he had left for the United States). It was an awkward situation. Vera had returned to her family because, she said, her in-laws were making her life miserable. When Jorge arrived, rather than force the point, he went to stay with Vera, creating some tensions between the families. He arrived in early spring, a time when there is little to do around the village. The weaving market is usually depressed following the major tourist holidays of Christmas and Easter. The planting season had yet to begin and there are no major celebrations on the local calendar. There were also few supplies to complete much work on Vera and Jorge's new home. In the end Jorge stayed about a month, spent time with his daughter, and enjoyed old friends, but returned to the United States where he remained for another two years.

Vera and Flor's situation is typical, although they are a little older than most children who continue to live in their natal home and turn funds over to the head of household to pool in anticipation of familial needs. Thus, an assortment of economic strategies (weaving, farming, migration, and food preparation) combine to maintain the Sánchez household.

Typical Household II, Mario Mendoza

Mario Mendoza (twenty and unmarried) lived and wove with his father and mother. He turned finished textiles over to his father, who sought buyers in Teotitlán. Mario, his father, and his mother weave together to support four younger children who attend school. Mario does not receive income directly from his weaving. If he wants money, he must ask for it from his father. This requirement reinforces the hierarchy in the home and emphasizes Mario's subordinate position. The situation is awkward for Mario. He had spent two years away from the village, working in the United States; during his sojourn he regularly remitted funds to support his natal family. His father and mother did not encourage his marrying. He thinks they fear losing his labor power and income to a new household.

Although he had a girlfriend and could manage his own household, Mario Mendoza chooses to remain with his natal family. Together, the adults made a good living by local standards. Their home was comfortable, and with the funds Mario earned as a migrant, it was well appointed. Mario and his father work off and on with the village's textile cooperative, the Artisans' Society, and have invested limited funds in an attempt to enhance their position in the local market. Mario purchased a good camera and was creating a well-photographed brochure of the family's textiles.

Typical Household III, Fernando and Emilia Aquino

I met Fernando Aquino (thirty-three) early in my stay. He was finishing his cargo assignment as the treasurer of the *Comité del Museo Shan-Dany* (the Shan-Dany Museum committee) and together, we would translate descriptive texts for the galleries (see Cohen 1989). We regularly discussed our lives, dreams, and hopes. Fernando described his experiences working in the United States and his intentions to return after completing his cargo. At the time, I did not realize that my key informant planned to leave in the middle of my project.

Fernando, his wife Emilia (thirty-one), and their children live in a compound near the center of town. The compound is large, and homes belonging to Fernando's parents and siblings also open onto a shared patio (a pattern noted by Hunt and Nash 1967; Parsons 1936: 66). Child care typically falls on women present in the solar (Fernando's grandmother and a teenage daughter), and someone is always available to watch, feed, and care for the children. In the solar, each nuclear family forms a separate household with an independent kitchen and budget. There is a fluid movement of children, food, goods, and cooperative support. However, inter-familial cooperation does not include commercial activities such as textile production. Weaving is a venture independently pursued by each family.

Fernando and his father have separate contracts with the same Teotiteco intermediary. Fernando and Emilia spend most of their time weaving on contract with their Teotiteco patron. Their oldest son (fourteen) also weaves. Together, they produce tourist-quality textiles of standard designs and sizes. Fernando farms one-half hectare of land that he received as collateral for a loan made six years ago. He had use of the plot for nine years (1986–1995); three more years were left on the contract in 1992. After the nine years, the loan was to be repaid in full. The contract was formal and was witnessed by members of the village's central authority. The formal status of the loan gave Fernando recourse if he had not been paid at the end of the agreed period (which he was). Had the loan not been repaid, Fernando would have had the opportunity to claim the land as his own, or work out a new contract and new payment or use schedule with the owner. The agreement worked to Fernando's advantage since he owned no land.

Fernando's father, Gregorio, owns one hectare of third-class land. Gregorio's land should ideally be divided equally among his children (four sons and six daughters) at his death (see Nader 1969: 348). In reality, the land will likely go to his oldest son. Daughters will receive minor property or wealth, and the remaining sons will divide additional goods. This formula maintains the land's integrity and limits the claims of daughters, who are now the responsibilities of their husbands' families. The youngest son (a boy of only fifteen years) will inherit the homesite before Gregorio's death. In exchange, he will care for his parents in their old age. Finally, the other sons will divide up remaining goods, including looms, animals, and some luxury items (see Nader 1990: 38).

Fernando returned to the United States in November 1992 to earn funds to purchase land for sale near Tlacolula's border with Santa Ana. He decided to leave for San Diego after harvesting a wilted crop of corn.

Fernando did not ask his brothers or friends to help with the harvest (aid he gave to his father without question). Instead, he paid four men to work two full days (each earned approximately five dollars for their efforts) harvesting the field and cutting and bundling the *zacate* (dried corn stalks) to sell as feed. The cost of labor, which included two meals each day (approximately twenty dollars total), was offset by the income that the zacate generated (approximately fifty dollars). This small-scale profiteering is typical of the area. It is one way to make ends meet. It is also a difficult way to try to improve a household's overall living standard or status (see Acheson 1972).

The decision to pay workers rather than to seek reciprocal aid may seem odd given the central role reciprocal relationships play in the village. However, in conversations, Fernando reminded me he was leaving for the United States. To ask men for support would be to place himself in a position of social debt that might be hard to repay in the short term. Furthermore, by helping his father, but completing his harvest with paid workers, he left his family with others owing it assistance. Emilia can collect these cooperative debts during Fernando's absence. This example again points to what we can call the pragmatics of cooperation. Fernando's actions are not so much an indication of the weakness of cooperative bonds in a changing world; rather, they are a sign of the ways in which Santañeros weigh the costs and benefits of new reciprocal ties. Cooperation is not an unlimited resource. It is finite and comes with real costs. Asking for assistance on a project means that at some future point, that assistance will be recalled. Thus, Santañeros need to weigh the choice to cooperate. In certain situations, like Fernando's, Santañeros may choose to formally hire workers rather than incur new social debts.

After completing his cargo service to the museum and training the replacement members of the comité, Fernando prepared to leave. A large *compromiso* (party) was thrown for Fernando by his compadre, who is also his uncle. These and other family-based, life-cycle celebrations (baptisms and weddings, for example) are taking the place of traditional communal events and *mayordomías* (saints' day celebrations). The celebrations are new ways in which a household commemorates and defines its status vis-à-vis other households (Stephen 1991b: 181). At the party, *barbacoa de chivo* (barbecued goat) was served with plenty of mescal. One of the community's brass bands was hired to play music, and relatives, compadres, and guelaguetza partners attended. The party, a two-day affair, was a success. Most *invitados* (guests) were drunk and crying as the compromiso ended to the sound of fireworks in the early hours of the morning. When Fernando left for the United States, we piled into our car for the ride to the airport to see him off.

With Fernando gone, Emilia was left in charge of the household. She continued to weave with her oldest son to keep up with their contracts. The oldest daughters (twelve and ten) helped in the kitchen when they were not in school. Emilia often took them out of school to help in the house and with the younger children, allowing herself time to weave. In addition, the entire family spent more time with Emilia's parents, where she could leave the children when necessary. Fernando sent money, but remittances were earmarked for the future, not to meet immediate needs.[9]

Male heads of households complain of the sacrifices they make for their families. They typically frame statements in the following terms, "I only do this [migrating, for example] for the good of my family, to give my children a proper home, to advance ourselves." Yet, for a wife and the older children left behind, there are intensified economic burdens and stresses. There is little evidence that remittances are unwisely invested on consumer goods by a household—instead, remittances are often hoarded for investment in major projects such as house building, business start-ups, and communal expenses. Wives and children struggle to make ends meet; and over the first few months of Fernando's absence, Emilia was hard-pressed. In the end she borrowed money from friends and relatives to cover her expenses.

Crisis Household, Emiliano García

Emiliano García had some success as a migrant in the United States. He earned a green card during the Reagan administration's amnesty program and returned to Santa Ana in 1989 with a car. However, three years later he had little to show for his sojourn. The home he hoped to finish with saved earnings remained half-built, and his family continued to live in two carrizo structures. His children were described as difficult and ill-behaved by neighbors and relatives. Both he and his wife had reputations as petty thieves among Santa Ana's shop owners. In spite of his reputation, Emiliano asserted his innocence and altruism:

> I taught my brother how to weave, I brought him to the United States, I gave him a car, I taught him how to speak English, and what does he do? He beats my kids, steals my zacate; he sold the car and now he is turning my mother against me.

I heard this story from Emiliano often. Typically his tale of woe was accompanied by a request for a loan. I spent time with Emiliano's extended family and worked with his mother on several occasions. I also worked closely with his brothers on community projects. My experiences with Emiliano and my interactions with others around him revealed the many games he plays in an effort to manipulate the significance and meaning of cooperation. While he is sincere, he stretches the truth to serve his needs and is guilty of petty theft. His mother does not allow him into her home because he and his children have stolen money. The money they legitimately borrowed is not repaid. When I asked Emiliano what he thought was going on, he answered that the loans were payment for services rendered. His list of these services changed from day to day, and their value often increased over time. To be fair, Emiliano's younger brothers did receive a car from him. They assumed (perhaps wrongly) it was theirs to do with as they pleased. Correctly anticipating that Emiliano would want it back later, they sold the vehicle and used the money to buy building supplies for their home. Much of the material they purchased, reinforced steel rods and cement, is now being used by Emiliano in the construction of his home. Emiliano's household, like the disaster households described by Acheson (1996), is marked by hoarding and ineffective investment. Emiliano used some funds to purchase heavy-duty farm equipment to start a small business as a hired field hand. Within months, the tools were broken, in need of repairs that he could not afford, and lacking fuel that was also out of reach.

When discussing Emiliano's actions with people beyond his immediate household, the responses remained consistently negative. Emiliano's misuse of altruism has led to a great deal of mistrust by others. Storekeepers do not advance him credit, he is not asked to serve on important committees, and his extended family has distanced itself from him. Here again we see that cooperative relationships are serious associations that are not lightly broken or misrepresented. The threat is not simply a personal one. It is much greater and goes to the heart of Santañero custom: the community will not long tolerate a threat to its traditions.

Successful Household, Alejandro and María Bautista

In the previous examples, we have followed the ways in which cooperative relationships (and in some instances, their illegitimate use) create the household as a physical and social unit. Cooperative relationships also are key elements as household members come together to expand into new businesses. María and Alejandro Bautista, a young couple with three small children, live in a large compound divided into three parts. One section is home to Alejandro's older brother, and the third to his brother's eldest son, who is nearly Alejandro's age. Alejandro's mother lives in the compound as well, in a room adjoining the eldest brother's home.

Alejandro's mother is a small-scale buyer and with a cousin, manages a stall in Oaxaca City's Mercado de Artesanías. Alejandro, his wife, his brother, nephew, and nephew's wife all produce textiles independently. They are skilled independent weavers and they often sell their textiles in the mercado. Ties to María's parents and siblings, who are also well-known local weavers, enhance the family's status and facilitate contacts with exporters and middlemen. Information on style changes, color schemes, and market demands allows Alejandro and María to plan for production. At times, the couple knows when to hoard tapetes in anticipation of a buyer; at other times, they sell, and even take a small loss, to avoid a drop in demand.

The adults in this compound (both men and women) have also spent time as migrants in the United States. Typically, one or two members of the family travel (usually a husband and wife together), and the remaining extended family members take on the added responsibility for child care and home maintenance. This accomplishes most goals, not the least of which is to allow the migrant to save earnings rather than spend them on family maintenance.

Alejandro and María work together, weaving, migrating, and caring for their children. Together, they have used funds saved from their sojourns and sales to purchase two sewing machines and open a tailor shop (Cohen 1998). The store runs much like a weaving workshop, with very little overhead and no hired employees. Alejandro describes the work as much easier than weaving, which places a great deal of strain on one's back. Combined with weaving, the shop helps the family generate enough income so that neither Alejandro nor María has had to think about migrating, an option to which neither looked forward.

Households and Cooperation

The five households described (three typical, one crisis, and one successful) cooperate to greater and lesser degrees in response to various needs (from basic maintenance and reproduction to economic expansion) and various goals (from the ambiguous actions of Emiliano, to the choices made by Mario, Fernando, Flor, and Vera). From these examples it should be obvious that decisions to cooperate are not irrational responses to deep-seated communal drives located in shared psychology (see the discussion in Goody 1993: 26). Individuals make decisions as members of households and in response to local history, individual and group needs, life-cycle stage, morality, and expectations. In addition, decisions are influenced by external economic, political, and social processes that include the market, educational systems, national trends, and macro-historical events (see Netting et al. 1984). Cooperation and reciprocity are thus the outcomes of choices made in response to a series of local and external processes and tempered by individual desires and expectations (see Turner 1994; Watanabe 1992). Alternative paths exist. Cooperation and reciprocal behavior are not deterministic social forces seated in the mind of homogeneous social beings. Flor could leave her natal home to live and work in Oaxaca City as many single women from rural villages have—as did one of her sisters (see Howell 1993b). Mario could stay in the United States, or marry and establish his own household away from the control of his father. But Flor and Mario remain in their natal homes and participate in the social maintenance of these households. They are not always content with their decisions. Mario is ambivalent about his position. He was proud of helping his family and caring for his siblings;

on the other hand, he was the butt of many jokes and often complained about turning income over to his father.

Flor and Vera, Mario, and Fernando and Emilia chose to cooperate as one way of guaranteeing the successful maintenance and reproduction of their households and families. They are responding to expectations and social pressures that they perceive as communal and which, in turn, motivate their decisions and actions. They cooperate because it is what they believe good Santañeros do. In doing so, they hope to please their families. They also know that rewards come to those who invest in locally sanctioned behaviors. Mario has gained a large measure of local status through his work as village secretary in the early 1990s.[10] Flor has a social network that a single woman living alone would likely lack. Fernando and Emilia have planned their reciprocal ties carefully to aid in household maintenance, while Fernando is working in the United States. Alejandro and María use their relationships to support the growth of their local business.

The altruism expected by a parent and framed in many statements about the ideal family is a sign of real household harmony. Nevertheless, children do not always react as expected to the demands of their families. There is evidence, physical, spoken, and implied, that supports the conclusion that children and young adults enact cooperation with little coercion (for example, Flor and Vera's actions and experiences). There are also real exploitative pressures found within most households. But, if cooperation were nothing more than exploitation misrepresented, few Santañeros would be persuaded to participate.

Cooperation in rural peasant communities is often described as exploitation masked by altruistic rhetoric and posturing (see Cook and Binford 1990; Peterson 1993; Stephen 1991b). First, there is the control of household finances by the male head of the family. Second, household funds are often distributed or shared unequally. Third, there is pressure on children to aid in household maintenance and reproduction through their unpaid labor in agriculture and textile production. Finally, perhaps the most blatant exploitation occurs when a father takes the money earned by a son or daughter working outside Santa Ana and refuses to redistribute the funds, instead using the money for his own entertainment.

One way children avoid familial demands and exploitation is to leave their home. A child can disappear with friends for a day, climbing into ranch lands to hide. Older children, typically sons and daughters over the age of eighteen, migrate and leave their responsibilities behind (although not without creating new sets of demands and responsibilities). The prospect of such an escape captured the attention of a young Santañero named Juan Sánchez. Juan had worked as part of an exhibition staged by the Shan-Dany Museum in the city of Tapachula.[11] He told me of meeting young women in the city, and of the opportunities that "abound" in this border city. It was a place where Juan thought a migrant would have "few cares" (and see Rouse 1991, 1992). The attraction was equal parts the allure of the new, the lack of familial responsibilities, and the change of pace from village life and full-time weaving. In addition, Tapachula was a boom town in 1993. Prices were low, and housing, work, and opportunities were plentiful. Add to this an ongoing fight between Juan and his wife, and the fantasy of Tapachula—the escape from household responsibility—was seductive.

There are also many Santañeros who go beyond the fantasy of escape and leave the village permanently. Women leave the village and families and strike out on new paths that carry them away from their subordinate positions in the rural household. Unfortunately, many of these women move into abusive and exploitative situations in unfamiliar urban settings as well. Many rural Oaxacan women move to the capital city of Oaxaca (sometimes as a first stage in a final migration to the United States). In Oaxaca City they enter a series of service and low-status jobs, perhaps attend school, and learn a trade. Many women remain in subordinate economic and social positions once in the city due to ethnicity and gender. However, there is an opportunity to exercise considerably more control over their lives and finances in the city than in a rural setting (Howell 1993a).

A new situation arises when Santañero children are born outside the village. Don Mauro has grandchildren who were born in the United States. These children maintain important social ties with their extended family in the United States and Mexico. However, their social lives are built around Los Angeles and Santa Monica, California, not Santa Ana and the goals of cooperation.

Another strategy used by some Santañeros to avoid familial and household demands is to ignore them. This is manifest in various actions, from choosing a new career outside the natal household, to outright resistance to the family's demands. Guadalupe (a friend from Teotitlán) left the village with her family's support, and completed a college degree in agronomy. Although she continued to participate in family celebrations, she no longer lived in the village. Distance did not eliminate, but it did limit, the burden her parents could place upon her.

Vera followed a more typical path for a Santañera. She moved in with the parents of her common-law husband after she became pregnant. She remained in their household and had her first child there. After her husband left for the United States, she worked as a member of her affinal family, contributing labor and earnings to the household as a weaver and homemaker. Claiming not to get along well with her in-laws, she returned to her natal home after her husband's departure. Now she works alongside Flor to support Don Francisco, Consuela, and Rosy. The active movement away from exploitation is an effective form of resistance, although one form of exploitation (by in-laws) is traded for another form of exploitation (by blood relatives), but one with which she is familiar. Vera's decision puts her in direct control of the money earned by her husband. Although she turns her earnings from textiles over to her father, she saves the remittances received from her husband and uses the funds to purchase building materials.

A Santañero can also exploit cooperative relationships by making an illegitimate claim of altruism and family support. To fictionalize one's altruism is difficult, as it demands the careful deployment of real action in support of the fallacious claims. To argue that your actions are cooperative can only work if at some point you have behaved in such a manner. For a Santañero to be considered altruistic, there needs to be some evidence of sacrifice. In the event real life catches up to illegitimate cooperative claims, altruistic posturing can backfire, as with Emiliano García.

These five examples are in many ways similar, but they are decidedly not equal. Flor and Vera's participation in cooperative relationships does not carry the coercive undertones of Mario's situation. Emiliano's experiences are quite different from those of Fernando and Emilia. The influences on patterns of cooperation include the life cycle of the individuals involved and the stage of their household's development, local and external economic forces, the gender of the individual household member upon whom we have focused, and the very desires of each social actor. Newly formed households have a very different set of needs than mature households. Expanding households in which children are young and cannot participate in effective social and economic reproduction are particularly difficult to maintain. Much of Fernando's decision to migrate is rooted in the high costs of maintaining a home with many young children. However, his experience as a migrant and with Emilia, and the recognition of just what the household needs to function effectively in his absence, all aid in his decision to migrate and to pay workers to harvest crops.

Gender roles and expectations that surround women and men also influence the structure of household cooperation (see Chiñas 1983; Mathews 1992; Stephen 1991b). Working with female artisans in Turkey, White tells us:

> . . . Women's labor—whether paid or unpaid—is conflated with social and gender identity and with membership in social groups such as the family. Labor is a constituent part of women's membership in the social groups that provide the basis for security and identity, which are fundamental prerequisites for physical and social reproduction (1994: 15).

Relative to Santa Ana, we note that though Santañeras are important as weavers, and may support their household single-handedly when their husbands migrate, their status is framed largely by its domestic functions (Bernal 1994: 53, 61; Roger 1980). Thus, Vera and Flor, like all Santañeras, are responding to what they perceive as social expectations. This does not mean they are unaware of the exploitation that occurs around them in the name of the family. However, for Flor, who has made the conscious choice not to marry, this status helps her fit into Santañero society and limits the social effects of her identity as a *soltera* (spinster), which reduces her access to the many reciprocal relationships that are only established at marriage.

Men, on the other hand, gain prestige as they move away from their natal homes, marry, and establish new households, following local patterns of life-cycle development (see Nader 1969). Mario is caught in an awkward contradiction. Although he is older, successful, and talented, he is not married, and he continues to live with his parents. His experiences and expectations make his situation less troublesome. With his father, he has used some of his income to experiment a bit as a weaver, moving away from mano de obra and toward more independent production using new designs. Finally, though he complains about his status vis-à-vis his father, he does not have to worry about building a home and supporting his own family. Remaining at home has other advantages as well. In 1996, his father paid for him and his nephew to return to the United States.

Conclusions

In this chapter I have surveyed cooperation's foundation in the Santañero household and family. To summarize, cooperation in the examples is exercised for different reasons and is framed in different ways. The decision to cooperate is influenced by gender, status, life cycle, local and external economy, education, and personal desires. Santañeros expect both men and women will support their families. However, expectations are gender-based. Although both men and women migrate or stay at home, weave or farm, men have more options, and women's actions are typically measured by their domestic function. Status also influences cooperative decision making. Households with high social and economic status cooperate by choice, not because it is crucial to survival. For Alejandro and María, cooperation is another form of investment, a way of enhancing success. The life-cycle stage of a household, along with its members, also influences decision making. Fernando and Emilia are positioning their household to succeed through the careful deployment of cooperative bonds. If their children were older, the situation would be different. Vera waits to begin life in her own home with her husband, and until his return, she divides her loyalties between competing demands of her parents and her spouse. Expectations also influence actions. Choices to cooperate have a pragmatic quality. Flor has a ready-made social network that is hard for the unmarried Santañera to establish.

The descriptions define the ways in which cooperation becomes more than a common story, a social template, or hardwired response that is uniform to all Santañeros. Cooperation is, in a real sense, a kind of social capital. It represents social relationships imbued with specific value and invested in the maintenance of self and family, prestige, and status (Bourdieu 1986). It is also cultural capital, conferring identity and creating a sense of belonging based on an assumption of shared knowledge (Piot 1991). For all the positive attributes most Santañeros associate with cooperation, we have also noted the contest and conflict that surround most relationships. A villager can choose to cooperate. Yet that choice is not simply motivated by deep-seated altruism. Questions of power, production, gender, and identity are part of the decision. A Santañero can also choose not to cooperate, but in doing so, he or she may opt out of many supportive relationships that can assist his or her household at points of stress.

Like Fernando and Emilia, villagers blend cooperative and noncooperative responses to meet their needs best. The importance of family-based reciprocal relationships points toward the value these ties hold, and the fact that such relationships cannot be dealt with lightly. A similar pattern is found in the actions and experiences of María and Alejandro, who successfully built a new business around the traditional values of cooperation. In this example, we note cooperation is not overwhelmed by new market forces. Here, reciprocal bonds of mutual aid become the foundation upon which new businesses are founded. Finally, Santañeros can also choose to cooperate, but not necessarily for idealistic reasons, as with Emiliano. How these patterns of cooperation are played out between households is the subject of the next chapter, as we examine interhousehold patterns of association including guelaguetza and compadrazgo.

Chapter Four

Guelaguetza and Compadrazgo

Interhousehold Cooperation in Santa Ana

Don Mauro invited Maria and me to attend a wedding during our first week in the village. He was a guest of the *padrinos* (godparents) of the groom, and thought we would enjoy the experience. Knowing very little about life in Santa Ana, I asked what we should bring to the celebration. Don Mauro told us to buy two bottles of mescal and four packs of cigarettes. Later we discovered this was the minimum acceptable gift to present a family as guelaguetza. Once at the wedding party (a three-night affair at the home of the groom's parents), the *huehuete* (a ritual leader) ushered us before the family's altar. The room reeked of mescal, *mole* (a sauce blending chocolate and chilies served over chicken), smoke, and people. The altar was glorious. It was covered with flowers, candles, and gifts. A young man and the parents of the groom formally greeted us. We presented the mescal and cigarettes to the parents and huehuete. The young man took out the newlyweds' guelaguetza book (a tablet that contains notes on the exchanges in which the family has participated) and entered our gift. Each night we returned with additional gifts to offer the family in honor of the wedding. For three nights we ate, drank, and danced to the music of Santa Ana's brass band and conjunto until very late, and we returned home quite early in the morning with tortillas stacked around leftovers.

OUR EXPERIENCES AT this and other weddings, compromisos, and community events typified the kinds of events and patterns of reciprocity that occurred regularly in Santa Ana. We often watched Santañero families on their way to the home of a compadre, friend, or family

Women preparing mole for a wedding

member for an event of some kind. Some celebrations were intimate affairs. *Todos Santos* (All Saints' Day) brought extended families together in
celebration. Family members moved from house to house visiting altars
decorated with breads, fruits, candles, and flowers. At each stop a spe-
cially prepared meal was shared, as were memories of times past and rec-
ollections of the deceased. Other events like weddings, funerals, and mayordomías could grow quite large. Hundreds of invitados would fill
courtyards, celebrating with food, drink, and music over one to three or
more days and nights (for a detailed account of ritual in central valley
communities, see El-Guindi 1986; Stephen 1991b).

No one in Santa Ana goes to a social affair empty-handed, not even a
visiting anthropologist. At some point in the past, or in anticipation of
the future, those invited to the celebration have (or will) help the family
throwing the party. The exchange may have occurred in the distant past
in conjunction with an earlier event. Support is also lent for the celebra-

tion at hand. No matter the time of the transaction, the contribution is noted in the family's guelaguetza book.

Interhousehold Cooperation

If cooperation and reciprocity were limited to immediate familial relations, they would not be ideal structures through which to construct local identity and a sense of community. Yet, cooperation is a core element of Santañero daily life and a key building block of the community as a social entity. Thus, to understand cooperation's importance to social reproduction, we must look beyond the confines of households and familial ties.

In Santa Ana, reciprocal and cooperative relationships involve families in extensive social networks that reach well beyond the social limits and geographical boundaries of any single household and the village itself. The relationships between families are important for practical as well as symbolic and ideological reasons. First, the ties between families are a safety net, a way to hedge against disaster. In the process, a moral economy is constructed, one that protects and defends villagers (see Scott 1976). This is particularly important for families living with little reserve social or economic capital (see Lomnitz 1977). Second, the many reciprocal relationships that link families, from short-term dyadic contracts to long-term guelaguetza and compadrazgo ties, are symbolic of Santañero communal identity (see Monaghan 1995; Watanabe 1992). Words, ideas, and actions create a template upon which social actors organize their lives and their practices. Actions reinforce words and beliefs. Reciprocal ties are modified and reinvented through an ever developing process of social change (Eriksen 1991). Finally, cooperative ties among families work at an ideological level and become powerful tools in the evaluation of social forces and social changes that are rooted in processes taking place well beyond the limits of the community itself (see Mallon 1983). In this respect, cooperative and reciprocal relationships become key structures through which Santañeros create themselves as a group and respond to global capitalism, national politics, and state policies (Cohen n.d.; Greenberg 1995; Monaghan 1995).

Informal cooperative relationships among villagers, as members of various households, follow a model similar to the dyadic contracts explored in detail by Foster (1961, 1963). These informal relationships link individuals from a variety of households into temporary alliances around particular activities and needs. People help each other, exchange goods and services, and go their way when the goal is reached or a project is complete. For example, a family plans a trip to ranch lands to collect firewood. Such a trip can take the better part of a day and is quite strenuous to complete on foot. Thus, most families search for a vehicle that can be rented for transportation. A family reaches an agreement with the owner of the vehicle; the owner receives a portion of the wood collected in exchange for his truck and time. The project is complete when the wood is delivered; the contract is dissolved, or perhaps becomes the basis for the next project. Nothing else need take place once formal repayment for services rendered has been met, and a dyadic contract need not be extended beyond the contracted event. However, it is typical in Santa Ana for temporary relationships to become the basis for longer term cooperative ties. Alternatively, short-term associations are often generated around and from long-term relationships.

People create informal reciprocal alliances with their friends and relatives because the community is small. In addition, to build trust one must take time and invest effort. Many villagers choose, therefore, to work with the same individuals through time, forming and reforming alliances as necessary. These informal relationships are often carried into new situations and can be the foundation for exchanges among migrants living in the United States (Kearney 1996; Kemper 1977).

It should come as no surprise that given such patterns of association, these informal contracts develop into formal social relationships including compadrazgo and guelaguetza. The cooperative relationships sometimes unite villagers into unlikely social combinations. Reciprocal ties bridge various social strata and different economic classes within the community. Poorer Santañeros may start as *peones* (unskilled workers) in service to wealthier village members. As their employment continues, their connection to the family grows to include formal relationships.

El-Guindi and Selby (1976) note that the Zapotecs organize their social universe into a hierarchical system of oppositional stages. Each stage (starting with the individual) is mediated by the next higher step (in this case, family). In other words, individuals who struggle with one another (as siblings often do) are unified within the household in relationship to other households. Households are joined by neighborhoods. The village is unified as well, in opposition to external forces, including the economic domination of Teotitlán and the growing influence of market capitalism. Formal reciprocal ties are often the glue that cements these relationships, and set the stage for ongoing cooperation and social practice (see Eriksen 1991).

Nader argues that such a model of cooperation explains Zapotec social order (1990: 30). For the Taleans (Talea is a highland Zapotec community north of the central valley), social life is replete with minor injustices. The tensions created from petty disputes build over time and can undermine communal solidarity and goodwill. However, working to mediate such tensions are "cross-linkages." Cross-linkages maintain *harmonía* (harmony or balance) by bringing Taleans of different social and economic means together. Such relationships create a level of social involvement that limits (but does not prevent) open contests over power and status (Nader 1990: 59). The results of such cooperative ties are not the end of problems among Taleans. Rather, the relationships maintain a level of equilibrium based on the ideal of harmony—the assumption that harmony exists although life is full of injustice—and in the end a balance is struck between the positive and negative of continued participation in the life of the community.[1]

In the Santañero household, we find individuals are often at odds with one another. High levels of tension exist among family members. Children fight over food and the affection and attention of a parent. Parents in turn struggle with budget constraints, the demands of other relatives, and their own emotional needs. Mediating these tensions are close cooperative relationships, the stories people tell, and the altruistic associations they hold with one another. These mediating factors build strong social networks and expectations from which an individual's extrication can be quite hard. Francisco Mendoza, a young new father, often talked about the weight he felt bearing down upon him in terms of growing familial responsibilities. While his mother, sisters, and in-laws all helped mediate the shifts Francisco and his wife were involved in, the emotional and financial burdens, combined with his own expectations, made for a difficult situation. Thus, the cooperative and reciprocal relationships that frame an individual's life are more than simply recipes for action. They are weighty structures for coping with change and for organizing, gauging, and rating performance.

Families stand in competition with one another even as they talk about and expect to create cooperative relationships. Each family is an independent entity. Each competes for access to markets for weavings and social status in the village, among other things. Like their Talean contemporaries (see Nader 1990), Santañero families are involved in constant minor disputes over money, social position, work, and the future (and see Parnell 1988). Brothers stop talking to each other over a loan gone bad. Daughters and sons avoid their parents and burdensome demands for financial support. There are also the typical arguments over love, life, and romance. Yet families are also cohesive units, creating stable and safe environments for social survival and success. Informal alliances produce formal relationships including compadrazgo and guelaguetza. These associations unite families, create cross-linkages, and mediate contradictions (Nader 1990).

Guelaguetza

As children grow older and prepare to marry, guelaguetza, a formal system of reciprocity and cooperation, begins to function in their lives, tying their household to others in the community. Guelaguetza (pronounced *ghelagetz'* in Santa Ana), or reciprocal giving, creates interfamilial support networks organized around exchanges of gifts and services (Acevedo and Restrepo 1991: 22–23). Guelaguetza is an institution of "total service." It carries with it strongly sanctioned obligations to give and receive which last over time (Mauss 1990: 13).

Guelaguetza relationships unify the various social and economic classes within Santañero society. The reciprocal relationships formed through the exchanges moderate the mistrust that often marks interfamilial relations. In other words, from a system marked by suspicion, grows a structure of support, if not complete trust (see El-Guindi and Selby 1976). Guelaguetza connections "cross-cut" differences and create common ground for the exercise and development of shared common identity.

Santañeros describe guelaguetza as a community tradition. They practice guelaguetza because "that is what Santa Ana does." Ricardo suggested one afternoon, "It is the custom here, it is how we help each other out. If I need something, well you can give it to me. When you need something, I can give it back." Ties of mutual aid are formalized in the guelaguetza book, guarded by each family, and typically found locked away for safety. All gifts given and services rendered are noted in the book. Throughout the life cycle of a family, the guelaguetza book fills with the history of its relationships; it is the story of a family's social assets as well as its social debts.

Guelaguetza relationships are founded upon marriage and create obligations between newly married couples and other families in the community. A wedding in Santa Ana is a grand affair. The ceremonies and parties in celebration of a wedding can last from three to five days, and may be attended by up to two hundred guests. A large wedding typically begins on a Thursday morning and continues through the following Monday night, when it culminates in a large dance.

A groom can spend between one and three years earning the money to help cover the expenses for wedding parties. The bulk of expenses associated with the marriage are met through guelaguetza. Before the formal ceremonies and parties begin, people start to talk about the event. As the date draws near, families bring goods for the party and *fandango* (dance). Donations are not usually a response to a direct request. Instead, one learns through gossip that a wedding is coming. A Santañero might hear that Pedro and Lupe need chickens for their wedding. If the couple are friends, family, or potentially helpful in a future relationship (for political support, for example), a household may decide to deliver a few chickens. Typically, families bring food, including eggs, bread, chickens, tortillas, chocolate, and pigs, and money. Services provided as guelaguetza include assisting in food preparation and covering the costs of the bands that will play at the party. People also lend a hand to clean and prepare the wedding site, usually the groom's home. Each gift has a relative value. Five chickens are worth more than a bottle of mescal, for example. Women arrive to cook the mole, *higaditos* (an egg dish prepared with meat and served in a spicy soup), and *chocolate atole* (a corn beverage flavored with chocolate). Men serve food, cut wood, and slaughter animals. By the end of the wedding, the newlyweds have built a large network of reciprocal associations and many social obligations. They find themselves in debt to their supporters. Wedding debts may take years to repay, and no one expects an immediate return on their contribution. Bourdieu (1977: 8) suggests quick repayment would nullify social relationships. The rapid repayment of debt is, in his estimation, the rejection of the giver by the receiver (and see Mauss 1990: 13). In Santa Ana the issue is moot, as few newlyweds have the financial means with which to repay their new debts.

The act of giving guelaguetza is complex and must be correctly executed. One does not go to a wealthy member of the community and ask for a particular gift. Neither do the givers expect to be lavished with praise for services or goods they have provided. Such patterns of action follow local ideas concerning *envida* (envy) and *respecto* (respect). To ask a wealthy villager for a gift places the person who makes the request in a precarious position. The action can be read as a sign of weakness, a mark of the requesting party's envy, or a failure to meet locally conceived ideals of reciprocity. The open request risks a negative response, and the implication that an individual or household cannot cover reciprocal demands can create jealousy. Knowledge of a family's inability to meet reciprocal goals also becomes a dilemma as a family struggles to cover its cooperative debts. In addition, the tables can turn on givers and receivers. If a request is denied, the result can affect the requesting party adversely. The denial leads to a decline in the requesting party's status. People begin to ask why others are withdrawing their support. The resulting *verguenza* (shame) of the potential giver who cannot or will not give and of the potential receiver who now feels slighted can be detrimental for all involved (see Kearney 1986: 101–103; Leslie 1960: 72; Nader 1969: 352).

What do Santañeros say about the debts they have to repay? Many villagers give pragmatic answers and point to the role guelaguetza plays in the maintenance of mutual support and the successful celebration of an event.

> It is a way to help a family economically, and if you have a party, everyone brings something to the fiesta—food, mescal, or bringing the band to a wedding. When I have something, they know and then I can bring it.

Guelaguetza is a positive social link among villagers seen in this light. However, there are other less affirmative opinions when people are asked about reciprocal ties. When I asked Valentino Aquino whether or not he participates in guelaguetza with other villagers, he gave a short terse answer: "No, it is too much money, I don't do it." Pedro Martínez added that he participates "only because I still owe some families."

Of the thirty-six men who talked about guelaguetza, six claimed not to participate, and five said that they only participated if they had a debt or were urged to contribute. Twenty-five men answered they regularly participate in guelaguetza. Only six of these twenty-five mentioned the goal or ideal of mutual support in their answers. The remaining nineteen men stated their participation was expected and so they participated, but nothing more.

Villagers do not avoid their responsibilities when it is time to repay a debt. I did not hear of anyone failing to repay a debt; however, I was part of an odd guelaguetza delivery in the spring of 1993. Héctor Jiménez and his wife owed the Martínez family a gross of eggs from their (the Jiménez's) wedding celebrated eight years earlier. Unfortunately, in the following years the two families had a falling out, and spent very little time together. When it was time for the Martínez's son's formal wedding ceremony, Héctor discovered that they wanted the eggs returned in kind. During the day of the fandango, we hauled a gross of eggs through the late afternoon heat to the Martínez's home. During our walk Héctor cursed the family, yet the minute we entered their courtyard, his demeanor shifted and became quite solicitous. We brought the eggs to the altar and went through a formal exchange of greetings and introductions. Out came the guelaguetza book and the returned gift was noted. We were fed black beans and *chicharone* (pork rinds), we toasted the couple with shots of mescal and beer, and then we left. We were not more than two meters from the gate when Héctor began to curse the family again. Héctor's attitude was not atypical, and it does point to the fact that most people prefer to receive gifts than to return their debts. It also reveals how obligations, made with the highest of goals, become burdens that can weigh down relationships, and how friendships crumble even as debts remain to be repaid.

A handful of families refuse to participate in guelaguetza and other cooperative relationship on religious grounds. They argue they should not be asked to participate in "heathen" acts, nor should they be asked to serve in the village cargos, citing their recent conversion to an evangelical Christian faith (I was never able to discover the church). In other words, the *evangélicos* (literally, evangelicals, but used here to describe converts to various Protestant faiths) in the community removed themselves from reciprocal ties to anyone who would not also convert. However, among these church members reciprocal relationships remained strong, and the three evangelical households in Santa Ana supported one another in a manner that paralleled that of their Catholic neighbors. Evangelical support networks also extended to include church members living in neighboring villages (and see Ramírez Gómez 1991).

Compadrazgo

The compadrazgo system as found in Mesoamerica evolved following the conquest and did not replace an earlier, lineal system (Nader 1969; Nutini and Bell 1980). Parsons proposes:

> If there was ever a larger kinship group among the Zapotec than there is today, a group larger than that of the bilateral blood family,

it has been substituted for by the compadre system which fulfills all the functions that would be expected of a kinship group outside of immediate family (1936: 60).

In addition, the compadrazgo system should be seen as a system; it is not an egocentric safety net (Nutini 1984: 403). Fictive kin networks parallel real familial relationships in their structure, permanence, and associated behavior. The resulting systems are long-lived and not short-term investments that one individual periodically makes in the life of another person. In other words, the *padrinos del bautismo* (the godparents of a child's baptism and very important compadres in any person's life) do not simply cover baptismal costs for an individual; the padrinos, in effect, become important long-term emotional and social resources for a child. Mintz and Wolf (1950) point out in addition, that the compadrazgo system is adaptable to a variety of situations, and can be carried into new social settings. Hirabayashi (1993, 1994) found such a process occurring among migrant Zapotec communities in Mexico City. Paralleling and building upon compadrazgo relationships were relationships he defines as *paisanazgo*. Paisanazgo relationships are built around shared geographic origins, traditional beliefs, and ethnicity, and become frameworks upon which to create new social relationships in new settings. Finally, Foster (1961) adds that compadrazgo relationships create links beyond the child-godparent bond, tying unrelated households to each other through formal relationships.

At the time of a Santañero child's baptism, godparents are chosen to stand as compadres. During a Santañero's life, many different compadres of varying importance and permanence are chosen. None are as important as the padrinos del bautismo. They are foster parents and guardians and they help in the overall training and support of a child. In return for the support of a compadre, the godchild frequently lends a hand around his or her padrino's home (see de la Fuente 1949: 168; Nutini 1984). Many Santañeros described their padrinos in affectionate terms, often expressing appreciation for the debts incurred on their behalf by padrinos.

Less formal, but no less important, fictive ties are created around many more trivial events and rituals. An individual may purchase school supplies, uniforms for sports teams, or clothing—or sponsor a small celebration in honor of a child—and in the process become a minor compadre to the child and parents (Foster 1979: 82–83; Lomnitz 1977: 160; Stephen 1991b: 190–191). Lesser compadre relationships are often built around

Men toasting one another at a celebration

real kin relations. Such ties contribute to the overall maintenance of the community and the reproduction of Santañero identity, adding yet another level of cooperative relationships to the creation of local morality.

Compadrazgo relationships are clothed in a powerful rhetoric of mutual support and sacrifice that reaches across generations, binding individuals to each other and fulfilling the needs (education, clothing, housing, etc.) faced by children as they grow. Compadrazgo is also more than a system guaranteeing a child's well-being. Working in central Mexico, Lomnitz (1977) notes three reasons for maintaining fictive kinship relations. First, compadrazgo aids in the maintenance of social ties. Second, it promotes social mobility in a community. Third, it supports social, economic, and physical protection among and between villagers.

Becoming compadres in Santa Ana, as elsewhere in Mesoamerica, "strengthens social ties between equals" and the label, compadre, is often used among close friends (Lomnitz 1977: 160). Walking through the village with Santañeros, the term "compadre" is constantly heard in conversation. Part of the exchange is to allow an individual to demonstrate his or her standing in the community to me, as outside observer. In addition, the use of the term "compadre," or more typically in Santa Ana, a shortened *comp'*, is one way an individual maintains his or her place in the community, and in the process, maintains the community as a social space.

The regular usage of *comp'* by villagers gives voice to the ideals of balanced, cross-linking, horizontal relationships among people of various social standing (see Lambek 1990: 659). The solidarity established through compadrazgo relationships and use of the term itself does not alleviate the inequalities (a family's standing, access to wealth, and community power) that pervade Santañero life. Nor does the structure of the alliances necessarily mean villagers can become equals at some point in the future (see Stephen 1991b: 193). However, returning to El-Guindi and Selby's model of Zapotec world view (1976), compadre relationships in Santa Ana establish structures of association that mediate the conflicts between individuals and households.

The presence of the term *comp'* in conversation is part of this process. Its use can reconcile social tensions and foster solidarity (see Donham 1994: 152). *Comp'* is a metaphor or symbol that engages an ideal identity in an immediate fashion. Maybe it is used and not meant—I certainly greeted people as *comp'* with whom I did not want to associate. Often informants would curse a fellow villager under their breath after an encounter. As such, the term may have little effect, and yet its usage remains important and points to the continual maintenance of culturally practical knowledge that marks most social interaction.

The bridges that compadrazgo relationships create between the various strata of Santañero society do not mean all villagers thereby are equals (and see Donham 1990: 180; Nutini 1984: 133). Wealthy members of the community tend to support more children, both rich and poor, and are requested more often to act as padrinos than their poorer neighbors (see Stephen 1991b).[2] Wealthy Santañeros use their support of children to build political allegiance and social prestige. This is a public pursuit. The wealthy family makes a sacrifice that is central to the ritual life of the village, and therefore, the investment (an investment in the core beliefs of the village) is on public display. The more children supported, the more obvious are the status of a family and its investment in local socially sanctioned behaviors. In return, the household supported becomes a resource to the wealthy household, one that can be used in the future. In other words, compadrazgo is about more than the welfare of a child; it also establishes alliances between adults and creates networks through which social status is exercised and ideals of community maintained.

Compadrazgo also reproduces structures of "symbolic violence" (Bourdieu 1990: 135–136; Wacquant 1987). Symbolic violence is found as wealthy and high-status villagers use compadrazgo alliances to legitimize their exercise of political and social power. The wealthy and high-status Santañeros display and celebrate their family's standing and good fortune through the many alliances they maintain. They use their positions and alliances to emphasize what makes them (the wealthy) high status in the community and different from the poor. Nevertheless, they do so in a way that is not blatantly coercive (Greenberg 1995). In other words, they frame their wealth relative to the social ideals of the community; compadrazgo mystifies and confounds local relations of power.[3]

Wealthy households use compadrazgo alliances as a foundation for political action. A Santañero interested in office can usually count on the votes of his compadres. Economic capital is therefore converted to social capital through these relationships.

Money without social standing is of little use in the sociopolitical life of the community. Wealthy villagers who contribute little to the community (ritual or otherwise) will have few opportunities to display their power. Thus, to become compadre for a child is one way to make economic capital legitimate and socially useful within the community (Greenberg 1995). The issue is not whether a person can be wealthy. It is the goal of many villagers to "advance" themselves—to earn enough money to leave behind subsistence agriculture and mano de obra. The real issue is whether or not the economic capital a Santañero earns precludes his or her investment in the social welfare of others (see, for example, Bennett 1989).

The difference in wealth among various Santañero families, expressed in the number of children a family is asked to support as compadres, is one indication of class in the community.[4] Other evidence of class includes what a family does to earn a living. Whether household members work in the village or as migrants will have an impact on their income and status as well. The migrant earns a higher wage, but lacking participation in the political life of the community, may not see his household's status increase as rapidly as the Santañero who remains in the village, but earns less.

The approach a family takes to weaving also influences its class standing. Mano de obra is a secure avenue to income but carries little prestige and a low monetary return. Independent textile production can earn a weaving household a higher return and signals self-reliance. Working as a merchant carries the greatest sense of independence. However, economic independence should not come at the expense of community support if the household hopes to see economic power translated to social standing. Thus, smart merchants, whether building a large- or small-scale operation, wrap themselves in the rhetoric and practice of reciprocal ties. Arturo García had become an accomplished buyer in just such a fashion. He willingly paid top price for tapetes. In addition, he bought regularly from weavers, even when the market was down. A cousin who sold to García commented he was jealous of his cousin, but he did not feel mistreated, and had broken some ties with merchants in Teotitlán to work consistently with him.

Compadrazgo relationships influence the positions one holds in the local cargo hierarchy and are, when taken together, also indications of status (for the individual and household) in the community (Cancian 1965; Wasserstrom 1983).[5] Economic, cultural, and social capital are linked in the creation of class identity in Santa Ana. No Santañero can move up the status hierarchy if he or she ignores any facet of the system (see Bourdieu 1990: 75). Similarly, the failure of a household to participate in cooperative and reciprocal relationships can reduce social standing in relation to other families and households in the community.

Given the role of compadrazgo in the maintenance of local hierarchy, why do poor Santañeros continue to participate? The answer would be difficult to fathom if, in fact, the relationships created were nothing more than a myth in the service of symbolic violence by wealthy Santañeros, or for that matter, simply a cultural ideal with little importance in daily life. However, this is not so; fictive kin ties "further social mobility and economic advancement" (Lomnitz 1977: 160). Santañero households seek wealthy members of the community to act as compadres for their children in the hope of future improvements. The consequences of such relationships include the creation of cross-linkages between different strata in the community (Nader 1990: 47). These "asymmetrical dyads" (Foster 1963) reproduce associations organized hierarchically (or vertically) rather than horizontally. In other words, it links people of differing statuses rather than of the same statuses and classes. These connections ensure poorer members of Santa Ana at least a nominal voice in political decisions (see Foster 1979: 82). This is particularly the case when representatives of Santa Ana's "ruling class" turn to the parents of their godchildren and adult godchildren for political support. At these moments, the children and their parents have an opportunity to make themselves and their demands heard.

Compadrazgo relations offer protection as well as safety from aggression, antagonism, and hostility. There are two primary paths through which protection is established in Santa Ana: first, through informal gossip and second, through control of cultural capital (see Bourdieu 1986). At points of tension, an individual can activate ties to compadres to solve problems. As a dispute moves beyond the immediate contestants to involve other people, tensions are usually mediated by friends and family (and see Haviland 1977: 67). If a disagreement continues, gossip and rumors—always moving through networks—are engaged in the service of dispute resolution (see Abrahams 1970; Gluckman 1963). As gossip spreads, individuals who may be tied to both factions in a dispute use their influence (typically based in social relationships) to help contestants reach a solution and limit open hostility (for additional examples, see Leslie 1960; Nader 1990; Parsons 1936).

Compadrazgo also offers protection to Santañeros as they grow older, and their economic capital and social role in the life of the village declines. Part of the decline is due to physiological change. An older weaver's eyesight worsens with age, a farmer's energy declines, and a tortilla maker's back and knees become arthritic. Yet, even as their economic power ebbs, a person's role as compadre may increase (Stephen 1991b: 193). This is an indication of the rising value of individuals' historical or cultural capital—that is, their value not in economic or monetary terms, but as recognized examples of cultural ideals. They are individuals who control sanctioned knowledge and hold experience in the construction and maintenance of social hierarchies (Bourdieu 1977, 1986). The villager, often an older woman, as described by Stephen (1991b), relies on growing fictive kin networks to maintain a household and to subsist, even as his or her "real" social networks slowly fade away (on aging and social alliances, see Sault 1985).

Fictive kin ties also reach beyond the confines of the village to link Santañeros with individuals outside the community (Stephen 1987b, 1991b: 193). Santañero weaving families establish compadrazgo relationships with international and local buyers. The relationships created invoke metaphors of cooperation, although not to the degree or in the same manner as inter-familial or, even necessarily, village patterns. The outcome is to add a layer of socially sanctioned relationships to what would otherwise be an economic contract (Holmes 1989). A patron knows that taking the role of a compadre often enhances his or her relationship with a client. His or her support also helps keep costs lower (by maintaining prices) and guarantees a steady supply of textiles. Thus, the relationship is not the sacrifice that many buyers make it out to be. Talking informally with merchants in Teotitlán, I often heard the buyers talk of their sacrifices working with contracted weavers. Some went as far as to show me poor quality textiles that they had been "forced" to purchase in order to appease a struggling weaver.

Santañeros are not bowled over by a metaphoric bond or the patron's use of cooperative ideology (see, for example, Harris 1964). Rather, Santañeros are well aware of the exploitation that takes place, and there is resentment of a patron's actions. Weavers know that they are paid less than they should be for their work, but the structure of the market makes it difficult for them to avoid mano de obra contracts (Cohen 1998).

Santañero weavers in unenviable contracts often told stories about a patron's "contracts with the devil" and rhetorically criticized the merchants for their actions (see Greenberg 1995; Shipton 1989: 28; Taussig 1980). Stories of deals with the devil are usually told in relation to Santañeros and Teotitecos who are economically much better off than the storyteller. Wealthy men go to an outcropping of rocks high above Santa Ana called *xhiacol'* or *piedras coloradas* (the purple rocks). There they meet the devil and enter contracts that guarantee their continued profits. However, economic good fortune is not without its price. As an informant told me, "Yes, they [the buyers who have made the contracts] make much money, but they cannot enjoy it. They suffer for their profit. They buy food, but are never satisfied by it. Instead they suffer. They are always hungry and usually sick." The story is a familiar one of ill-gotten profit that brings its holder no good in the end.[6]

The presence of such tales does not indicate that Santañeros believe there is no legitimate way to accrue wealth. Nor does it indicate an irrational aversion to profit. Rather, stories of contracts with the devil signal the importance of the local moral economy and that moral system's ongoing integration with new market relationships (see Bennett 1989).

Greenberg notes a similar situation among the Mixe of Oaxaca. Like the Santañeros described here, the Mixe use stories of contracts made with the devil and concepts of "good" and "evil" money to deal with ongoing economic change and to critique the participation of local peoples in the developing formal economy.

> In contrast to an anonymous market economy in which merchants may charge whatever the market will bear, the Mixe merchant is constrained by the norms of reciprocity to respond to his clients in the same way they treat him, that is, with respect, fairness, and even generosity (1995: 77–78).

Villagers who claim a person has entered a contract with the devil, are, in effect, suggesting that the person in question has failed to live up to local social norms. There is also a threat of ostracism that follows along with the stories. A Santañero entering a contract with the devil cannot count upon support or assistance in times of need. Finally, through these stories, villagers voice their disappointments as well as their jealousies over profits never achieved and wealth never recognized.

Contracts with the devil are the antitheses of compadrazgo relationships. The contracts are cooperative ties manipulated for self-aggrandizement and lack any pretense of cooperative support and interfamilial networking. These stories are therefore critical comments on wealth and its incorrect usage. They point to the difference between economic and social capital within the community. Economic wealth becomes social capital, and the basis for respect and prestige, only when it is invested correctly (Greenberg 1995; Scott 1986).

In the case of Santa Ana, correct investments are those that maintain some cooperative goals. The force of these stories questions the choice of economic profit over socially sanctioned action, and many villagers choose to "steer a course that does not repudiate those [cooperative] norm[s]" (Scott 1986: 234).

Many Santañeros will respond with minor acts of resistance to actions they consider beyond the realm of correct and proper action. This is easiest to note among weavers who maintain patron-client relationships with Teotiteco textile merchants. In these situations, resistance can take a number of forms. A weaver may make a purposeful mistake in an order, steal yarns and wool, or delay finishing contracts to upset a buyer's schedule. The weaver may use the formal status of a compadre or his patron-client relationship to persuade his patron to buy tapetes when the demand for textiles is low, by arguing that the continued sales will support the compadre's godchildren.

These minor examples of resistance achieve little direct material gain. They do not alleviate inequalities of power in the community. However, their enactment is important and shows that the population is neither lulled by the ideology of patrons, nor mystified by the symbolic violence of the wealthy. Resistance limits exploitation to a small degree. More important, such actions work to "deny claims made by superordinate classes or to advance claims vis-à-vis those superordinate classes" (Scott 1986: 32).

The stories about contracts with the devil and the minor acts of villagers' pilfering from abusive patrons confirm practical knowledge in the community and highlight the perception of improper practices among the wealthy. The resulting confirmation of local cooperative goals then becomes a foundation upon which villagers more successfully build institutions for the resistance of exploitation. In fact, this is what I found in Santa Ana; and in Chapter Six, I note that Santañeros have established a weaving cooperative and are developing closer ties between themselves and the state (again based upon the logic of reciprocal cooperation), all of which aids the community in its struggle to escape the dominant market position of Teotitlán (Cohen 1998). Thus, everyday forms of resistance become the basis upon which exploitative relationships are effectively countered.

Promesas

The cooperative bonds created through compadrazgo and guelaguetza are paralleled by the promesa that an individual makes to a saint. In making a promesa, the Santañero establishes an asymmetrical dyadic contract with a supernatural being (Brandes 1988: 62). The contract is asymmetrical in that the saint or supernatural being is much more powerful than its human counterpart. Like the dyadic contract, the promesa is a pact that exists over a set period and between two individuals. Promises typically have specific purposes, including support in a large construction project, assistance at work, success at school, or a cure to an illness. In exchange for supernatural support, the individual promises service to the saint. The pledge of service is usually fulfilled by throwing a fiesta, assuming support of a mayordomía, or serving in a religious cargo.

The contracts with the devil discussed above follow a pattern nearly identical to the promesa. In the former, the individual asks a supernatural being, in this case the devil, for support in a venture. The rhetoric of cooperation is invoked in the association and a reciprocal relationship is established—a soul is traded for success. When working with the devil, however, the relationship is described in negative and abusive terms. The outcome of such associations is never anything that will aid others. In fact, it is said that the individual in such a relationship will often suffer and see any riches earned or successes achieved collapse and end in ruin. A promesa, on the other hand, is a positive relationship. It is achieved through piety and sacrifice. A promesa rewards the individual with good fortune, a cure to a disease, and so on.

Adults are not the only Santañeros to make promesas. Children, like their parents, can make a pledge for any reason. Young adults who are involved in one of Santa Ana's two dance troupes, groups that perform during the village's two main fiestas, frequently dance as a way to fulfill their promesas or the promises made by a parent (J. Cohen 1993). The promesa is further evidence of how Santañeros, even at an early age, learn the cooperative relationships they will be asked to enact throughout their lives.

It may seem odd that a society as pragmatic and as embedded in a cash economy as Santa Ana would continue to practice the promesa, or for that matter, believe in contracts with the devil.[7] The functionalist argues that the promise is an important custom that helps assure psychological well-being—in this respect, the promesa acts like the magic which Trobriand Islanders use to protect their boats (Malinowski 1984). But the promesa is not something that can be explained strictly as a way to reduce anxiety or as a compensatory action (see Tambiah 1990: 72). The use of the promesa does not indicate that the population places its hopes in false truths and miracles that bring psychological reassurance. Neither are stories of contracts with the devil "magical" excuses for social inequalities.

The opening statement of Chapter Three was part of a discussion I had with Aron Sánchez concerning economic reality in Santa Ana and the importance of a promesa. A person's network of social relations can mean the difference between survival and prosperity, not just economic wealth, but cultural and social security. And, as we have seen in this chapter and the discussion of guelaguetza and compadrazgo, wealth is not defined or situated in a strictly economic realm. Santañeros work in a system that places value on cultural and social forms of capital in addition to economic capital. The symbolic links created between an individual and saint in a promesa reproduce practical knowledge and a pattern of association

Danzantes

that permeates Santañero social life in the form of guelaguetza and compadrazgo. The promesa emphasizes the ideals of cooperative relationships, and their positive attributes—just as contracts with the devil emphasize negative processes at work in the community. In a promesa the Santañero elevates his or her position to something more than the mundane, through association with a supernatural being, and does so within the logical schema of local ideas concerning cooperation.

Conclusions

In this chapter I followed cooperative relationships among households. Compadrazgo establishes social relationships and bonds that build upon familial ties between individuals who may or may not be related. Guela-

Las Malinches

guetza creates an alternative set of alliances among families, based on reciprocity. Piot (1991) argues that the act of giving bestows a kind of "immortality" on the giver, providing a central reason for exchange. He is correct in part, for the guelaguetza book is a virtual record of a family's entire history of alliances. It creates a sense of permanence and belonging for both giver and receiver. However, these relationships also accomplish a great deal more.

Compadrazgo and guelaguetza have a pragmatic quality. Both sets of relationships create a sense of security that offers protection to those involved. The alliances created are part of the structure through which Santañeros enact practical knowledge and social norms. A family's status is gauged through its relationships. Class differences are objectified in the number of guelaguetza and compadrazgo relationships a household can maintain. A villager interested in a position in the community authority needs to build his place as compadre and sustain guelaguetza relationships to gain the status and prestige necessary to win an election. A Santañero's alliances also become the basis for his power bid, when he calls on the support of his many associates (see Sahlins 1963: 289).

A final question we can ask is whether guelaguetza and compadrazgo relationships are declining as Santañeros become more a part of a cash-based economy. It appears that both types of relationships will continue in the community, but with changes. Gifts of cash are replacing goods and services when it comes to guelaguetza exchanges. Larger consumer goods (stoves, refrigerators, etc.) are now given at weddings, but are not usually framed as guelaguetza. Consumer goods hold a position essentially equivalent to the wedding gifts given in the United States. A reciprocal relationship is created, but it is not framed as concretely as guelaguetza. The gift is not part of an exchange of equivalents. In an odd twist, newfound wealth among villagers has led to more compadrazgo relationships (working with Mixtec population, see Monaghan 1995). It is not that Santañeros have nothing better to invest in. Rather, the change in compadrazgo and guelaguetza indicates a higher level of disposable income for some families. In response, new minor compadre roles are created. In addition, celebrations are becoming larger and more elaborate. Larger parties call for more compadres as well as increased guelaguetza. In the next chapter, I explore how these patterns are created and reproduced at the level of the community; and how cooperation is changing in response to economic development and local involvement in capitalist markets.

Chapter Five

Cooperation and Community

Tequio, Cooperación, and Servicio

JEFF: So why do you blow that conch shell?

TEODORO: It is to call people down to give tequio. We are going to get started tomorrow morning at around 6:00. So far only a few people have said they will help.

JEFF: What is the project?

TEODORO: We are going to clean the streambeds around the village in preparation for the rains next month.

JEFF: Does this happen every spring?

TEODORO: Well, it is supposed to be done every spring and again in the fall, but this is the first time in almost three years that we have cleaned them.

JEFF: Why haven't you cleaned the streambeds over the last few years?

TEODORO: Nobody wanted to give up their time to help.

JEFF: Do you think many people will help tomorrow?

TEODORO: Well, I hope so, but I don't know. People don't really like working. It takes two or maybe three days, and when you get home, you don't want to do anything else.

I DISCOVERED THE importance of community cooperation (te-quio, communal labor; cooperación, monetary donations to village projects; and servicio, community service) early in our stay in Santa Ana. Porfirio, who would become my assistant later in the year, and many other Santañeros asked Maria and me to teach English classes. It occurred to us that we could meet people more quickly as volunteer teachers. It also created a useful identity for us. What we did not realize was how important our identity as teachers, and therefore participatory members of the community, would become during fieldwork.

I presented myself before the *Comité del Pueblo* one afternoon in September of 1992 to discuss the possibilities of teaching English as a form of community service, and in a very limited way reciprocate the hospitality and support of the village. I spoke with the *presidente municipal* (the equivalent of the mayor), his *regidores* (counselors or advisers to the president), the secretary, and the treasurer in the municipio's main office. The village's municipal offices stand along the northern tier of Santa Ana's main plaza and overlook the community's basketball court, dance space, and commons. Porfirio and I walked out of the midday sun and into the cool, dark room to meet the president and his committee members. Along the walls hung large portraits of famous Mexicans: the child-heroes of the Chapultépec battalion; Benito Juárez, the architect of the constitution and a local favorite born in the highland Oaxacan village of Gelatao; and Salinas de Gotari, the president of the Republic at the time.

The village president sat behind a large steel desk, the Mexican flag to his back. The officers of the municipio sat along one wall on folding chairs and were arranged according to rank and office. Everyone took a seat after formal introductions that included handshakes and salutations. Porfirio did much of the talking, adding linguistic flourishes in Zapotec and Spanish that I could not follow at the time. After some debate among the committee concerning old and ongoing business of the municipio, the president looked over his desk toward me with concern. He asked why I wanted to teach English classes in the village. My answer was one that I had rehearsed with Porfirio and it went something like this:

> I want to give service to your community. You have been kind enough to allow us to stay here for the year, and we want to repay you in some small way. I know that most men give service to the village from time to time, and in return for your support in my work, I would like to give these classes as my service to Santa Ana.

A regidor asked, "Would you charge for these classes then?" I responded, "No, I see this as a service; we want to give something to Santa Ana." The response brought smiles and nods of agreement. Our discussion turned to the logistics of teaching. After a short debate, we decided to use a classroom in the morning school, just to the north of the plaza. Classes would meet twice a week in the late afternoons on Tuesdays and Thursdays and would be open to the entire community. Children from about eight to eighteen years of age and a few adults signed up for classes at the municipio's office. In less than a week, we had more than thirty students divided into two classes, one for children less than ten years of age, the other for teenagers and young adults.[1]

We shook hands with the president and his advisers again as we prepared to leave the municipal offices. Porfirio and I praised each committee member for his wisdom, sponsorship, and support. Regidores voiced their approval, "Yes, this is the way it should be." At that moment, Maria and I gained a new and lasting identity in Santa Ana as *maestros* (teachers).[2] We were transformed from the odd gringos living in Don Mauro's house on the hill (sharing little in common with our neighbors), to members of the village (although we never lost our status as outsiders and oddities). We became part of a locally defined social system. Like all Santañeros, we gave service to maintain our membership in the community. Our status in the community became the basis of many jokes, as friends and informants would make up elaborate stories of my chances at becoming village president, in "maybe ten years," according to Vicky and Gloria.

Community-Based Cooperation

Santañeros talk a great deal about cooperation. Sometimes discussions and stories focus on the family and suggest what is considered correct models for behavior. For example, the tale of the *llorona* (the weeping woman), whose passions and selfish actions lead to the deaths of her husband, children, and herself, holds a blueprint for correct behavior in its plot, and emphasizes the troubles that befall persons (particularly women) who make the wrong decisions (see Mathews 1992).[3] Other stories highlight interhousehold cooperation and the goals of compadrazgo and guelaguetza. In the last chapter, I noted how the talk of miracles, promesas, and contracts with the devil emphasizes the values of proper action, the benefits that come from familial alliances and networks, and the dangers associated with the subversion of local morality and practice for self-aggrandizement.

Santañeros also talk about community-based models of cooperation. One version of community cooperation and its role in the creation of local identity is found in Chapter Two's discussion of Santañero reactions to the Mexican Revolution. Working together, Santañero fighters triumphed over attacking Carrancista forces. We cannot be sure that the instrumental actions of the villagers in reaction to the attacking army were truly decisive. What is important is the way the story symbolizes the community's continued unity and identity based upon the goals of co-operation and reciprocity. To this day, the story of Santa Ana's role in the Revolution remains an often-told tale of local practice and the defense of the community against external aggression.

Cooperative Structures and Geography in the Village

Tequio, cooperación, and servicio express the ideal of community coop-eration. These three social contracts are the basis upon which villagers (as representatives of households and families) construct alliances between themselves and the community, and in the process create Santa Ana as a social place (Kuper 1992; Watanabe 1992). The networks and patterns of association resulting from these relationships establish cross-linkages be-tween the various strata of Santañero society. High-status Santañeros as well as people with little prestige involve themselves in community-based relationships. These relationships mediate the divisions, social tensions, economic class, and political contests that mark village life.

Santa Ana has always been a small community. And, as noted, Santa-ñero society is marked by local class and status divisions. These divisions are revealed in the changing structure and makeup of houses in the village as well as by shifts in residency patterns among Santañeros. Historically, more powerful local families have clumped around the central plaza and the church, and particularly to the west of the plaza. Additional differ-ences were present between families living in the village proper and those Santañeros residing in the mountains above the community. The divi-sions redeveloped within the village proper and between the village and the ranch settlement of Las Carritas following the Revolution. Currently the village is geographically divided into two essentially equal *secciones* (sections) and three new *colonias* (suburbs) that are located above the vil-lage proper.

Section divisions had an effect upon political conflicts in the past; how-ever, they currently have little impact on or relationship to political, so-cial, and economic divisions in the village. Social contests are organized around factions built upon extended household networks (tied together through kinship, compadrazgo, and so forth) and occur between and within the sections and the new colonias. Tensions are founded on differ-ences in class, wealth, power, education, and religion (with the recent conversion of some Santañero families to evangelical faiths). The lack of strong section identity and pronounced section conflict is likely due to the increase in the village's population and the movement of young householders onto new village lands.

Barrios, Colonias, and Secciones

Social conflicts in rural Mesoamerica are often tied to a community's geographical divisions into barrios (Hunt and Nash 1967: 258). Conflicts typically manifest themselves in the political and ritual actions of barrios vis-à-vis each other (Hunt and Nash 1967: 162). In such settings, the barrio is essentially the equivalent to what North Americans call a neighborhood association, and is characteristic of most peasant Indian communities in Mexico (Hunt and Nash 1967; Nader 1969). The barrio's authority structure is a local parallel to the community's authority at large (Hill and Monaghan 1987: 12). It has a managing body and organizes work groups and ritual celebrations (Nutini 1984: 348). Its official committees function as savings and loans, financing neighborhood improvements (Nader 1990: 46). The barrio also defines the limits of endogamy, and can demarcate social and political alliances. This is especially true in larger urban settings (Murphy and Stepick 1991; Vélez-Ibañez 1983).

Santañeros do not use the term barrio to describe the divisions of their community.[4] Instead, as noted, Santa Ana has two sections divided by a north-south axis that runs directly along the rear of the church along Avenida Independencia and Calle Matamoros. The solares to the west of the plaza are in *sección uno* (section one), and compounds to the east of the plaza and church are in *sección dos* (section two). Households from the poor and marginal to the rich and dominant are found in both sections. Neither section is associated with any definite patterns of wealth, status, or economic success. Furthermore, marriage ties, compadrazgo, and guelaguetza relationships regularly cross section boundaries.

The current structure of the community's population and changes that occurred over the last century may have destroyed formal barrios—if indeed they ever existed in the village. Five factors influence the insignificance of geographic divisions. First, Santa Ana's population has remained relatively small throughout its history, limiting the size of local factions. Second, the community was a satellite settlement of Teotitlán del Valle for much of its early history, and internal divisions were overshadowed by disputes with Teotiteco leaders. Third, the 30 percent drop in the community's population following the Mexican Revolution and movement of families into the ranch left the population in flux. Fourth, in response to these changes, many families lost or severed ties to particular parts of the village. Fifth and finally, the rise in population since 1970 has led to a construction boom and the creation of new colonias on village land. Santañeros are moving to colonias above the central village and creating new geographic divisions that are not part of the current secciones or any historical barrio pattern.

One marked difference between Santa Ana and surrounding communities is the lack of antagonism expressed and enacted between the two village secciones. When I asked Santañeros about the meaning and status of their section, the majority answered that it was no more than a spatial reference. Section identity was a way to organize Santa Ana on the ground but had little meaning in local political affairs. Don Librado made one of the most interesting comments concerning the secciones. He said there had been tension between the sections in the past, but currently they "function only to maintain equal representation on committees for all Santañeros. We pick members from both sections to fill positions so no one part of the village will feel ignored."

There is evidence that political activity was marked by open and sometimes violent sectional conflict in the 1960s. While informants acknowledged these problems, I was not able to learn much concerning what occurred. Some stress was due to the presence of multiple political parties in Santa Ana during the 1960s, with fighting among the various factions. The village has been unified behind the PRI *(Partido Revolucionario Institucional)* since the late 1970s. This unification coincides with a rise in local infrastructural development that includes road construction, access to electricity, and the refurbishment of the central village plaza. Most Santañeros professed their support of the village authority's policies enacted since the 1970s; however, as discussed in the next chapter, disputes can arise quite rapidly.

Tensions between secciones are also mediated through the concerted effort of the village's political hierarchy. At elections, candidates for positions are chosen from each section, and most committees are filled with a mixture of representatives from both sections one and two. The presidents for most committees are also chosen alternately from the two sections. The structure of these committees cross-links the secciones and unifies the village as a political entity.

There was a division between families living in the ranch and those living in the village before the municipio's population was consolidated around the central plaza in the 1960s and 1970s (see Chapter Two for details). This segregation had a limited effect upon Santañero marriage patterns. Families in the ranch were physically separated from village households, and were by all accounts largely self-sufficient. Part of the division between ranch and village was due to circumstance and the difficulty of movement between locales. María Cruz described her choice of a marriage partner as follows: "Why did I marry him? His family lived in the ranch, and frankly we did not know families in town as well." In addition, families living in the ranch were characterized as poorer, typical "rural cousins" to the relatively more urbane village population.

A new set of geographical divisions has emerged between Santa Ana's secciones and the three colonias established to the north and up-slope from the main village. We lived in the central colonia, north of the main plaza and a twenty-minute walk up the slope along Calle Leona Vicario, which continues into the Sierra along a well-worn cattle path. The easternmost colonia is the oldest of the three new neighborhoods and includes homes built over the past fifteen years. The solares in the colonia were marked off along two horse paths, Plan de Ayala and Miguel Cabrera (both streets become paths, continuing to Diáz Ordáz and the mountains). The central and western colonias are relatively new and most homes were no more than five years old in 1992–1993.

The majority of lots in the colonias were originally either empty municipal lands not held by individuals, or marginal garden plots held by individuals before the current building boom. The community authority began to lease empty lots in the colonias as the population increased.[5] According to Fernando Mendoza, Santañeros who want to garner favor with members of the authority in the hopes of leasing land often go to great pains to participate in the political life of the community, betting that their actions will be rewarded by the authority.

There are growing social tensions between the families living in the colonias and the rest of the community over access to electricity and water and the quality of roads linking the colonias and the village proper. Electric lines have been run to most homes, but water remains available only from wells (all of which are found in the village proper). A water storage facility located above the western colonia serves homes in sección uno, but is not connected to colonia households. Families living in the colonias are beginning to voice concerns over the lack of services available in their homes, even as development continues in the village. If the expansion of the colonias continues with little improvement in community services, one might anticipate growing dissension between Santañero families living in the colonias and those in secciones uno and dos.

Factionalism in a community can quickly lead to divisive and violent conflict (see Dennis 1987; Greenberg 1989). Cooperative structures like tequio, cooperación, and servicio mediate these oppositions.[6] But community associations do not simply correct and resolve the contradictions inherent in Santañero society and create harmony where it does not exist. Nor can we describe tequio, cooperación, and servicio as only reproductive of "symbolic violence," or oppressive ideology (Bourdieu 1977; Harris 1964: 30). Rather, at any given moment, community cooperation is marked by disputes as are its familial and household counterparts. Social life includes both contest and commitment in its creation, construction, and reproduction.

Tequio

If guelaguetza is the tie that binds families to each other in mutual aid and reciprocal support, tequio is its equivalent at the level of the community. Tequio is based on the ideal that citizens should support their village and is defined as "collective work that is organized around projects of the formal municipal authority" (Acevedo and Restrepo 1991: 23). In other words, it is based upon a sense of civic duty. Tequio is typical of most poor, rural communities in the state.[7] Yet, Santañeros see their collective action as uniquely their own. It is part of the package of behaviors that villagers use to identify themselves in contrast to other communities.

All married adult males between the ages of seventeen and sixty participate in tequio, although as indicated earlier, it is often difficult to find and organize a work crew. Even so, nearly every week there is tequio in the village. Projects range from the trivial to the complex, from painting school chairs to major road maintenance. An easy job might be carried out in the shade of the central plaza late in the afternoon during a few hours squeezed between work and a late meal. Other tequio can be much more difficult and can include backbreaking labor in the hot sun; one crew cleaned area streambeds, and another repaired and extended the village's piped water system. Although it is often difficult work, most Santañeros praise the notion of tequio and maintain it is an equitable form of communal investment that guarantees legitimate membership in the community in return for labor.

Santañeros talk about their participation in tequio as altruistic action taken on behalf of the community. Tequio is "something given to the community." Santañeros who do not participate are likely to become the object of gossip and the subject of village sanctions. Persons who decline tequio can be sanctioned and fined or given short prison terms. Jail time is served in one of Santa Ana's two cells on the north side of the central plaza. Anyone incarcerated is displayed for the entire community to see. Some tension surrounding the status of the evangélicos in the community is associated with their choice to avoid tequio and other forms of community service. They claim no need to participate in tequio because they no longer involve themselves in the life of the village, and nearly every year there is a conflict over the demands of community and religious freedoms in the community (Cohen n.d.).

Real benefits come to villagers who volunteer to serve in work crews. When it is time to refinish school chairs, the leftover paint goes home with those who worked on the project. It is not uncommon for a bag of cement to "fall off the truck" and end up in a worker's solar. Santañeros who clean the streambeds are given first choice on the brush and wood that is cleared away. The wood is not free, and a fee is paid to the *Comité de las Buenas Comunales* (community projects committee). But the fee is small, and the wood, already cut and quite accessible, is a good fuel source. Doña Minerva bought nearly three months' worth of firewood through her son's participation in tequio.

Tequio is under new pressures due to Santa Ana's changing economic and social reality. Two problems challenging tequio's usefulness are migration and the technological training needed for advanced development projects. First, the rise in the number of men leaving the community as migrants results in a decline in the number of workers available for work crews. Second, technological innovations and materials may demand more training than most Santañeros may possess. An additional factor that may become more of a problem in the future is the expansion of formal-sector employment in the community. If work schedules become less flexible, and Santañeros begin to earn hourly wages, they will lack the free time necessary for tequio obligations.

Santañeros who hold salaried positions (teachers, government workers, and day laborers commuting to Tlacolula) have begun to pay friends and relatives to fill their tequio obligations. Many migrants who are out of the community for three or more years also hire workers to cover tequio. Finally, some weavers who cannot afford the time away from their looms are paying for replacement workers during periods of intensive production. The rate for a day's tequio in 1992–1993 was around thirty

Table 5.1 Tequio Commitments in Santa Ana

Give Tequio	Pay Worker	Pay or Work Depending on Time	Cover Tequio (son is migrant)	Commitment Completed (over 60)	Total
28	2	2	2	5	39

thousand pesos (approximately ten dollars), and was commensurate with a standard low wage paid for a day's work at the time. The wage paid for tequio service had dropped to only fifteen nuevos pesos for the day in 1996, a wage that was only about one-fifth its value in 1993 (although still near the minimum wage for a day's work). For a Santañero who has committed himself to tequio for a day, the decision to hire a replacement worker to serve in the work crew can be a wise investment, particularly if the villager stands to earn more than fifteen pesos at his regular job. The credit for the project goes to the Santañero who pays for the work. The use of paid labor in projects brings the possibility of a new class of Santañero workers who will make their living primarily through contracts to cover the tequio commitments of others. However, in 1992, the number of villagers paying others to work tequio was low, and only two of thirty-nine respondents surveyed had paid for replacement workers (see Table 5.1).

A different problem emerges when a project is too difficult for the community to use tequio effectively. During the 1992 building of a new day school in the village, cooperación replaced tequio and the village collected funds to support construction. The state government granted the community supplies to build the new day school early in the year. The funds for construction materials were supplied through President Salinas de Gotari's Solidaridad program and the state government. In accordance with project policies, labor was to be provided by the community.[8]

An empty site on the western edge of the town was chosen for the school. Cement, steel rods, electrical wiring, and plumbing fixtures were delivered. Work began; however, the diverse composition and skill of the tequio crews at any given time made it nearly impossible to complete the project following the traditional pattern of communal labor. The project involved specialized equipment, skill, and months to complete. Instead of depending on tequio alone to meet the needs of the project, a contractor was hired from Tlacolula. He came to Santa Ana with his apprentices and crews to do most of the work. Santañeros contributed labor as their schedules and skills permitted. In addition, families contributed money to support the project. Their assistance was noted by the treasurer and the secretary of the municipio as tequio.

This pattern of government-provided supplies and the use of paid wage labor, tequio, and cooperación to cover village development projects continued in 1996.[9] Four major projects had begun in 1995, and each used paid work brigades in combination with nationally supplied materials and locally collected funds. The most ambitious of these projects is the development of a large freshwater reservoir on village lands. Less dramatic, but no less important, projects include paving roads, replanting trees on village mountain lands, installing a village-wide sewer system, and purchasing a new bus with state funds.

A second issue inherent in the changing nature of tequio is the difference between working communally and paying someone to do communal work. Sending money to Santa Ana to employ a fellow Santañero to cover tequio while working as a migrant in the United States is different

The new village bus purchased in 1993.

from living in the village and participating in the daily life of the community. The difference creates what Mauss (cited in Bloch and Parry 1989: 5) describes as "possession at a distance," where a relationship stills works to invoke social ties and responsibilities, but does so in a new and different way. Here, the social contract that tequio establishes between a Santañero household and the community is being replaced by a business contract between an employer and employee (see Holmes 1989: 31). In other words, tequio, which is a work relationship defined by a moral imperative, becomes an employer-employee relationship defined by market forces and issues of supply and demand.

Cooperación

Cooperación is a form of taxation, although most Santañeros will tell you they pay no taxes. The treasurers of various committees will call all of the heads of households to the plaza from time to time to collect cooperación. Treasurers keep the books for their committees, and funds are usually held in the Banamex bank branch in Tlacolula. It often falls upon the treasurer to cover missing funds if a discrepancy is found. *Alumbrado Público* (Public Electricity) collects fees for electricity every other month. The fee includes a set charge that covers the community's streetlights. Festival committees associated with the church collect throughout the year in support of fiestas. One-time contributions are made for projects such as the reservoir and sewer system. During our 1992–1993 stay, money was collected for a deep well under construction to the northwest of the community (thirty thousand pesos, or ten dollars, per household). For the January fiesta, households contributed twenty thousand pesos to cover expenses that in the past would typically be paid for by the mayordomía, who traditionally sponsored the event (and see Stephen 1990).

Santañeros will tell you they cooperate to maintain the village and their place in it. Cooperación has been around for a long time. Older informants remember their parents contributing in the past, but only in recent years has it become of central importance. Don Beto told me, "When I was a child, oh, your family had maybe a centavo to give, a centavo. We cooperated, but for a centavo it means nothing. Today, you might give twenty thousand pesos [seven dollars]—now that is some money." As our discussion continued, he suggested the emphasis on cooperación is based on rising incomes in the community, the technological demands of villagers, and shifts in what the community wants through local develop-

ment. The list of contemporary programs supported through cooperación includes the expansion of the electrical grid, the construction of a
sewer system, building projects, and arts programs.

Santañeros usually said they had few problems dealing with the growing emphasis on cooperación. They did not see their payments as a form
of taxation, describing their payments as "monetary tequio." Additional
discussion revealed that the majority of villagers were not entirely comfortable with the idea of cooperación, or with its increasing role in the
community. People complained about the cost of cooperation, and contributed only grudgingly. Some men went as far as to hide in their homes
or leave the community around the time contributions were collected,
perhaps escaping to Oaxaca City for the day or taking their livestock into
the mountains.[10] Another complaint is that wealthy households pay no
more than anyone else. It is quite easy to see who is more and less able to
pay for projects. A family living in a large home is obviously better off
than a family living in a one-room cane house. Cooperación places a pro-
portionately larger burden on the poor, much like a regressive tax. The
increase in cooperación is part of the changing local economy and of the
increased association of Santañeros with international markets (and see
Wilk 1991: 172).

The shift from tequio to cooperación is both subversive to sociocultural orders, and "an instrument for their maintenance" (Bloch and Parry
1989: 22). New relationships built around the contribution of money
mark a shift away from participatory action. In the example of tequio, we
find there are new challenges to the cooperative structure of society. The
shift toward contract relationships reduces long-term social networks between individuals and families and both emphasizes and objectifies economic and class differences. In addition, cooperación is increasing while
social and political action moves from a *caciquismo* (informal rule based
on social prestige) style of rule, and toward a more professional model of
management (see López-Cortés 1991), challenging the cooperative basis
of local government. Nevertheless, the use of cooperación maintains a
developmental and programming framework that would otherwise be
marked by increased state involvement in local affairs.

The decline in structures like tequio threatens to undermine an integral
way in which cooperation is practiced within the community. This is not
necessarily a problem when other social contracts remain strong or new
patterns of association are developed. In Santa Ana, guelaguetza, com-

padrazgo, and informal household ties continue to link individuals and families to each other. Chapter Six outlines innovative ways in which Santañeros are responding to ongoing change in their community.

Servicio and Community Politics

While we wait for the officials to line up, let us review some of the projects carried out for this community. We have the construction of the primary school José Vazconcelos. The president of the municipio, along with the community, carried out this project. Also our community began a project to bring potable water into the village. We have the extension of electricity, the repavement of our road, and the rehabilitation of the plaza, palacio municipal, and the recovery of the treasures of our past. We have a market for crafts, a post office, a library. Now we also have the new school. Thus, we have many projects for the community carried out by the municipio and that help Santañeros to advance. We also have the remodeling of the plaza, for the benefit of our community and future citizens of our community.

Emcee praising the outgoing municipal government,
January 1, 1993.

Servicio describes the many political commitments that an individual makes to his or her community as a representative of a household. Service is the work a Santañero gives while holding a position in one of Santa Ana's many political and religious committees. These *nombramientos* (elected or voluntary positions) are described as *cargos* (burdens) by the men and women who hold them, owing to the pressures they can place on an individual's time and finances. Traditionally, these positions were held by men, and women played informal, nonofficial roles. In 1992–1993, women held leadership positions on only one committee, associated with a commodities food program. By 1996, women had begun to hold more diverse positions, although their numbers overall remain quite low.

Some positions require minimal effort and little money and are completed over a short period—usually one year. Other cargos may demand full-time involvement and last for three years. Full-time positions include high-ranking offices like municipal president and carry a great deal of prestige. Such positions typically mark the high points in a Santañero's political career.

A Santañero's status is determined by the cargo committees and positions he or she has held on those committees. The efforts and energies invested in a committee are often indications of the prestige associated with and embodied in service. Unlike some communities where there is a separation of the religious and civil hierarchy, Santañeros move back and forth between the two. Some cargos, such as sponsorship of mayor-domías or care for the village church, are fully voluntary and confer high status on their holders (see Royce 1975). On the other hand, a minor po-sition like *vocal* (voting member) of a school committee demands little time and carries little status (see Wasserstrom 1983: 246).

The cargo systems emerged during the colonial period in response to expropriations by the Catholic Church and by the state of communally controlled lands and restrictions by the Church on communal support of local practices (Chance 1990: 29). The *cofradías* (religious brotherhoods) gave way to civil-religious hierarchies following the Mexican Revolution and increased village autonomy. The most recent shifts in the structure of the system are toward strictly religious hierarchies, as civil government falls under tighter state control and is bureaucratized (Chance 1990: 33).

Cargo systems are microcosms of local community relationships and are marked by competition and contest over positions (Cancian 1965: 135). An individual's and his or her family's status is the foundation for cargo service. It is through continued service that status is enhanced, maintained, and re-created through time. Thus, the number and ranks of the positions a villager holds are one indication of a person's standing in the community. Competition for various offices can be fierce at times. This is especially the case when the number of men vying for office out-numbers the total cargos available (Cancian 1965: 126–128). On the other hand, some cargos are difficult to fill. Men complain of the time and money they are asked to invest in service, and in many villages the num-ber of individuals interested in service is in decline (Cancian 1992). High-ranking offices often demand a near daily commitment of time and en-ergy. Here again, then, we note the push and pull of communalism and social rules that both empower and restrict practice.

The cargo system in Mesoamerica generates coalitions that unify a community in response to external economic and political domination (Greenberg 1981). In times of tension and national stress, community members limit their external involvement and create "closed corporate" systems for self-defense (Wolf 1957, 1986).[11] Closed, or judicial and agri-cultural corporate structures, defend the community's population from the exploitative grip of national governments and markets. These "closed" structures open as a village's population associates with external markets, national politics, and global economics (Wolf 1957: 12–13). The ongoing development of ties between local and national economies continues until the very structure of the cargo system, and the definition of what constitutes a community, are transformed. In place of a closed, corporate system in which social networks mediate internal difference, we find that an open, noncorporate entity is created. This open, noncorporate system is characterized by increased class-based differences and a decline in the presence of effective and functioning cross-linkages (Cancian 1992: 185).

Anthropologists have proposed many explanations to account for the structure and meaning of the cargo system since Wolf's pioneering work. Harris (1964: 30) argues that the structure of local hierarchies, and in particular religious cargos, accomplished little more than effecting the exploitation of a population already pushed to its economic limits. The Catholic Church exploited peasant communities through the extraction of economic capital, while working under the guise of faith, church celebrations, and village-based fiestas. Rather than building cohesion through mutual aid, Harris maintains that the cargo system masked what villagers would otherwise have labeled "blatant abuse." In other words, a case of symbolic violence in service to state and religious hegemony was clothed in the rhetoric of cooperation and reciprocity (Bourdieu 1977).

Alternatively, Dow (1977) argues that the cargo system works primarily to redistribute wealth within the peasant community. While not claiming that peasants are "irrational," Dow maintains that they exist at a stage removed from capitalism and lack a real class system. More recently, Wasserstrom (1983) argues that the structure of the cargo system is rooted in the historical relationship of the peasant community to regional economies, state religion, and politics. Thus, communalism is the result of the dialectical and sometimes antagonistic relationship of the local social system with the external social, political, and economic systems (Wasserstrom 1983: 246).

What these models lack is first, a sense that native and peasant populations understand their position vis-à-vis the state. As should be apparent, Santañeros (and I would argue, most Mesoamericans) are not blind to the machinations of the state. Cooperation has its coercive functions at the local and state levels; however, it is also a system that works. Second, rural peasant and indigenous communities are marked by class-based differences. These differences may be expressed in terms that are not as blatantly economic as in urban, Western society; however, they do exist and are rooted in the hierarchical civil and religious cargo systems found in most rural communities.

What is needed is an alternative model that captures the history, the contested nature of status, and the contemporary "location" of the community in a changing economic, social, and political reality. In other words, once we understand the history of the cargo system (see Chance 1990; Wasserstrom 1983), we must examine how the system is modernized and adapted to new situations (see Smith 1989). In this approach, the cargo system becomes one structure through which a community delimits and "cleanses," or purifies, external social, economic, and political forces and negotiates local differences. Cooperative structures thus become models through which global changes are translated into indigenous practices and morality and local status is created and contested.

Patterns of familial cooperation create bonds between individuals but do not necessarily resolve conflicts. Household associations, generated through guelaguetza and tequio, parallel familial patterns of cooperation, creating cross-linkages that mediate oppositions, but do not miraculously resolve them. Cross-linkages do not preclude exploitation of one household by another. Such structures do not prevent the exploitation of Santañeros by nonlocal actors (from Teotiteco intermediaries to state politicians, from development specialists to international exporters), nor does the presence of cooperation necessarily mean that redistribution will always take place.

The outcome of community cooperation leads to a conundrum about the definition of altruism and self-interested behavior (see Wilk 1993). Defining the motivations for participation in community-based forms of cooperation is as difficult as determining when an action is altruistic or selfish. Choosing altruism over self-interest risks misrepresenting the nature of social practice, which often falls between these two poles. However, a practice-centered approach, one rooted in understanding the setting, structure, and multiple meanings of action, allows for the exploration of Santañero systems of cooperation as tools through which villagers deal with their changing needs in a changing world. Thus, tequio, cooperación, and servicio are community-wide relationships that aid in the maintenance of social solidarity and integrity, even as they are coercive and contribute to status contests. Cargo systems, then, are not immune to radical changes given new economic realities. Rather, they are a site where local cultural practices meet changing economic realities and through which new patterns of cooperation and action are established (and see Robben 1989).

Cancian (1990, 1992) notes a precipitous drop in the number of cargos and cargo holders as a result of political and social decentralization in Zinacantán, Chiapas. Decentralization of social and political control exercised by Zinacantecos over outlying hamlets, the growing dependency of local workers on external markets, and declining employment contribute to the rapid decline of the cargo system (Cancian 1990: 69–71). The cargo system in Santa Ana (which is subject to many similar constraints and changes) has not declined in a similar manner. The number of mayordomías has dropped from nine to three due to lack of annual sponsorship. However, there has been an increase in the number of civil committees and familial rites-of-passage ceremonies celebrated locally (see Stephen 1991b).

Santañeros talk about civil cargo service in much the same way they talk about religious cargos. They are serving the community, and through participation they establish status in the village. In Zinacantán, on the other hand, new committees reflect the geographical division of the municipio into a village and hamlets. Service in a new civil cargo adds to the tensions already at work against cohesion (Cancian 1992: 194). Many new committees in Zinacantán and Santa Ana reflect a growing association with state governments, and some committees are directly sanctioned by the PRI (Chance 1990: 33). However, Santañeros talk about their actions in intimate terms: "This is what I do for my community." Informants seldom mentioned the ties to the state, and instead used new civil cargos to "reconcile in some measure those inequalities that modernization has created" (Wasserstrom 1983: 239). Lacking the local divisions of Zinacantán, and with Teotitlán as a nearby and powerful opponent, Santañeros appear able to maintain their system and invent new ways of cooperating that continue to create important cross-linkages within the community.

Cargos and Status in Santa Ana

I have argued that servicio creates cross-linkages between various strata in Santañero society, and that these linkages do not preclude inequality. Contests about status and prestige revolve around religious and civil cargos. At the top of the status ladder, in terms of prestige and responsibility, are four committees: the *Comité del Templo* (church committee), *Comité del Pueblo* (the village committee that is equivalent to the county commissioners), the *alcaldes* (a board of three men who adjudicate disputes), and the *Comité de las Buenas Comunales* (resource management committee).

The Comité del Templo maintains the church and guards the community's sacred well-being. Unlike the other committees, the Comité del Templo is voluntary and is usually filled by older Santañeros who have already held high-ranking positions. Since 1990, the church committee has been responsible for mayordomías that are no longer sponsored by individual families. There are only three family-sponsored mayordomías

The January saint's day in full swing

celebrated in the community—two in January, the other running from the end of July to early August. In the past there have been as many as nine mayordomías in Santa Ana annually. In Zinacantán a parallel decline is defined in relation to rising incomes and local involvement in the national economy (Cancian 1992). Zinacantecos are earning more money, but have less economic security and are investing more of their income in the management of private enterprises rather than in the maintenance of community cargos (see Stephen 1990).

Mayordomías in Santa Ana have also disappeared; however, in their place are growing community-wide and communally financed events. The January and July/August saint's day celebrations (once fully supported by mayordomía sponsorship) are now supported by individual families and by the Comité del Templo (which collects funds annually from village households), and have become community-wide celebrations that carry a carnival-like quality (see A. Cohen 1993). The religious features of the celebrations are downplayed, outside of church rituals and family-sponsored masses, while civic pride is emphasized. The church committee collects funds from all households to support the mayordomía, and all members of the community are invited to partake of the festivities which include two dances, performances by the *danzantes,* parades, a two-day rodeo, fireworks, and a special show of children's art at the Shan-Dany Museum.

The Comités del Pueblo and de las Buenas Comunales, and the alcaldes, make up what is known in the village as *La Autoridad* (the authority). The Comité del Pueblo functions like a county commission in the United States, overseeing the daily functions of the municipio. Governed by a president, the committee includes a treasurer, a secretary, and seven regidores. The regidores cover the office each day of the week if the president is unavailable. Buenas Comunales is also a ten-member committee, and oversees the management of Santa Ana's public lands and resources. It works out the details of community projects, such as the location for a new well. These committees serve three-year terms, typically working a few days each week on local projects. The presidents of the municipio and Buenas Comunales work nearly full time, forsaking farming and weaving. Migrants help support Santañero involvement in committee work. Remittances from family members living away from the community often cover the costs incurred. In an interview, a former president of the municipio told me he could not fulfill the requirements of his office if it were not for the three hundred dollars in remittances sent back almost every

Table 5.2 Minor Committees Found in Santa Ana

Committee	Function
Comité del Escuela, matinal y tarde	Morning and afternoon school committees
Comité del Kinder	Kindergarten committee
Alumbrado Público	Public lights
Mejores Materiales	Project materials
Comité de la Casa de Salud	Health clinic committee
Junta Patriótica	Oversees national holidays and elections
Comité de la Casa del Pueblo	Traditional arts committee
Comité de Auga Potable	Drinking water committee
Topiles del Templo	Church security, bell ringers (two men)
Vigilancia	Police
Comité del Museo Shan-Dany	Shan-Dany museum committee
Transportación	Transportation, maintains buses
Comité de la Capilla	Chapel committee

month by his sons working in the United States (and see Smith 1992).

The alcaldes in Santa Ana adjudicate local affairs, whether common or criminal. The three alcaldes decide disputes between villagers and can discipline people who violate written and implicit community codes. Alcaldes are typically men who have been president of the municipio or have served on many high-ranking committees. Their standing in the community is often above reproach and their decisions cannot be challenged. This final point is important, because alcaldes are sometimes called upon to sanction committee members who are in abuse of their positions. While it seldom happens, they can, and have, removed some committee presidents from office.

I counted at least thirty-five major and minor committees in the community in 1993. Their structure follows the pattern noted. Each includes seven men: a president, a treasurer, a secretary and four *vocales* (voting members) whose terms of office are one year (see Table 5.2 for a selected list of committees). New committees are regularly created as needed or as required. One of the more recently formed committees was organized around migrants living in the United States. The committee was established because of the deaths of two Santañeros in the United States during 1991. At that point, migrants working in the area (southern California) pooled their resources to return the bodies for burial. Villagers living in the United States decided they should formalize their actions and established the committee following the crisis. No committee can be created or make decisions without the support of the Comité del Pueblo, alcaldes, and Buenas Comunales.

Generally, men serve on committees, and men cast the majority of votes at village elections. Women have the right to vote and to serve on committees, but most women do not attend elections.[12] In fall 1992, I observed the local elections throughout a September day, and only three women voted. In contrast, men were collected and brought to the plaza, by force if necessary, to vote in the elections. By noon there were more than one hundred men in the courtyard of the municipio. The crowd argued over the proper course for the community's future. Women have a right to run for all offices, and in some communities they have taken positions in the central authority. However, Santa Ana's government remains dominated by men. When nominees for a position were not forwarded quickly enough, one of the members of the *Junta Patriótica* (election board) threatened to enlist women for offices. This quickly brought nominations from the floor. A few women had begun to serve on committees as voting members and treasurers by 1996. One of the first women to serve told me she had replaced her husband who had left the country as a migrant. While I was unable to survey many men on their feelings concerning women serving on committees, at least a handful felt it would be a change for the better. They suggested that women were likely to be much better at managing committee funds, and much less likely to waste committee time with alcohol and arguments.

Village elections are conducted as an open ballot.[13] After nominees agree to run, their names are listed on a blackboard in plain view. At this point, candidates or their supporters can make statements promoting their election. Following the speeches, each Santañero walks to the blackboard at the front of the room. Before the entire group, the voter takes a piece of chalk and marks his choice. This often leads to landslides in favor of particular candidates. Most voters climb on the bandwagon and vote for the leading candidate, as voting continues and a clear winner becomes apparent.

A Santañero must be married and over the age of eighteen to participate in committees and vote. Before a young man marries and reaches the

Election day 1992

required age for service, he spends time as a *topile* (police officer). The topiles are charged with the safety of the community. Most single men begin their committee work as topiles patrolling the village after dark with their friends. Young men are eager to become part of the security force. It is a legitimate excuse used to evade household responsibility and escape parental involvement. There are Santañeros who never advance beyond this stage of service. However, Santañeros who restrict themselves to such positions earn little status in relation to other villagers and are often described by terms usually reserved for children.

Children who become members of one of the community's three dance troupes gain early experience with servicio and the responsibilities of cargo work. The church supports two dance troupes that perform at community fiestas. A third secular dance troupe is part of the *Casa del Pueblo* program (a state arts project). To become a part of a troupe, the individual makes a promesa (see Chapter Four) to dance for three years (see Brandes 1988: 63; J. Cohen 1993: 153). The church troupes and Casa

Table 5.3 Cargo Positions Held among Santañeros Age 20 and above

| Age | \multicolumn{14}{c}{Number of Cargo Positions Held} | | | | | | | | | | | | | |
	1	2	3	4	5	6	7	8	9	10	11	12	13	14
20–30	5	3	1											
31–40		2	6	1	1	1								
41–50	2	2	1			1	1	1						
51–60			1	1		1	3	1			1	1		
60 and above									2			1		1

del Pueblo group are affiliated with national arts programs that organize performances and exhibitions throughout the country. Working with the programming board at the Casa de la Cultura in Oaxaca City, Santa Ana's committee sent local dancers and the village's band to Spain on an exchange organized in conjunction with the 1992 Olympics.

A Santañero's responsibilities and prestige typically increase with age as he or she moves through various positions and committees. The office of president carries the most prestige, and is followed in order by treasurer, secretary, and vocal. A villager will earn very little status by filling such positions in minor committees. Santañeros who have excelled in school are usually elected to the posts of secretary and treasurer, and often they serve before they are married. Many men with young children take positions in a school committee as one of their first cargos in order to represent their children in decisions about schools.

Finding older Santañeros who have served in five to ten cargos during their political careers is not unusual (see Table 5.3). Nearly every man I surveyed began his service as a topile around eighteen years of age. From this first position in the community's police force, most villagers move on to act as vocales in various cargos. They begin to run for or volunteer to take on more prestigious positions, gaining status and political power in the process (Cancian 1965: 87). Aron Mendoza, an independent weaver, had served on seven committees, including the position of vocal for *Transportación*, Comité del Templo, Alumbrado Público, and *Comité de la Casa del Salud*, and secretary for both the municipio and *Mejores Materiales* by the age of forty-two.

In the past, men could choose not to serve on formal committees, and work as teachers in the adult literacy campaign instead—something Don Mauro did twice. A position as teacher carried cultural capital beyond the social prestige associated with most cargos. Such a position was a material statement of the intelligence and education attained by the individual and his knowledge of national culture. Presently, education is organized by the state and instructors are professionally trained.

A Santañero is allowed to retire from cargo service after reaching sixty years of age. Many older men go on to fill additional positions as alcalde or become members of the Comité del Templo. Sometimes villagers serve well past retirement age. Santañeros will often sponsor fiestas (large and small) in the community following their formal retirement from committee work.

Cargos are ranked according to status and the burden associated with a position. Service is marked by conflicts and contests. Some villagers choose not to work, and others seek easy positions. Disputes erupt around policies, workloads, and projects. Yet Santañeros use their committees to unite villagers into a coherent entity, and mediate the intervention of outsiders. In this respect, the community becomes another level in the hierarchy of unified oppositions in Zapotec world view (El-Guindi and Selby 1976). The oppositions that mark interhousehold relations are mediated through the cargos and establish new sets of oppositions, those between Santa Ana and the state.

The cargo system stands in contrast to state hierarchies. The local management of village affairs and the resolution of household disputes by alcaldes limit state intervention, and are avenues through which villagers resist external political domination (Nader 1990). However, changes in the demography and income of the community as well as increasing demands by villagers for more services, and the resulting increase in ties between state and local systems, threaten the independent and cooperative nature of Santa Ana's political hierarchy.

Although it is in fact a coercive system of ranked and contested positions serving the political needs of the community, the cargo system is structured upon the rhetoric of cooperation and voluntary self-sacrifice. Thus, it is wrapped in the trappings of what Gramsci defined as civil society, or the private and personal equivalent to government and the state (Gramsci 1988: 420). The involvement of the state in local affairs and the professionalization of politics (as cargo positions in the municipio and other high-ranking committees become full-time jobs) move the structure of local government away from the informal patterns of the cacique and toward formalized bureaucratic management (see Holmes 1989: 31, 42).

It must be pointed out that the wealthy and powerful in the village typically hold the most prestigious committee assignments. Many additional positions are filled by their cronies. By filling committee presidencies and treasury positions, they control the capital collected for various projects and events, and therefore the community itself.

Elites' control of cooperación, powerful committee positions, the definition of area development projects, and the distribution of state funds, leads to claims of abuse by those villagers who are less well-off. Members of committees, especially treasurers, are often accused of stealing community funds (Tendler 1983: 5). Whether the accusations are real or not, this indicates that cooperation, for all of its benefits, is also a source of conflict within the community. Moreover, civil society, although an alternative to state control, becomes a structure for exploitation and manipulation of poorer villagers by their wealthier, more powerful, neighbors. It should come as no surprise that in this world of cooperation, there is little trust, and even close relatives often accuse each other of economically or socially devious behavior.

Conclusions

In this chapter I have outlined the cooperative relationships that Santañeros create in service to their village. Tequio, cooperación, and servicio are relationships through which the social contests and reciprocal commitments founded in interhousehold relationships are constructed and reproduced at the more inclusive level of the community. Santa Ana is more than a geographical location on a map. It is a group of people involved in the daily negotiation of society and identity. One way villagers forge, maintain, and reproduce their identity is through cooperation. The process of identity formation does not occur in a vacuum, and Santañeros are not isolated from global markets, national politics, and the influence of extra-local social forces. These influences are manifest locally in the increasing presence of consumer goods, the involvement of weavers in transnational markets for their work, the movement of Santañeros to and from the United States as migrants, demands for infrastructural and educational improvements, and growing economic prosperity.

Cooperation then, must be more than a symbol. In the village it is. It is at the core of a practical system Santañeros use to make sense of their changing world. In the process, cooperative relationships are updated and reinvented. There is a declining dependence on tequio in response to changing demography and increasingly specialized technology for projects. In turn, villagers rely more heavily on cooperación. The reliance on monetary support for community projects objectifies growing economic differences in the village. The structure of the political hierarchy is also going through changes. In the past, political power was founded upon a person's prestige and status. Control was organized through the influence and management of cooperative networks. Currently, political cargos are undergoing a process of professionalization. How these changes are played out in the community, and the future place of cooperation in village life, are the subject of the next chapter.

Chapter Six

Cooperation, the Politics of Leadership, and Civil Society

Señores, señoras, jovenes, niños — in the name of the constitutional government I accept my position as president from 1993 through 1995. It is my honor to serve. I am dedicated to you. Before anything I want to thank and assure the observers from Oaxaca that we will work as hard as others before us. You rest assured. Have confidence in us. The ex-president Librado Aquino has given us a mandate for today, for loving service to our community. During my three years I am ready for any responsibility, and to carry out any projects for the community. The former committee worked with the Casa de Salud, constructed the deep well, and a system for potable water. They renovated the central plaza and rediscovered our history. Through Solidaridad, the community was linked with our president, Salinas de Gotari, and the governor of our state.

We will work together with the people of the pueblo to move Santa Ana forward, and to guarantee a proper education for our young. From tomorrow there will begin a new era. We will work to improve streets, buildings, and our general health. Our tourist center will be important to our community and our plans. We will work with Buenas Communales to protect the environment and animals. We will be in contact with members of our community who have migrated to the other Latin countries and the United States of America; they are a part of us as well. This way we will be organized together and will always be in communication. These and other projects we propose to the community to consider as we give our service to everyone. Former presidents and the dear pueblo of Santa Ana del Valle, call my name, keep me informed, I wait to work with you and with the authority of the community and to progress together.

—Municipal President, Cristoforo Cruz, January 1, 1993

THE PREVIOUS CHAPTER noted three shifts in the structure and practice of cooperative relationships among Santañeros. First, participation in tequio is dropping and the structure of work brigades is changing. Households pay hired replacements to cover tequio, and projects may demand technical skills and require time commitments that are difficult to meet through voluntary brigades. Second, cooperación is increasingly important as a means to support community projects and fiestas. Third, the cargo system's foundation in formal social networks and the control of local caciques has given way to a more bureaucratic system tied to state guidelines. The outcome is a society in which wealth, class, and work are becoming more important than an individual's experience, social status, and familial background.

Changes in local social practices are in response to many different factors: an increase in migration, a shift in the demographic structure of the adult population, the involvement of Santañeros in a cash-based economy, and the overall rise in the community's population. These forces are also linked to changes in local expectations among Santañeros, who now want access to markets and new goods as well as the public utilities and services typically associated with urban life—electricity, plumbing, water, and so forth (and see Alarcón 1992).

Santa Ana's political hierarchy finds itself involved more directly with the state in response to increasing demands of the population. The growth of state-local relationships leads to the professionalization or "rationalization" of the political system (see the discussion of Weber in Holmes 1989). In other words, locally defined social networks based upon indigenous beliefs and morality decline as local society is reorganized around contracts and the rules of bureaucratic law. Local elites, and particularly those closely involved with state programs, mobilize and direct the population, encouraging economic development and rational decision making (see Holmes 1989). In the Santañero example, this includes entrepreneurial investments by independent weavers, rising mano de obra work, migration, and capital-intensive development (expanding the electrical grid, for example), rather than focused investment and reproduction of traditional social relationships. Nevertheless, in Santa Ana, the movement toward professionalism and the process of rationalization that characterizes local-state and local-global relations have not destroyed locally defined cooperative and reciprocal social practices (and see Granovetter 1995; Greenberg 1995; Watanabe 1992). Thus, social disenchantment (the decline of traditional practices), characterized by "rational discourse" with the state, does not "penetrate the strata upon strata of traditional sensibilities that preoccupied the rural populace" (Holmes 1989: 145). In Santa Ana, local practices are not replaced wholly by new, rational systems. New patterns of reciprocal and cooperative associations build upon traditional structures as local society continues to change.

We are left then to ponder: How are Santañeros able to define a local social system based in "traditional" ideas of cooperation and reciprocity that remains practical and important, given the ongoing changes in their world? Before examining the three cooperative alternatives which Santañeros have created in response to ongoing economic and political change —the Shan-Dany Museum, basketball clubs, and a weaving cooperative— it is important to explore further the professionalization of the cargo system. The cargo system is the point at which local and state forces come together most powerfully. It is also a point at which we can focus on the social fallout from the growth of professional politicians.

The contrasting experiences and effectiveness of two men, Tonio García and Cristoforo Cruz (both past municipal presidents), illustrate how politicians both succeed and fail as they reformulate and reinvent themselves and social practices according to locally defined rules and personal goals for the future.

Electing a President

Santa Ana inaugurated a new government, including the Comité del Pueblo, in January 1993. Elections for the municipal president, his seven regidores, the secretary, and the treasurer, along with members of all of the community's one-year committees, were held in September 1992. Election day was marked by debate concerning the qualities of leadership needed in a municipal president, given the rise in out-migration and demands for new services locally. Speakers mentioned important factors to consider in the nominating process. Personal experience and reputation were most important. Community status and an ability to work with state officials were also important attributes for the future president.

Three candidates were nominated to run for municipal president after a morning of debate. The first nominee was Cristoforo Cruz (age, forty-nine). Cruz was a successful sometime migrant who lived in a large home with modern appliances and owned vehicles and one shop (a shop selling dry goods and stationery). He was living with his son in San Diego, California, and working in construction during the elections. He agreed to run for the office of president over the telephone.

The second nominee was Bonifacio Aquino (age, fifty-six). Aquino had never left the community for an extended time and worked as a farmer and a successful contract weaver. He was respected for his many years of cargo service to the village, rather than for any particular success in business.

The third candidate was Ricardo García (age, thirty-eight). García was an independent weaver who exported textiles directly to a gallery in the United States. He had recently completed a cargo as community treasurer. Young and successful, García was also the son of Tonio García, an important village leader who had played a central role in the revitalization of the central plaza and the founding of the Shan-Dany Museum.

Juan Sánchez (a state worker who commutes to Oaxaca City daily) rose in support of Cristoforo Cruz when the director of the *Junta Patriótica* asked for endorsements. He said:

> We need leadership, activism, and in this Cristoforo Cruz has proved himself repeatedly. Remember when we paved the road into our town? Who put together the plan? Who engineered the bridge [a two-lane bridge spanning an arroyo about a kilometer outside town and on the way to Tlacolula]? Cristoforo Cruz did these things. Now we must ask him to return to the community again.

No one stood to speak on behalf of the other candidates. An older man suggested Aquino was a good citizen and deserved the position as a sign of respect for his dedication to the village. Other Santañeros mumbled angrily that Ricardo García was too young for the responsibility of the office. One man sitting nearby stated that Ricardo was nothing more than a puppet for his father. There were also rumors that García embezzled community funds to support his export business during his tenure as village treasurer. There was no substance to the rumor and the village's books were in order. Nevertheless, such statements are one way to gauge the tensions that revolve around filling high-status political offices.

Once the men were nominated and debate had ceased, the three names were written on a blackboard that stood at the front of the gathered electorate. Santañeros came forward to place a check by the name of their choice. Voting was open and everyone watched as the line slowly progressed and the chalk marks increased. Cruz built an early lead that became a landslide by the end of voting. Cruz learned of his election victory over the phone. He was to be the next municipal president and it was time to return to Santa Ana after a two-year absence.

The new government was the subject of nonstop gossip during the months between the September elections and January inauguration. People remembered what they liked and disliked about Cruz and his associates. Jealousies surfaced and uncertainties about Cruz's abilities were voiced. In his favor was his success as a migrant worker and businessman. Cristoforo Cruz had made a small fortune working in construction in California, and had sent money home to open a store at a busy village intersection. His mother (a part-time textile buyer) and his wife managed the store and sold a few tapetes. Theirs was also the only establishment in the community that advertised in English and invited tourists to browse.

Cruz's success worked against him. Most villagers were envious of his good fortune. For some, the envy went beyond the emotional. It became *muina,* a physical affliction brought on by intense jealousy (on various emotional responses in Zapotec communities, see Kearney 1986: 70; Nader 1969: 352). Others went so far as to talk about Cruz's accomplishments as if they came at their (the villagers') own expense.

One interviewee pointed out that Cruz had a large, well-built home with many appliances which were just becoming available locally (refrigerators, a water heater, and so forth) and spent his money on home improvements rather than on the village. A second informant suggested that Cruz's lapse in caring about the village was due to the years he had spent as a migrant. For this man, Cruz's election was an opportunity to correct what he perceived as Cruz's slighting of communal needs. Other villagers criticized Cruz and his wife for not supporting godchildren (although the Cruz family maintained many ties). Independent weavers complained that Cruz's wife and mother paid too little for textiles and earned profits as if they were Teotiteco intermediaries, not locals. Listening to informants, it seemed Cruz was trapped. On the one hand, many villagers wanted him to return to the community to limit his successes, or at least force him to invest that success into the development of the village. On the other hand, others thought Cruz should be respected for his success and the many important positions his family held in the village.[1] They also looked to him to effectively manage the village.

Tensions mounted around the time of the inauguration of the incoming authority. A new story circulated concerning the fitness of the president and his men. The election of two evangélicos to positions as regidores was one point of uncertainty among locals.[2] Rumors spread that the evangélicos were morally corrupt. One informant swore that the converts swapped wives with each other. A second rumor declared that Cruz had himself converted. People noted he no longer drank alcohol, a sure sign of change. In an interview, Cruz told me he gave up drinking for his health and still considered himself Catholic. There was little truth to the rumors, yet innuendo was difficult to escape. Cruz apparently never did pick up a drink throughout his tenure.

Cruz's attitude toward drinking was critical, given its ritual and social significance in the community and Zapotec society in general (see Nader 1969: 355; 1990: 276). Alcohol is shared equally among friends and co-workers (including politicians). Sharing alcohol and the mild inebriation that follows guarantees that no person within a group remains sober and therefore able to take advantage of a drinker (Kearney 1986: 76). Ritualized patterns of drinking also correlate with the goals of reciprocity and cooperation. To decline an offered drink is to insult the person making the presentation (Kearney 1986: 77). Refusal brings social tensions that may exist below the surface in most settings into the open. The rejected drink becomes a symbol of the rejected man who offers the liquor. Thus, the exchange of alcohol is yet another activity whereby social and cultural cross-linkages are established and maintained among Santañeros. Santañeros drink at most social events, including weddings, funerals, and committee meetings. To decline a toast or a drink is to decline participation in a social event or contract and to face retribution that can run from mild censure to vocal and public condemnation (and see Mauss 1990: 13).[3] Many men who publicly criticized Cruz's actions, said in private that it made sense for him to remain sober, given his health and the demands of his job.

Cristoforo Cruz and Tonio García

Cruz's term of office began midway through the three-year term of the Comité de las Buenas Comunales. Buenas Comunales was led by Tonio

García, Ricardo García's father and a central figure in Santa Ana's development. Terms of office for the Comité del Pueblo and Buenas Comunales are staggered to guard against two inexperienced presidents entering office in the same year. Cristoforo Cruz and Tonio García were compadres who had spent years working together in the 1970s to have the road into Santa Ana paved.[4] Tonio García, ten years Cruz's senior, was an important friend who aided Cruz during his early migrations to the United States.

García developed strong ties with state officials in Oaxaca City during his tenure as municipal president (mid-1980s). His foresight and management of village affairs are credited with the purchase of the community's first microbus for service between Tlacolula and Santa Ana. He gained state support for the founding and development of the Shan-Dany Museum and refurbishment of the plaza. He also installed the village's basketball court on the plaza and brought in benches, a market area, and a band shelter.[5] Finally, he was the first community leader to begin to update the antiquated water system.

García operated according to the rules of Santañero politics. He also learned how to manage in state politics to accomplish village goals. He was masterful at manipulating local reciprocal relationships to his advantage. García used compadrazgo and guelaguetza relationships to build authority and create consensus through gentle prompting and carefully deployed charisma, alcohol, and socially sanctioned pressure (and see Scott 1989).

I watched him operate occasionally. He would arrive at a household with a bottle of mescal and stay a few hours to talk. Later he would leave, having gained the support of another family. When it was time to work with politicians from Oaxaca, he was equally adept. He ingratiated himself and the village to state workers through constant praise and electoral support, building upon government programs that matched locally collected funds peso for peso. García maintained a steady flow of government monies into development projects.

One afternoon while sitting in the plaza, I asked García whether he felt he had traded any of Santa Ana's independence in exchange for state support. He shrugged and said, "Sometimes when you sleep with the dogs, you get some fleas." He added that a few fleas were not so terrible when the alternative was to remain in Teotitlán's shadow.[6]

Tonio García had been out of the office of the municipal president for seven years when he was elected to head Buenas Comunales. Meanwhile, his position in the community had not diminished. He and his wife were compadres to many children. They were present at most weddings and funerals, and at official celebrations he held a place of honor among former municipal presidents. His nomination and election as president of Buenas Comunales in 1991 was a show of the community's respect and esteem for his ability, as well as of his continued interest in local politics and social power.

García's term as the president of Buenas Comunales ran from January 1992 through the end of 1994. Cruz took office in January 1993 and would serve three years, through the end of 1995. Thus, for two years, Cruz's term of office would coincide with García's term at the helm of Buenas Comunales. Some of the tensions that developed between the two leaders were likely due to the changing structure of local politics, the changing definition and use of status in the village, and the growing relationships building between the community and the state. Other tensions came from the pressures placed on local leaders by villagers and outsiders competing for their attention and support. Still a third area of tension was rooted in the stresses of two people who were vying for a position of authority and power in a limited political universe.

Cristoforo Cruz and Tonio García were driven leaders and successful men. Each had held multiple high offices in the village and were accorded respect by most Santañeros. Each leader manipulated local consensus to meet federally defined standards. What is interesting for the discussion, given the parallels in their lives, is that García remained a far more successful politician. Thus, I am interested less in understanding the fight between the current and past president, and more interested in why Cristoforo Cruz's administration was plagued with problems while Tonio García enjoyed widespread support as the leader of Buenas Comunales.

Cruz's administration was confronted with skepticism by the village even before his term in office began. Word circulated among villagers that two early actions to be taken by the municipal government would be a ban on all public drinking and the elimination of the village's chronic problem with stray dogs. Villagers were not consulted, town meetings were not called, nor did Cruz meet with families informally. Instead, a plan of action was formulated by his committee and announced. Santañeros were left with no way to respond to the projects. In formal as well as informal discussions, I found few Santañeros who were angered by Cruz's plans. Cleaning the village streets of stray dogs was a decision most villagers applauded. The strays were a nuisance and often scared people at night. Ridding the plaza of drunks was also generally supported (particularly by young men and most women). Many people felt Santa Ana would look more attractive to tourists if inebriated villagers were not evident. Nevertheless, the municipio's leadership, and Cruz in particular, came under intense criticism. People were bothered by the way the decision was reached. Older villagers in particular felt they had been slighted by the committee's decision making and in turn were resistant to Cruz's goals. In other words, men and women in the village wanted to be consulted before the programs were initiated. The local formula had not been followed; villagers were left feeling slighted.

While Cruz struggled to promote programs that appeared to have general village support, many villagers were thrilled to hear that Tonio García had obtained another state-funded project for the community with little fanfare. INAH, along with the support of the Union of Oaxacan Community Museums, planned to build a children's museum in Santa Ana.[7] The project would be funded by INAH and the state, and the museum would bring visitors (although most likely they would be school-age Oaxacans and not tourists) to the community on a regular basis.

What is important to note is how Tonio García succeeded where Cruz failed. García used connections with state officials and his position within Buenas Comunales to manage village decision making and build consensus. García and his committeemen flattered Santañeros for their foresight and did not simply announce that the community would be the site for the new children's museum. García slowly brought informal conversations around to the relationship of Santa Ana and the state (typically over a bottle of mescal). He mentioned the state's interest in the community as a site for the new children's museum. Then he would pause and wait for his audience to voice an opinion. García would compliment villagers on their wise decision making and their skills in helping him develop the Shan-Dany Museum, and further emphasize the value of Santa Ana to the state and the respect given Santañeros by INAH. He moved the conversation in the right direction gently, toward village support of the new museum (something that was not guaranteed, given the many people who opposed the community museum). A decision negotiated between García, local leaders, and the state came in the end to look like a decision reflecting the opinion of the village as a whole. A sense of pride and importance was created among Santañeros, and in April, the state governor's wife came to Santa Ana for a ribbon-cutting ceremony that inaugurated construction. (The children's museum remained unfinished in 1996. A second project, to build an overnight guest house for visitors to the village, had been successfully completed with the support of INAH and the Union of Oaxacan Community Museums.)

The difference between Cristoforo Cruz's and Tonio García's actions reveals much about the exercise of power in the community and the changing place of cooperation in village politics. Cruz and García are both wealthy men. The former made his fortune working in the United States over the last ten years in construction work. The latter also spent time working as a migrant, in the 1960s and 1970s. Over the past ten years, García supported himself as an independent weaver. He worked with his son to become a successful, small-scale exporter.[8]

García and Cruz live in large homes with many modern conveniences. Yet their power is not based strictly on economic success. Authority is the combination of affluence, social standing, and the network of social relationships open and available for support (Bourdieu 1986; Scott 1989). Lacking economic wealth, a Santañero does not find himself able to become a leader. He cannot afford the costs of compadrazgo, nor the weight of important cargos. But affluence does not necessarily translate into social status. A Santañero must invest in the community.[9] This is not a demonstration of the irrationality of community members, nor is it an indication of an innate peasant-leveling mechanism (see discussion in Granovetter 1985; Wilk 1996). Rather, Santañero culture and economy are founded in the logic of their cooperative world view and social practices that remain effective and serve as an alternative to state processes. This does not mean Santañeros are altruistic, and as noted throughout this text, cooperation is contested and reciprocal relationships are full of tension. However, self-interest and personal affluence do not threaten the system if neither comes at the expense of the community (see Barth 1992; Bloch and Parry 1989; Granovetter 1995; Greenberg 1995).

García's experience and success are an example of the way in which status, affluence, and cooperation combine to create local authority based around traditional ideals, even as the village grows enmeshed in external social, political, and economic processes. García consistently manipulated cooperative relationships with other Santañero families to political ends. He knew the rhetoric of cooperation and he put it to action in the many formal and informal relationships he maintained. This was not a one-way process. People sought out his assistance and they knew he regularly invested in compadrazgo relationships. In return, villagers knew their support would be requested at critical junctures in the political life of the community.

The dyadic contracts García held with state officials further increased his local status. He was (and is) a leader who could get a job done. Social and economic capital came together in his hands and in the service of personal power. This was not simply an example of symbolic violence—in other words, García's actions were not the abuse of power disguised as altruism (see Bourdieu 1990; Rothman 1978). Few Santañeros would have supported García if his only motivation had been to gain political control or personal wealth. Instead, his participation in communal activities held advantages for the village and local households as well as for his own social and political ambitions (see Hardin 1993).

Cristoforo Cruz is similar to García in background and wealth. Yet his status in the village and support among Santañeros remained problematic before and throughout his administration. One issue was Cruz's limited experience in office. A second was his lengthy and frequent absences from the village. Surveys in 1996 indicated that migration does not necessarily influence effective village participation in and of itself. However, when a migrant is involved in multiple trips over long periods, as was Cruz, the effect can be a decline in status and influence (see Conway and Cohen 1998). Influence drops as the migrant attenuates ties to other villagers and households. When another villager is paid by the migrant to fill his tequio or cargo position, the opportunity to perform communal service in public is also lost. Status within the village also declines as distance and time remove the migrant from local decision making and leadership.

Cruz entered the office of municipal president with an activist platform that he felt would benefit the community. He rapidly proposed a series of programs (from removing drunks from the streets to expanding access to water) but spent little time discussing the projects with villagers. He was attacked for his style and approach to problem solving. Few people complained about the choices he made in terms of community projects. Nevertheless, Cruz placed himself into a difficult situation and found little support among his constituency.[10]

In response to growing criticism from the community, Cruz held town meetings, began to attend more local events (although he continued to refuse alcohol), and used informal discussions to frame public policy. The projects he promoted had not changed: He advocated the construction of a sewer system (a project that began in 1995), joined in support of the children's museum, and organized the purchase of a new bus for the community.

García's success and Cruz's troubles are indicative of the issues and contests that surround the manipulation of social, economic, and symbolic meaning within the community (see for example, Feierman 1991: 31). Wealth alone does not guarantee success or the prestige necessary to plan future projects. Cruz did not propose anything so outlandish that the community would reject his recommendation. Rather, the problem developed from the way in which he made proposals. His standing in the community, already problematic due to his years away from Santa Ana and rejection of ritual drinking, was further questioned through actions that did not meet local standards. In other words, the decisions or plans were not problematic; instead, the decision maker became the problem. Culture is "a way to comprehend the rational, not an abstract rationality divorced from the world of living people and set against the latter as its judge, but the rationality of living" (Dirlik 1990: 394–95); and as part of a cultural system, the conceptualization of prestige or status does not exist in a vacuum (see Smart 1993). Cruz's original approach was, in effect, "divorced" from the actual world of the Santañeros. His method of decision making conflicted with local standards; it was only when he began to follow local custom that community support was forthcoming.

Leadership is a quality that is not lightly conferred on the individual. It develops in the negotiation of social knowledge. The Santañero born to high status, like the individual who earns his or her social place, can only maintain and enhance that position through success in continued social contests. To deny the contest, or to set a new standard with little or no debate, undermines the tacitly agreed-upon social system that informs practice and action (see Robben 1989: 10–12). Cruz's status was built upon a shared morality rooted in cooperation and reciprocal systems that link the various layers of Santañero society and, in the process, create the community. Yet the president's actions, once he was in office, undermined the very patterns upon which the office was built and effectively pulled the communal rug from under his own feet.

The public, traditional structure of Santa Ana's cargo system stands in contrast to the bureaucratic demands of the state. Cruz's governing style sits uneasily at the intersection of these contrasting systems. He was elected to office following traditional rules based on locally defined status requirements. His approach to government followed a micromanagement model that placed little emphasis on informal consensus building through the manipulation of strong social networks. His administration moved public discourse into a private arena. Decision making in the community is based upon public debate, and the informal discussion of policy is based around social drinking. The public qualities of decision making work to mediate illegitimate, or nontraditional, political practice and encourage "consensual participation" (Hardin 1993: 236) by the general population. Cruz denied Santañeros their forum, and in return, the population was wary of his decisions and policies.

Santañeros continue to create and re-create traditional structures of civil society based around the goals of cooperation and reciprocity, even as political leadership becomes rationalized. For Cruz, this meant holding public meetings on community projects. He also began to attend public events. Regidores openly participated in communal drinking, and Cruz loosened his objections to public drinking.

New Patterns of Cooperation I: The Shan-Dany Museum

Museums are often described as staid repositories that reflect the past and preserve the present chiefly for the wealthy (see Alexander 1979; Harris 1990; Stocking 1985). However, museums also become "crucibles for forging citizens who see themselves as part of civil society, as important members of a valid social order" and "compensate for the failures of other institutions" (Karp 1992: 25).

The Shan-Dany Museum fills one gap left by changes in the local structure of authority and community social life. It documents and authenticates community traditions as the cargo system is rationalized and cooperative relationships become less crucial to immediate survival. It also aids villagers in the process of self-definition (Cohen 1997; Morales Lersch and Camarena Ocampo 1987). Since villagers are leaving Santa Ana as migrants and turning to new economic strategies, the Shan-Dany becomes an important new forum for the negotiation of identity, value, and status (see Gaither 1992: 61) and for continued economic growth (Vázquez Rojas 1991: 179).

The museum's bulletin captures the rhetoric of cooperation, and introduces the village to visitors as an ideal place. The goals of cooperative harmony are highlighted in the first sentence: "This museum is the product of the collective effort of the people of Santa Ana del Valle, Tlacolula, Oaxaca, and the National Institute for Anthropology and History" (CMSD 1992: 1). This opening statement emphasizes the local ideal of cooperation. It also extends the cooperative metaphor and goal of reciprocity to include the relationship between Santa Ana and the state. The museum builds an additional layer of complex social interaction, easing and mediating the tense and often distant relationship that characterizes linkages between village and state.

The museum reinforces cooperative goals through its structure and its focus on community traditions, with an emphasis on the "material objectification of cultural practices" (Robben 1989: 16). Cooperation is objectified and presented in the Shan-Dany's displays, which include a collection based primarily on familial donations by the community at large. The galleries capture a picture of local life that presents traditional activities. It documents daily life and notes the importance of the cargos and the place of the mayordomías in the Santañero celebration of identity. The cooperative ties that frame textile production are also highlighted. The museum bulletin states:

> The members of the community elect their authorities and give service to the village in accordance with proper traditions. They practice tequio and guelaguetza and maintain the celebration of mayordomías and festivals. Conserving and enriching their traditions, they are dedicated as much to labor in the field as to weaving serapes, *cobijas* [jackets] and other woolen objects (CMSD 1992: 4).

Cooperation is also created in the actions of Santañeros associated with the museum. People donate materials to the Shan-Dany throughout the year, and they describe their connection to the museum in intimate terms. The majority of the artifacts in the collection are from the village homes, and Santañeros are acknowledged throughout the four museum galleries for their contributions. The museum committee conducted oral history projects to document Santa Ana's past, and in the process, created a living trust for the village. Students use the archives and museum's collections in school projects.[11]

The Shan-Dany's collections represent the traditions, history, and identity of Santa Ana. They present the community as an uncontested social arena where life is peaceful. Missing from the walls of the collection is the mention of such issues as migration, the exploitative nature of textile production, tensions with the state, and the regular daily contests that surround daily life in the community.

The museum presents the village as uniformly peaceful; however, the reality of Santañero social life is quite a bit more complicated. People of various social positions, ages, and genders respond to the museum differently, and conflicts arise around the interpretations presented in the Shan-Dany history and identity. The Shan-Dany celebrated its fifth anniversary in 1991. A group of women performed a short play that quite openly criticized migrant village men for leaving their families.

The plot follows a hardworking Santañera as she watches her husband leave for the United States. She faces supporting her household and children alone. The husband is portrayed enjoying himself in the United States. The wife works hard for her family back in the village. She gives her husband an ultimatum upon his return—he must choose between Santa Ana and his life in America. When he decides to leave the village again, the Santañera interrupts and takes command of the situation; she forcefully throws the man from their home and warns him not to return. He returns home and begs to be taken in by his family as the play draws to a close. Observers reported that the performance left men and women feeling uncomfortable. The demands of migration are difficult to balance against the needs of the family. The women involved with the play reported feeling a sense of pride and satisfaction upon voicing their complaints in public for the first time.

The Shan-Dany became, at least for that day, a site at which women and men could openly voice private concerns. Women described the burden of familial support and education that falls more heavily on their shoulders when left by husbands looking for work. Husbands ventured to describe their experiences (sometimes quite terrifying) in the United States. Community festivals and museums open new possibilities for a population to discuss its present and review it past, and to do so in a public way (see Lavenda 1992). Santañeras used the performance and the museum's setting to begin the difficult and ongoing process of enfranchisement (see Gaither 1992: 61).

The Shan-Dany was one of the community's first committee-run projects to allow women as officers. When I first visited the Shan-Dany in 1987, my hostess was the Shan-Dany's secretary. Committees associated with the museum, the *Grupo de Artesanos Solidarizados* (a weaving cooperative)and the *Casa del Pueblo,* also included women in the late 1980s. The Grupo de Artesanos Solidarizados gave way to the Artisans' Society of Santa Ana in the 1990s. The Casa del Pueblo is part of a state-run arts program that combines arts education with projects to preserve local material culture, traditional dance, and song.

The programs and projects of the Shan-Dany and Casa del Pueblo

Noisemakers atop the church, Easter 1993

highlight the growth of state involvement in Santa Ana. The stories described within the walls of the Shan-Dany frame the relationship between Santa Ana and the nation in cooperative terms, and in many ways it is a reciprocal relationship that benefits both the local community and the state. INAH allows the museum committee and the Casa del Pueblo a good deal of independence in programming (see Morales Lersch and Camarena Ocampo 1987). However, in return for support, children and teenagers affiliated with the Casa del Pueblo perform at state functions, primarily dance exhibitions.

The Casa del Pueblo participants do not perform dances that are strictly Zapotec or even from the state of Oaxaca. Rather, the group performs a codified selection of folk dances that come from throughout the country. The dancers also wear various costumes related to each particular dance, whether it is from the Sonoran Desert or the Gulf of Mexico. School students also participate throughout the year in social and cultural programs sponsored by the museum and Casa del Pueblo. Programs usually have a national flavor and are organized around secular state holidays and national healthcare programs, and typically include minor competitions for small prizes supplied by state agencies. Thus, the Casa del Pueblo becomes a setting in which Santañero children learn state culture even as they participate in the construction and celebration of community (see Corrigan and Sayer 1985; Lavine 1992).[12]

Mexican history and ideology are illustrated in Shan-Dany's displays and throughout the Union of Oaxacan Community Museums member museums (a group of eleven museums organized to lobby for the support and training of member village committees and programs). The Shan-Dany stresses indigenous art, dance, and the Mexican Revolution. San José el Mogote, a museum in the Etla district, documents the demise of the hacienda system and pre-Columbian history. Suchquilitongo's museum (on the Pan-American highway north of the central valley) describes the village's cargo system and fiesta sponsorship. The museums collectively illustrate the breadth of Mexican history, from early prehistory to contemporary indigenous life. This picture of indigenous life is not made solely for internal (Santañero) consumption. The issues of social change addressed by the women of Santa Ana and their play concerning migration do not appear. Taken as a group, the museums focus on member communities as Indian or peasant and as literal symbols of traditional closed corporate community systems for tourist as well as local populations to enjoy (see García Canclini 1993).

The Shan-Dany creates a set nationalistic image of local culture; at the same time, Santañeros are empowered through the museum. It is a focus for organizing political and economic action. The Shan-Dany creates a sense of what is authentically Zapotec. Villagers use the aura of state support and sponsorship (INAH's certification that the Shan-Dany is legitimate) in their struggle with buyers from Teotitlán as well as with a popular press, which usually pays them scant attention (see for example, Freundheim 1988).[13] The museum bulletin objectifies traditional weaving, indigenous designs, and production technology:

The production of textiles in Santa Ana del Valle has a long history. In the Prehispanic period textiles were made of cotton on backstrap looms [a method used by Mixe Indians today]. This method was employed in the 15th century when the inhabitants of Santa Ana paid tribute in embroidered cloth and plain shawls to Moctezuma. In the 16th century Dominican friars introduced sheep and

Spanish foot looms. The techniques learned then exist today with few modifications.

It matters very little that few Santañeros weave as did their ancestors, dyeing with natural sources and spinning their own yarns, or that many weavers in the community may have only learned their art recently. The documentation in the Shan-Dany Museum wraps the community in history and tradition that can be juxtaposed against what tourists might hear in Teotitlán and the realities of production for export. For every story Teotitecos tell of Santa Ana's lack of quality, the museum makes a strong statement to the contrary.[14] The Shan-Dany also confers a sense of authenticity to designs that are problematic at best. The motifs found in most Santañero textiles are influenced by international demands, not local aesthetics (see Wood 1996). In 1993, the designs of Navajo Indians were more important than anything that could be associated with local traditions.

The Shan-Dany's committee also promotes local textile production. A *promotor* (a business consultant) employed by INAH helps the committee plan programs that will increase the sale of tapetes for Santañero weavers. Through INAH programs, the Shan-Dany has sent a touring exhibit of weaving technology, dye sources, and samples of tapetes to many cities in Mexico and California (Cohen 1989).[15] However, these programs typically help independent weavers who are already well established (Black 1991: 148; Tendler 1983: 25–26), due to the time and capital required for producing tapetes for an exhibition. A weaver contributing pieces to an exhibition must have enough capital put aside to cover the costs of sending work on the road. The time between the start and end of a show and the lag between the organizing date and payment for textiles makes it difficult for mano de obra producers who work on contract to participate.

Many Santañero contract workers are unable to contribute to the exhibits and describe the museum as an institution for the wealthy. In this respect, the Shan-Dany becomes a site for new conflicts between Santa Ana's emerging classes. The wealthy who can afford to weave independently and wait for payments are more likely to give textiles than weavers who depend on mano de obra and the demands of intermediaries and patrons in Teotitlán. In addition, some villagers (including the president of the 1993 museum committee, who wove on contract) felt that there were better ways to invest the community's resources. Perhaps, if the exhibitions are successful and the collections become an integral part of community life, the Shan-Dany will foster a sense of inclusion and enfranchisement for all villagers—as it has begun to do for women in the community. However, it currently continues to divide independent and contract weavers in the community (Lavine 1992: 142).

New Patterns of Cooperation II: Basketball Clubs

Another new structure for the expression of cooperative ideals in Santa Ana is basketball. Basketball is pursued with great seriousness in the region. Most villages in Oaxaca have at least one official court for games and many clubs, some of which are supported by wealthy merchants and shop owners.

In Santa Ana, a court, with the phrase *artesanías y deportivos* (arts and sports) emblazoned on the backboards, sits in the central plaza.[16] A game is played nearly every evening. Usually young boys and girls begin the games after school is dismissed in the afternoons. Older boys and men replace the youngsters in the evening. The benches around the plaza fill with spectators, and matches continue well past dusk. There is nothing trivial about basketball in Santa Ana. Games are serious, and sometimes a great deal of money is gambled on the outcome of a match.

Teams are usually long-lived. Most are organized around men who have grown up as friends and who maintain cooperative relationships with each other. Team members organize around a captain, but leadership is informal, and teamwork is important (and see Allison 1981). Younger men organize their teams in school and carry their rosters forward as completely as the pull of migration will allow. Team membership crosses class and status lines. In this respect, basketball works much like compadrazgo, establishing cross-linkages between the strata of Santañero society. The growing status and wealth differences noted in Chapters Four and Five are also mediated by the teams (see Allison 1981; Mandle and Mandle 1990). Players are involved in contests and commitments on the court that parallel everyday life. Success is only possible through teamwork and cooperation.

The structure of reciprocal ties that begin in the family and extend through ever larger social units are reproduced in large tournaments. Teams from around the valley and mountains surrounding Santa Ana show up to compete. A prize, usually a goat that is later cooked for a team's celebration, is donated by one of the teams, the municipio, or an association of supporters. Competition begins early and continues round-robin throughout the day. Villagers cheer first for their own team, especially if there is a member of their family playing. If that team loses, they cheer for a friend's or associate's team. If that team loses, they begin to cheer for any Santañero team left in the competition. Thus, club cooperation creates a new structure around which local identity is celebrated and alliances maintained.

New Patterns of Cooperation III: La Sociedad de Artesanos de Santa Ana del Valle

An additional focus for villagers involved in the reinvention of Santañero social life is the weaving cooperative established in the village following the founding of the Shan-Dany Museum. *La Sociedad de Artesanos de Santa Ana del Valle* (the Artisans' Society of Santa Ana) replaced the Grupo de Artesanos Solidarizados in 1987 as a cooperative entity with the specific goal of expanding the community's access to the export market for textiles (see Cohen 1998, 1999). Formal status and organization as a cooperative allowed Society members to request government grants. More recently the group applied for low-interest loans from sources such as BANFOCO (Bank for Cooperative Development) and state-run tourist programs. Santa Ana's status as an indigenous community also meant the Society's members could work with INI (Instituto Nacional Indigenista) programs and promoters.

The founders of the cooperative were independent producers and men and women trying to escape patron-client relationships with buyers in Teotitlán and to more effectively control the textile market. Cooperative members who had depended upon contract work hoped to become independent producers through the Society. Independent producers hoped to move into direct export relationships with U.S. intermediaries. Thus the Society's role was primarily to spread risk more evenly among Santa Ana's weavers (and see Attwood 1989). The goal of participants was to attract potential buyers; the Society more closely resembles a buying cooperative than the artisans' cooperatives that have come to typify local development in the Americas (see Hendrickson 1995; Nash 1994; Tice 1995). In fact, as particular weavers succeeded, they frequently left the group to work with their new contracts. At least two of these families moved into direct competition with the Society over textile exports to the

United States and the control of Santa Ana's market. Many other weavers who continued to struggle as marginal independent or contract producers have slowly dropped out of the group, leaving a core of twelve members in 1992, a total maintained through 1996.

Many Society members are related by blood and marriage. The more active participants include the families of two brothers, and of one brother's eldest son. Five additional families have members living in the United States who remit funds to support household production. All of the families have the capital necessary to support independent production and cope with difficult periods in the market. Two families are headed by women who participate in the Society and are also part of a government-funded, statewide women's cooperative organized through DIF (*Desarrollo Integral Familiar*—Family Development Programs). Finally, one Society family maintains a stall at the Mercado de Artesanías in Oaxaca City. They are dissatisfied with the low visitor attendance there and hope the cooperative will become a good alternative for growth.

The Society petitioned a number of state organizations, including FONART (*Fondo Nacional para el Fomento de las Artesanías,* a national program for the development of craft production), and received a grant to support the purchase of larger looms in 1990.[17] Society members also pooled money to buy pre-spun yarns directly from factories in Puebla, Mexico. Buying yarn directly allowed co-op members to avoid the intermediaries in Teotitlán from whom most village weavers buy their wool. Buying supplies directly from producers reduces capital outlays, but accomplishes little in terms of breaking the sales and export control by Teotitlán. Selling tapetes directly to exporters as a group is a more important issue in the development of the local economy. Unfortunately, the Society has had a limited effect on sales and has not increased local control of production or decreased exploitation of the weavers (and see Tendler 1983).

In 1988, the Society established a small weaving market on the west side of the central plaza in an open, airy section next to the Shan-Dany Museum. Lines strung across the market area display whatever stock is available for sale, and a small shed stands in one corner for storage. The price of tapetes includes a 5 percent markup that goes directly to the co-operative to cover its expenses. Marcos Sánchez, a Society participant, is using some of the co-op's funds to put together a color catalogue of Santañero textiles. When sales are slow and the co-op cannot meet rent, as happened twice in 1993, members contribute personal funds to cover the cooperative shortfalls.

Each Society member gives a day's service to the market every two weeks, following the normal pattern of cargo service (the time served at the market has increased as membership in the Society has declined). Members are also organized into an informal hierarchy for administrative purposes. Heads of households, both male and female, hold voting rights, and decisions made by the Society must be approved by its members.

Beginning daily around 10:00 A.M., a Society member hangs the current supply of textiles for sale in the market. A range of work is usually available, from small servilletas to elaborate high-quality wall hangings that may cost hundreds of dollars. The Society representative pauses for lunch in the early afternoon, and finishes the day's service at 6:00 P.M. Some days a tour bus unloads for a brief visit to the museum and market. On these days, typically Sundays (the market day in nearby Tlacolula), the Society may make a few sales. However, I watched days and weeks go by when no one visited the co-op store. Cooperative members also free their schedules by having older children work the market in their place. If a tour bus arrives while members are absent, a child runs off to fetch an adult member of the co-op.

Society members established direct export relations with galleries in Texas and Colorado in 1991 and 1992, respectively. These connections developed as exporters came to Santa Ana to visit the cooperative. Weavers use their access to galleries in the United States to avoid intermediaries in Teotitlán, and earn higher incomes.

The development of these ties to exporters fosters a sense of independence among weavers. Dealing directly with exporters is a learning experience as well; Santañeros are discovering the value of their work and what they can legitimately ask for in payment (Tendler 1983: 51).

The growing relationships between the Society and foreign buyers have soured some villagers' feelings about the cooperative. Santañeros who have dropped out of the Society, or were never able to afford to participate, often accuse the cooperative and its members of poor business practices. Some of their complaints are realistic; others are contemptuous and indicate that the Society cannot support all villagers.

In general, cooperatives do not help those villagers most in need of help because poorer members of a society cannot afford the costs of participation (Black 1991: 148). In Santa Ana, where poorer weavers are trapped in contracts with patrons in Teotitlán, this is the case. Contract weavers typically only make enough to meet weekly expenses and have little money, time, or materials left to pursue membership in the cooperative. Thus, one outcome of the cooperative is to contribute to the economic inequalities among villagers, emphasizing the difference between those weavers involved in mano de obra and those who produce independently (see Cohen 1998).

Mistrust, at least in the case of the Society, is rooted partly in the opposition of rhetoric and action. The ideal of the Society as a cooperative carries much of the rhetorical baggage associated with local models of cooperation. In effect, we would expect the Society to be another layer of social practice used to reinvent Santañero cooperative world view. In reality, the Society does create and reproduce cooperative action, but it is also built around the economic strength and weaving ability of independent families. The Society also emphasizes status differences in textile production and highlights the flexibility of more successful independent producers who can effectively participate in the Society. As such, the Society is an extension of traditional reciprocal relationships and all of the ambivalences that come with such relationships.

Participation in the Society is generally enacted for self-interest—increased market share, access to exporters, and so forth—especially for those weavers who are successful. The prosperous members of the Society will say things like, "The co-op advances all of us." Yet, at the same time, they do not work to assist struggling members to exploit the market better. Thus, Alejandro can tell you, "Oh, those people say they cannot afford to participate, but really they are only lazy." On the other hand, Bonifacio says, "Well, I would participate, but I don't have anything to give and anyway, Alejandro and his brother won't sell my tapetes because they only want the market for themselves."

The struggling weaver translates his or her disappointment into accusations of unfair business practices among other Society members, or the favoring of a family member's work over weavings of the person in question. In contrast, the successful Society members see a lazy weaver who complains too much. Thus, the differences in skill and production style are slowly becoming differences in class and are beginning to divide local weavers into distinct social groups. Nevertheless, among those active and successful Society members and those who are related to one another, the goals of cooperation are adhered to as the members work in support of each other (see Granovetter 1995). The group also builds confidence and

Watching the rodeo during the 1993 fiesta.

helps weavers realize their potential (Tendler 1983: 4). Thus, the Society reproduces the reciprocal structure of Santañero society in its organization. But these structures are exclusive, rather than inclusive, and many weavers do not benefit from the Artisans' Society.

Conclusions

Cooperation continues to play an important but changing role in Santañero social life. Political control and authority are no longer defined in strictly reciprocal terms. Cristoforo Cruz's original style of management upon his election, although quickly replaced by something villagers felt was more traditional, was a sign of the growing professionalization of village leadership. The job of the president is no longer an honorary position, awarded after years of service. It demands skills and training that are not always easy to find in a local population. Yet, at the same time, leaders must be able to produce and reproduce local social models. Too drastic a change results in the failure of a president and his projects.

Cooperative relationships are changing and are being reinvented in the community. The museum, basketball clubs, and the Artisans' Society all create local patterns of cooperation. At the same time, each emphasizes changes in Santañero society, increasing interaction with the state and global markets, and growing class-based and economic differences within the community.[18]

The reinvention of society does not always succeed or go as planned. Cooperation has proved difficult to organize in the Artisans' Society. Nevertheless, local reciprocal practices continue to impact on the structure of most social relationships. As new divisions in Santañero society develop around income, production, and authority, other structures mediate these divisions—basketball, the museum, and perhaps in the future, the Society. This is not to argue that Santa Ana is free of conflict and tension. It is to point out how conflict and contest are managed and mediated, and the ways in which practical knowledge and the logic of cooperation are applied to new situations.

Conclusions

Santa Ana in the World and Cooperation

in Southern Mexico

To abandon the persuasive simplicity of geocentric, functional, and determinative models of community is difficult. Such approaches assume cultures are rooted in specific places and are identifiable by essential and
shared traits that remain unchanged over time (see Watanabe 1992). In
these determinative models, community is a "superorganic" outcome of
forces that exist beyond the control (and often the consciousness) of individual actors (Durkheim 1964; Kroeber 1952: 51).

It is tempting to argue that Santa Ana is a community based only
upon geographic, determinative, and essentialistic models. The village
seems rooted in the ancient history of Oaxaca. It is nestled in the foothills of the Sierra. Social life is marked by "indigenous" crafts, clothing,
language, and so forth. Furthermore, Santañeros are involved in actions
that appear to have more in common with a pre-Columbian world view
than with the forces of modern capitalism. On the other hand, essential
models of Zapotec society and culture deny the complex economic, political, and social processes that distinguish Santañero history. Geocentric and deterministic models dismiss the external forces that influence
Santañero social practice as inconsequential. What is more important,
these models disregard local variability, class conflict, and the ways in
which Santañeros respond to change and reinvent themselves in the active pursuit of social life.[1]

A practice-centered approach pays attention to the production of local
knowledge and the ways this knowledge is used in the construction of
communal identity (Wilson 1993). It also accounts for the economic, po-

litical, and social constraints that define and influence social systems and link local and global processes in ever more complex ways (see Hannerz 1992, 1997). Using a practice-centered approach, we begin to understand how Santañeros create their community symbolically as well as strategically. We discover that cooperation is not deterministic or hardwired, nor is it just a poetic idea describing a mythic quality. It is an active (and often ambivalent) force in social life. It is one part of a set of relationships that villagers use to interact and understand themselves and the world. The ethnographic moments that illustrate a practice-based approach are messy when compared with the security of essentialistic and ahistorical models of Zapotec society; however, understanding the strategic use of cooperation also reveals the dynamic ways in which life is enacted and community created.

Cooperation is a powerful force in Santañero social life. Santañeros organize and judge action, create a sense of shared identity and purpose, and establish parameters through which community is defined, through cooperative and reciprocal relationships. Furthermore, they establish this sense of community with individuals and households with whom they may have little in common and of whom they may be quite suspicious.

Cooperative and reciprocal relationships grow from the choices individuals make as members of households, secciones, labor brigades, village committees, and so forth. By understanding the use and abuse of cooperation, we can begin to make sense of the ambivalent juxtaposition of cooperation and conflict, and the trust and suspicion that opened the introduction to this work. At its most basic, the contradictions found among Santañeros grow from the uncertainties that surround social practice (Moore 1975; Turner 1994).

People do not have to cooperate with one another. A Santañero always has the option of declining the offer to cooperate. What constrains actions and can mitigate suspicion and mistrust are the perceived social rewards which cooperation and reciprocity have for those who choose to participate. In other words, reciprocal actions in the past and present underwrite (but do not guarantee) their reproduction into the future. It is the reproduction of these patterned responses through time that creates community.[2]

Cooperative and reciprocal ties work at multiple levels to build and rebuild social relationships among Santañeros. These relationships are founded upon familial ties created in the daily life of the Santañero household. Formal and informal relationships, alliances, and contracts create systems of support that aid individuals as members of house-holds through time (Barth 1969, 1992; Granovetter 1985).

The alliances created in the family extend beyond the household as guelaguetza, compadrazgo relationships, and dyadic contracts, and be-come long-term structures through which individuals create themselves as social actors. The resulting relationships are a form of social capital that the Santañeros rely upon throughout their lives. In contests over status and power, these relationships are held in reserve and used strate-gically to create self, household, and community (see Barth 1992; Grano-vetter 1985).

Cooperation comes at a price in Santa Ana. Few acts are done for solely altruistic reasons (Axelrod 1984; Wilk 1993). The burden of cooperation often includes exploitative relationships. A child works for little or no pay in his or her father's workshop. A Santañero requests political allegiance in return for the sponsorship of another villager's child. Yet, the costs of cooperation do not outweigh the benefits most villagers believe it brings. Some of these benefits are quite serious—a poorer family knows its alli-ances with other households can guarantee its children will be fed and crisis averted. Powerful members of the community seem in little need of the aid and support of poorer men to establish status. However, it is chiefly through the manipulation of cooperative alliances, compadrazgo, guelaguetza, and servicio that status and prestige are created (López-Cortés 1991; Smart 1993).

Cooperation reproduces local hierarchies even as it creates cross-linkages between the strata of Santañero society. For example, the Santa-ñero who herds sheep for a living is not often asked to fill a high-ranking cargo. This is, in part, a response to family history, circumstance, and experience. A sheepherder, typically a low-status, low-income individual, has little time to learn how to manage cooperative structures, given the demands of survival. Most low-status households also have a history of marginality in the community and lack a legacy of cooperation upon which to build status (see Sullivan 1990). These factors combine to limit, but not to prohibit, participation in the local system. Instead, low-status households benefit through association, by playing into the needs of wealthier villagers. Cooperation is not the same thing for all Santañeros or for all village households. At a practical level, what low-status Santa-ñeros know about cooperation is different from (and is applied differently to) that of their wealthier counterparts. From one point of view, the re-sults are cross-linked households that choose to participate (sometimes consciously, often tacitly) in locally defined practices that create local society and community. An alternative analysis would point to this pattern of interaction as blatantly exploitative and an example of the exercise of power by the wealthy over the weak.

Understanding the conflicts involved in Santañero social practice points toward the role of cooperation in the production and reproduction of authority. Authority is reproduced in the relationships of household members. Children work together, yet also compete for the attention and esteem of their parents. Parents use the language of altruism to maintain control over the labor power of their children. In the community, authority is reproduced in the structure of the cargo system, Santa Ana's political hierarchy. The cargo system is not just the exercise of raw or unbridled power—it mediates and tempers hierarchies (Nader 1990). Recognizing the cross-linkages that mediate hierarchy does not mean that the system is free of conflict. The tensions and contests inherent in the structure of cooperation are obvious in the ambivalent attitudes which Santañeros have toward their participation in compadrazgo, guelaguetza, servicio, and cooperación.

Cooperation is also under new pressures, and new relationships are stressing old patterns of alliance. The rise in cooperación places increased importance on money and cash-based contractual relationships within the village. The decline in tequio and the loss of individuals to migration also reduces physical participation in the "life" of the community by Santañeros. Investing money is different from investing time and labor. Personal, immediate relationships become distant and survive with little "real" involvement (see Bloch and Parry 1989). These changes in participation do not destroy the importance of cooperation in Santañero society. However, the differences drive the growth of class divisions, convert morally sanctioned actions into monied relationships, and begin to objectify status differences within the village.

The increase in local incomes combines with rising educational standards and the demand for goods and services to revitalize the village. Households have the funds to contribute to infrastructural improvements. Villagers are looking for consumer goods and services typically found only in the city. Local entrepreneurs respond to increased demand by investing in local businesses. Many social scientists argue that such changes bring a rapid decline in participation in the traditional social practices that typify peasant communities (see Barabas 1995; Cancian 1992; Kicza 1993; Redfield 1950; Reichert 1982). Many of the economic changes observed by these researchers are ongoing in Santa Ana as well. The population is increasing at a rate well above the national average; the economy is growing more monetized; and finally, the state and global markets penetrate ever deeper into the very fabric of Santañero households. Nevertheless, Santañeros continue to cooperate.

Several factors mitigate the decline of community noted by Cancian (1992), among others. First, the location of much of Santa Ana's economic growth remains focused outside the village. Santañeros leave to earn capital necessary for investment. This is not to suggest there are no class differences among Santañero families. Rather, it is to point out that much economic growth in the village is due to the actions of individuals away from their home community, typically as migrants, and thus does not appear to come at the expense of local social relationships.

Changes in the textile industry have not affected the economic structure of the community. There is not an overabundance of intermediaries vying for a shrinking market, as there is in Teotitlán. Few weavers are moving into independent production that would increase local competition. There is little change in local technology, and much production continues to take place within households and around kin-based networks (see Cook 1978; Stephen 1991b). Finally, the Artisans' Society has done little to curtail exploitation by patrons and merchants living outside the community. Thus, local production remains focused on subsistence even as Santañeros grow more a part of a global "economic ecumene" (Appadurai 1990).

Cooperation in Santa Ana remains largely unchallenged by the logic of external economic practices and therefore remains an important force in local affairs (see Granovetter 1995; Stark 1992: 9). On the one hand, economic growth and market expansion into Santa Ana are not yet localized or manifest to the extent that they challenge indigenous systems of authority and control. On the other hand, much of the ongoing changes are mediated by local entrepreneurs and people who are invested in traditional practices. Thus, the force of change is mediated or translated in a way that largely interfaces with local practices and expectations (Greenberg 1995).

Cooperation in Santa Ana is a structure through which Santañeros localize the state and global processes. The cargo system is founded upon local ideas of prestige and status built on the manipulation of cooperative relationships and alliances, even as the demands of service change and become increasingly bureaucratized. Santa Ana's government remains structured around the metaphors of local practice, and not in the violent coercion that is often associated with the increasing penetration of the state (Gramsci 1988: 420). In addition, the control exercised by the alcaldes restricts the penetration of the state into local affairs.[3] Furthermore, reciprocity, tequio, and the goals of servicio mediate the growing involvement of the state in the management of the community, as exemplified earlier in the discussion of local development projects.

Cooperation is also instrumental in the definition of Santañero identity. Though most villages in the valley and region practice many of the same kinds of social relationships, Santañeros think of themselves as unique in their practices (and see Eriksen 1991; Robben 1989: 60). The generalized goals of cooperation create a sense of belonging for Santañeros which is largely unproblematic. The stories people tell are given weight in the daily practice of cooperation and reciprocity. More than just a story people tell, cooperation is objectified in social practice and action.

Villagers use these practices to pragmatic ends in the hope of exploiting the tourist market for textiles (as well as each other in the exercise of local power). Cooperation and the stories of the community combine with the objective statement of authenticity in the Shan-Dany Museum to create an aura of tradition marketed to tourists looking to buy Indian crafts. The museum is also a rallying point around which villagers organize themselves in opposition to other communities like Teotitlán. The exploitation of Santañeros by Teotiteco patrons motivates the creation of solidarity between Santañeros and sustains the stories villagers tell about themselves.

The stories of cooperation that people tell are a reference point against which to judge actions (local or global). Cooperative relationships in Santa Ana are not reducible to one or another typology nor to a determinative set of social rules. To define cooperation as leveling and redistributive (Dow 1977), stratifying (Cancian 1965), or exploitative (Harris 1964) limits understanding how Santañeros use these relationships in the practice of everyday life. Cooperation has redistributive qualities; it unites a diverse population and the growing social and economic classes within the village. Cooperation and reciprocity obscure the exploitative nature of many relationships and the ways in which Santañeros use cooperative relationships to reproduce local hierarchies. Finally, cooperative relationships make sense of the world and organize Santañeros for action.

Santañeros have devised various ways to meet the demands of everyday life throughout history. As their world changes, so have their strategies.

Twenty years ago, cooperation was an important part of a family's survival. Subsistence agriculture left little room for error, and a farmer depended upon others for assistance and, if a crop failed, sustenance.

Cooperative relationships have become less crucial to survival as incomes have risen, and new, less marginal production strategies have become available in recent years. State programs, controls, and development policies; global markets; and the interplay of production, migration, and ideology all impact upon the structure of practical knowledge and action in the community (Donham 1990: 161). As these influences wax and wane, local culture and social life change—as do practical knowledge and cooperative relationships.

The ongoing debates and contests that surround cooperation are an anthropological exercise for the Santañeros involved. It is a kind of "roundtable" run, not for academics, but for the community and its members. In this debate, Santañeros vie to define themselves, their community, and their place in the world. They also dispute conflicting definitions and begin to organize for their futures. Don Mario lamented the death of his padrino early in our stay; Señor Valeriano was a powerful member of the village and had played an instrumental role in the 1970s when electric lines were first run to the village. Don Mario recalled the way Señor Valeriano stood up to the objections of older leaders, people who argued that electricity was unnecessary and would only become a new cost to families already finding it difficult to make ends meet. Señor Valeriano persevered, and convinced the older, more traditional village leaders that change could be positive and that electricity would not signal the end of a way of life. Instead, as Don Mario recalled, electricity allowed villagers to begin to produce more textiles under better circumstances, which led to a slow increase in incomes.

It was a surprise to listen to Don Mario talk about future plans for the village after hearing him tell this story of Señor Valeriano's work. Don Mario had become a member of the ruling class in the 1990s and regularly influenced, and sometimes disrupted, village plans. Contemporary leaders coaxed and cajoled Don Mario, flattering him as they tried to win support for new projects.

The progressive supporter of Señor Valeriano was now himself described as a traditionalist. Listening to stories about the past and watching the present unfold, it is a little easier to recognize the ways in which systems shift over time. Yet, even with these changes, much of what has taken place in Santa Ana and among Santañeros is nothing more and nothing less than the ongoing negotiation of status, identity, and purpose in an ever-changing world. What pulls the system together and creates a sense of shared identity and community are the rich practices—here the cooperative and reciprocal practices—that come to represent the group.

Don Domingo, one of my closest informants, talked about the changes he had seen in his life. He recalled going to Tlacolula by oxcart and Oaxaca City by train—how the trip to the city took a day and how he was possessed with fear as he left the confines of the village. How vastly different the world has become. His children and grandchildren live in the United States, and he eats foods he never dreamed he could afford. He hopes for a future that is richer both economically and socially, and marked by more positive political change than in the past. The structure of cooperation has allowed many of those changes to occur without destroying Santañero society. The ongoing construction and reorganization of cooperation guarantees that the community will continue into the future.

Notes

Notes to the Introduction

1. Durkheim clearly creates a deterministic universe when he defines a social fact as consisting of "ways of acting, thinking, and feeling, external to the individual, and endowed with a power of coercion, by reason of which they control him" (1964: 3).

   Marx and Engels, in *The German Ideology,* make a similar argument when they use a determinative structure to describe communalism and cooperation in relation to divisions of labor.

   The social power, i.e., the multiplied productive force, which arises through the co-operation of different individuals as it is determined by the division of labour, appears to these individuals, since their co-operation is not voluntary but has come about naturally, not as their own united power, but as an alien force existing outside them, of the origin and goal of which they are ignorant, which they thus cannot control, which on the contrary passes through a peculiar series of phases and stages independent of the will and the action of man, nay even being the prime governor of these (McLellan 1977: 170).

2. John Watanabe (1992: X) clearly states this perspective:

   I firmly believe there is a reality "out there" amenable to analysis and explanation, predicated on such undeniables as power and control, privilege and property, life and death. At the same time, individuals imbue this reality with an indeterminacy that often subverts "ultimately determinant" political, cultural, historical or personal imperatives.

3. Concerning the place of history in the contemporary analysis of Latin America, Roseberry states:

   We must understand the interaction between non-capitalist and capitalist modes in Latin American history across five centuries in terms of what existed before contact, the nature of contact and the transformation of social relations that resulted, the new relations and dynamics that were instituted, the contradictions engendered by those relations, and the manner in which those contradictions were resolved and, in turn, set in motion new contradictory relations and dynamics (1989: 168).

4. Paisanazgo is a sense of common origin, and a set of socially integrated relationships that exist among migrants and parallel cooperative relationships in home villages. Paisanazgo provides the migrant with an identity and set of relationships through which he or she can understand and deal with new and changing situations. Hirabayashi asks why migrants do not invent new structures to secure their position and create a sense of identity. And in response he argues that they choose to participate in paisanazgo, because whether real or rhetorical, its language "helps pave the way for alliances and actions" (1993: 113) in a way that is known and familiar.

5. Berry (1985) and Shipton (1989) find similar patterns of association working in west Africa. Cooperation and reciprocity remain central to many societies due largely to economic uncertainty among individual actors. Berry suggests reciprocity does not alleviate the tensions resulting from unequal access to wealth and power, as these tensions always exist and conflicts often arise over economic inequality. However, reciprocal ties among individuals and households mediate economic inequalities, and thereby reduce stress and conflict (Berry 1985: 13). White (1994) takes this point a step further in her discussion of kinship and the control of women's labor in Turkish craft-producing communities. She describes the rhetoric of kinship as part of the process through which Turkish women are robbed of control over their labor power. Cooperation among women becomes a way to overcome their economic marginality. Cooperative relationships bind women together to face and perhaps resist the exploitation of merchants, husbands, and fathers.

6. The rise of personal business investment does not necessarily signal a collapse of cooperative networks. Alvarez and Collier (1994) note that Mayan truckers working in and around Zinacantán, and between Zinacantán and Mexico City, establish new networks of cooperation based on ethnicity and revolving around the control of information (see Alvarez 1994). These new networks create an alternative model upon which social solidarity is established. Furthermore, the Zapatista uprising has connected with an evolving pan-Mayan movement that is establishing an entirely new set of social networks, based upon shared ethnicity (in the broadest sense) rather than local identity (see Nash 1996; Watanabe 1995; Wilson 1995).

7. By way of comparison, Holmes (1989) notes a similar change, albeit over a much longer period of time, in his work in eastern Italy (and see Polanyi 1968; Weber 1946).

The contracts [authored by businesspeople and politicians] gradually superimposed on traditional social relations a "rational" cultural schema, one that substituted for material and symbolic reciprocities and personal piety a new, abstract calculus. This reification of traditional social ties rendered them "economic" and subject to bureaucratic logic and formula (Holmes 1989: 31).

8. In Santa Ana, "president" is used to describe the individual we would describe as mayor. Alcalde, often translated as "mayor," is used to describe the three men who act as justices of the peace within Santa Ana and adjudicate local disputes.

Notes to Chapter One

1. Transnationalism is used primarily in the description of the "multi-stranded social relations that link together (immigrant) societies of origin and settlement" (Basch et al. 1994: 7); however,

in a broader sense the term is used to indicate the role and dynamic tensions generated by global capitalist hegemony, the hegemonic forces within each of the competing core capitalist states, the hegemonic constructions generated by dominant forces within peripheral states, and the active agency of the world's people as they live lives stretched across national borders (15).

In terms of Santa Ana, I expand the concept to include links established through migration, markets, communication, and the media.

2. Evidence of the oldest settlements in the central valley and examples of some of the earliest domesticated corn in Mesoamerica were found at San José el Mogote, a village in the Etla arm of the valley, whose prehistoric roots date to the early formative period (Kirby 1973).

3. For readers familiar with earlier work on the region, the town of Mitla (described in detail in Parsons 1936) was also an important post-classic site located at the end of the Tlacolula, or eastern, branch of the central valley.

4. Cook and Diskin suggest that the years covering the construction and completion of the Pan-American highway (the mid-1940s) mark a period during which the traditional structure of the market system, based upon limited national integration, began to become more a part of the modern national economy (1976).

5. The market cycle rotates from the capital city on Saturdays through Tlacolula on Sundays, Miahuatlán on Mondays, Ayoquezco on Tuesdays, Etla and Zimatlán on Wednesdays, Ejutla and Zaachila on Thursdays, and Ocotlán on Fridays (Cook and Diskin 1976).

6. During the months of December and January, it is typical to find young children dressed for what looks like a New England winter. It also seems as though the entire village has the flu.

7. A reservoir to support irrigation in Teotitlán, constructed by the government in 1968, supplies some water to farmlands. A second smaller reservoir was built to the east of the community in 1975. However, poor construction has limited its usefulness (Lees 1973; Stephen 1991b).

8. The issue is more than simply one of irrigation, as most villagers suggest. The problem includes overuse and inappropriate farming practices on marginal land. Perhaps a benefit of the growing dependence on migration, weaving, and wage labor will be to take a bit of the burden off of this land, inadvertently giving it a chance to recover.

9. Santañeros characterize the Mixe (another ethnic minority in Oaxaca) as *muy Indio* (very Indian). The description parallels that of the stereotypical Indian in North American popular culture. The Mixe can talk to animals, live a more natural life, and are very superstitious.

10. Political unrest in Tlacolula throughout 1995 and 1996 has opened a new opportunity for legal landgrabs by Santañeros. At least two families have used the disputes among Tlacolula's political factions to purchase land at a low cost in the hope of turning a profit in the future.

11. Although the ranch has been abandoned for years, a committee still takes care of the chapel in Las Carritas.

12. In Teotitlán a similar geographic division between populations living around the center of the community and households built above the village in the foothills of the mountains has become a formal social boundary between barrios or *secciones* (neighborhoods or sections) of the community. Most Teotitecos maintain that a household's section is an indicator of class and community standing. Those families living in households around the central plaza, sections one and two, are of higher status.

13. The Bracero Program (1942–1964), also known as the Emergency Farm Labor Program, brought Mexican migrants legally into the United States on formal contracts, primarily as agricultural workers. The program was begun to increase the United States' farm labor population, which had dropped in response to the Second World War (Cockcroft 1983).

Notes to Chapter Two

1. For comparison, if we go to 1920 and the census with the earliest information on the structure of the village workforce, we find that 267 of 380 economically active men were involved in agricultural production. Weavers included 76 men and 14 women. Additionally, 13 men were listed as teachers. The remaining 24 workers were muleteers, professionals, and miners (SEN 1934).

2. Working adults include men and women above the age of fourteen.

3. Embriz estimates that 80 percent of Oaxaca's municipios are losing population to national and international migration (Embriz 1993). Surveys in 1996 indicate most Santañero households have firsthand or secondhand experience with migration. Of fifty-four households surveyed, only seven—or just under 13 percent of the households—had no connections to migrants outside of the community.

4. The 1990 census does note that some Santañeros no longer live within the community. The census includes in its number 36 migrants (14 men and 22 women) living outside the community, but within the boundaries of Mexico; an additional 22 villagers (17 men and 5 women) are listed as residents of other countries (INEGI 1992b).

5. Clements (1996) notes that the shifting patterns of exchange and use can have a much longer history than originally thought. In her work with cotton weavers, production for exchange dated back to the middle of the nineteenth century as nationals touring the region purchased locally made goods.

6. The 1990 census counts 4,430 people living in Teotitlán. Of this total, 796 are weavers. Of weavers in the community, 175 are employed by another Teotiteco, 524 are independent producers (more than likely involved in mano de obra), 5 are patrons (probably an undercount), 48 work without pay, and 44 would not give answers (INEGI 1992b).

7. Making this number particularly difficult to gauge is the mobility of most unpaid workers, who move from job to job within their households, move from school to work, or assist in weaving when time permits.

8. There are some Santañeros who do not have the capital necessary to purchase a loom or repair one that is damaged. These individuals will often rent looms and workshop space, or earn a wage while weaving on someone else's loom.

9. Often the final price for tapetes is agreed upon before a contract is finished. However, it is not uncommon for a patron or buyer to pay less than the agreed-upon price at the time of delivery. The buyer will make excuses about the lower price, including overhead costs. The buyer may go so far as to accuse the weaver of the theft of yarns (there is the accusation that yarn that was to go to a contract is missing). Weavers are left with little recourse and often accept the price, complaining bitterly later.

10. State tourism programs financed and opened the Artisans' Market in the early 1980s as an alternative structure to the larger city market located off the zócalo (central plaza of Oaxaca City). Planners felt tourists would prefer the cleaner surroundings of the Artisans' Market to the older, more crowded central market.

11. Two friends visited this man looking for a particular style of tapete. They reported (and this parallels statements given by Santañeros) that his asking price was nearly double what they had expected and even higher than prices found in Teotitlán.

12. As a former employee of INAH suggested to me in 1992, "Teotitlán and Santa Ana do the same things, produce weaving of the same quality and standard, from the same materials. The problem is that Teotitlán is imperialistic, while Santa Ana is poor."

13. The introduction of the new currency in 1993 eliminated three zeros (ones, tens, and hundreds) from the old rate. Thus, three thousand pesos (approximately one dollar at the time) became three nuevos pesos. Centavos were also reintroduced. The exchange rate remained unchanged until 1994.

14. Unpaid or underpaid labor does occupy the time of the unemployed and underemployed workers and can be the foundation upon which to begin a household business (Cook 1984: 191). However, the high rate of unpaid labor also inhibits economic development and capital expansion (see Acheson 1972), and carries with it a high degree of exploitation and self-exploitation.

15. Other indicators suggest the state is in a difficult position in terms of growth and development. Oaxaca has one of the highest rates of illiteracy in the country (12.4 percent of the population), one of the lowest rates of employment (only 39.2 percent of the population), the second highest rate of unpaid labor (6.2 percent of all workers), and one of the highest rates of participation in agricultural production (52.9 percent) in the country. The state also has the one of the lowest percentages of houses built of materials considered sturdy—that is, brick, cement, and wood. Only 29.9 percent of the population has access to sewers. Finally, the state has the lowest rate per capita of use of gas for cooking, which leads to the continued overcutting of woodlands for use as fuel (INEGI 1992b).

During the debt crisis (1982–1988), the inflation rate reached an average of nearly 90 percent. The rate in 1987, the worst year on record, topped 159 percent (*Economist* February 13, 1993: 3). During this same period, the gross domestic product of the nation fell at an annual rate of 4 percent (Pool and Stamos 1989: 101, cited in Stephen 1992). Wages have not kept pace with the increases in inflation. They have dropped in relation to prices by nearly 50 percent since the mid-1980s and are only beginning to recover (Carlsen 1988: 36, cited in Stephen 1992: 74).

16. Most marriages begin as *union libres* (common-law marriages) and children are typically born before a formal wedding has occurred. A first migration is often undertaken to finance a formal wedding.

Notes to Chapter Three

1. A factor that aided understanding the importance of cooperation was the small, modest set of reciprocal relationships Maria and I became involved in during fieldwork. These relationships also proved instrumental in field research. Reciprocal associations with one family were often an avenue toward new opportunities for meeting prospective informants, and for following social networks on the ground.

2. Aron and his wife lived down the hill from Maria and me. Their home was on the path we followed into the village proper. We regularly passed their home several times a day, and it was seldom that we did not spend a little time talking on any given day.

3. While I am not an expert on the social construction of self, it is interesting to note that Santañeros embody cooperation in their image of themselves as biological and social beings. The soul and the body, in other words, the spiritual and the corporeal, are cooperative structures that bring the ideal of reciprocity into the very constitution of the individual. At birth the relationship between spiritual and corporeal is tenuous; it is almost as if a struggle is taking place between motivating forces within the individual. It is only as a person grows as a social being, becoming a part of Santa Ana's social world, that his or her soul becomes "securely ensconced" (Leslie 1960: 45). Throughout life there are threats to the body and soul, perhaps the best known being *susto* (soul loss), where the spirit is frightened out of the body (see discussions in Kearney 1986; Rubel 1984). As might be expected, susto is more dangerous to children whose souls lack the strong cement of the adult.

4. Leslie, working in Mitla in the 1950s, tells us:

   The man or woman who was married to a diligent worker was considered well-mated, and the admonition to be industrious fell easily from the lips of parents. Much prestige attached to wealth, and townspeople admired the sophistication of the facile entrepreneur, but the poorest and most humble individuals commanded the respect of the community if they were industrious (1960: 72).

5. Vera and Jorge are considered "legally married" by most villagers although they had yet to celebrate their wedding. One reason Jorge migrated to the United States was to earn the funds necessary to finance a formal wedding. An informal marriage and children, followed years later with a formal wedding, is a typical pattern for many Santañeros.

6. This is a family that rarely eats meat. Typical meals consisted of beans and tortillas. Additional proteins were infrequently provided by *tripa* (tripe) which remains a low-cost, low-status food.

7. CONASUPO is a state-run market program that provides subsidized prices on many household goods.

8. Tortilla making can be more profitable than piecework and mano de obra. Working with a woman in Oaxaca City, Cook and Binford note,

   It took her two days to make one hundred tortillas, which she sold for one peso each in a Oaxacan City marketplace. Working on her embroidery for two to three hours daily, it took her approximately one month to finish embroidering a dress for which she was paid 110 pesos (1990: 174).

   While they identify tortilla making as labor intensive, it is part of the domain traditionally framed as female, and often incorporates the assistance of daughters as unpaid laborers.

9. This is an example of Stephen's (1991b) point that migration moves women into new positions as primary providers in their household. Unfortunately, women's work remains defined as primarily domestic. The challenge for Santañeras is to build awareness of their important role in the maintenance of households as breadwinners and not simply as caretakers.

10. The secretary's job is primarily as a scribe for the community and dates to a time when the illiteracy rate among villagers was high.

11. The exhibition of Santañero textiles was part of an exchange program organized and funded by INAH. The program carried a truckload of weavings to Tapachula for a two-week exhibition and sale.

Notes to Chapter Four

1. I was always struck during interviews by the various ways in which Santañeros voiced a similar idea of balance. Trade-offs were constantly made and new balances created. It sometimes reminded me of a children's story I had heard, titled *Fortunately, Unfortunately*. The plot followed a man through a day of minor disasters—or unfortunate events. Each crisis ended in a fortunate outcome. A plane crashes, but our hero has a parachute. The parachute breaks, but he lands in a haystack, and so on. Santañero life had a similar quality. Crops fail, but you weave. Weaving does not earn enough, but you migrate. Migration causes you to leave the family, but as a migrant you are with relatives, and so forth.

2. In conversations throughout my fieldwork, I noted that many villagers would name the same group of individuals as compadres. Most often the names belonged to Santa Ana's elite and included former and current members of the village authority. Following the elections in September for municipal president, many informants mentioned their relationship with Cristoforo Cruz, the president-elect.

3. Stephen (1991b: 192) notes, "The mean number of godchildren per household in 1986 was 9—some had none, while one had 246" in Teotitlán. While I do not have figures for Santa Ana, there is no reason to believe these totals are atypical for the region.

4. Rather than a strictly economic definition of class (see Deere 1990: 12; Marx 1906: 791), my approach is closer to that of Gledhill's (1994: 138). Gledhill states:

> The actual rather than theoretical consciousness of members of a class is the product of practical historical experiences of living in the world. This involves all the different dimensions of power relations and not simply the economic ones (and see Weber 1946: 193).

Gledhill's suggestion fits the ethnographic reality of Santañero society better than a strictly economic definition, in that differences in wealth are often insignificant among the majority of village households (and see Amariglio et al. 1988: 490–492; Mousse 1988: 90–91).

5. Levels of education indicate status as well. Literacy is prestigious, and finishing school is a sign that an individual has the time and financial support to pursue an education.

6. Some informants talked about enchanted money as well. Enchanted money is not earned through direct labor. It is money that does not return on investment and "won't feed you well. You will be hungry if you use enchanted money to buy your food." The category is similar to evil money, or "money of the wind" noted by Greenberg (1995).

7. Some informants appeared quite embarrassed by questions concerning contracts with the devil. One gentleman assured me that once electricity arrived in Santa Ana, the number of supernatural problems plaguing the community decreased. He attributed this outcome to the lights that might scare away dangerous beings.

Notes to Chapter Five

1. The classes met from October to May, with only a short break at Christmas. As texts we used books supplied by an expatriate American teaching in Oaxaca City.

2. Many people did not seem to understand that I was an anthropologist and not just an English teacher. From time to time, I would be asked who sent me to the village to teach English. Some people assumed I was involved with a government project to train workers in a foreign language. Others knew I was an anthropologist but were astounded to see me weeks or even months after our

original meetings. There seemed to be some consensus that two weeks was more than enough time to learn about Santa Ana.

3. The story of la llorona is replete with examples of minor errors in a woman's behavior. These failures add up and lead to the destruction of self and family. Thus, the plot places an extra burden on women to avoid even minor errors in their actions. The complete story builds a terrifying image of the costs of mistakes for Mexican women (for overview of the la llorona tale and its structure, see Jones 1988; Mathews 1992).

4. If the secciones were at one time barrios, it is likely that they were divided into four parts, creating the four barrios typical of most settlements in the area (see de la Fuente 1949: 28–29; Hill and Monaghan 1987: 18).

5. Leases are contingent on the actual use of the land. A family who pays for a lot and then does nothing to improve the land (build a home, start a new garden, etc.) can lose its lease after one year.

6. For comparative examples of community alliances and reciprocity among the Zapotec communities, see Nader (1990), working in the highlands; Higgins (1974) and Murphy and Stepick (1991), working in *colonias populares* (new settlements established by the working poor) of Oaxaca City; Hirabayashi (1993), working among Zapotec migrants living in Mexico City; and Nangengast and Kearney (1990), working in the United States with migrant associations.

7. The term *tequio* became part of government-sponsored projects funded by President Salinas de Gotari's Solidaridad program. After granting a community funds for a project's raw materials, the government encourages villagers to take part in tequio to supply most of the labor.

8. For a brief introduction to Solidaridad programs, see "A Survey of Mexico: Into the Spotlight," an insert in *The Economist* (February 13, 1993). The program has been accused of practicing paternalism, co-opting local community political structures to the PRI *(Partido Revolucionario Institucional),* and perpetuating the "Mexican tradition of rule by a strong man." At the same time, Solidaridad has brought many important and needed improvements to rural Mexico, including access to electricity for over thirteen million rural Mexicans, and running water to another eleven million (see Schulz and Williams 1995).

9. The COCEI *(Coalición Obrera Campesina Estudiantil de Istmo* or the Coalition of Workers, Peasants, and Students of the Isthmus), a Zapotec activist group working in the Isthmus of Tehuantepec, uses tequio to organize marches and governmental protests. The COCEI helps peasant families obtain credit in exchange for support (see Campbell 1993; Royce 1993; Rubin 1987).

10. The central authority found itself in an embarrassing situation in early 1993 as the newly elected treasurer was one of the men who had avoided contributing

funds for well over a year. When the president announced at a community meeting a new policy that would penalize those households which avoided contributing, there was an uproar and many villagers suggested that the treasurer be incarcerated until he paid his cooperación. The treasurer reluctantly made the outstanding contributions.

11. Santa Ana's development through history follows Wolf's (1957) model of the closed corporate peasant community. One exception, I argue, is that corporateness is a more fluid, cyclical process than Wolf allowed (although see his reconsideration of corporateness in Wolf 1986). During periods of economic expansion (the late nineteenth century under the Porfiriato and currently) Santañeros became more involved with national and international markets and culture. In periods of stress and warfare (during the Revolution and immediately following its conclusion) the village became more isolated. Currently, the village has opened. In the future, perhaps the population will once again slip into a period when they draw in upon themselves, severing ties with external influences.

12. An informant told me that more women voted in the last presidential election (August 21, 1994) than ever before. In our brief phone conversation he mentioned the work of the semi-autonomous *Instituto Federal Electoral* (Federal Electoral Institute) to register voters for the elections. The IFE registered men and women to vote and encouraged the population to take part in national, state, and local races. Women responded locally by voting in large numbers for the first time.

13. National elections, like the local races, are conducted by open ballots. Some informants suggested that the village authorities marked all ballots for the PRI in the last election without asking the population to vote. This did not seem to disturb Santañeros, and most felt the elections were rigged for the PRI and that a protest vote would do little to help the community.

Notes to Chapter Six

1. Statements both in support and critical of Cruz may signal the ways in which Santañeros try to manage their envy and mistrust of one another. Kearney (1986: 70–78) notes that creating communal bonds and reciprocity often reduces the envy that exists among villagers. Perhaps Santañeros were trying to convince themselves to trust Cruz.

2. The community organized to oust the evangelico families from Santa Ana in 1991. The evangelicos cited their conversions and movement away from social networks based around Catholicism as effectively removing them from the demands of community support. Santañeros argued that they must participate in Santañero social life—specifically the payment of cooperación, participation in tequio, and community service—or they should lose their rights to live in the pueblo. The situation became so problematic that a judge from Tlacolula was

finally called in to mediate the impasse. He recommended the evangelicos maintain their right to live in the village, but only if they would serve on civil committees, contribute tequio, and pay cooperación for all nonreligious collections. Two evangelicos were elected to fill positions as regidores of the municipio in 1992 in accordance with the judgment. In 1996, I learned that the fight over service and between evangelicos and traditionalists had become an almost yearly event.

3. Miller's (1993) work, *Humiliation,* provides a fascinating discussion of what occurs when gift giving backfires, as well as the jealousy and envy that exist below the surface of most exchanges.

4. They used the term *comp'* with each other in conversation.

5. Even though the market area was an important addition to the village and facilitated the sale of food locally, it replaced the public washing area. With the closing of the village's only public area for washing clothes, women effectively lost an important venue for talking.

6. García was a good example of a peasant intellectual, or a person who "mediates the relationship between domination and discourse, between the active creation of political language and long-term continuity, and also between local society and the wider world" (Feierman 1991: 5). He was able to operate in two similar, but different forums—the local one based on manipulation of cooperative bonds and the national one founded on state patronage and support of PRI's status quo.

7. The Union of Oaxacan Community Museums is made up of the managing committees of the eleven community museums found in Oaxaca. Santa Ana's committee chairman holds the position of president of the Union because the Shan-Dany was the first community museum founded. Tonio García was president of the municipio when the museum was established in 1985 and remains in touch with INAH officials as a consultant for new museums.

8. Some Santañeros suggested Tonio García's real purpose in backing the construction of the museum was to better exploit the market for archaeological artifacts and attract possible buyers to the village.

9. Scott (1989: 149) argues that prestige is never bought by an individual. It can only be conferred to an individual by others. Granting status is thus a mark of correct behavior (and see Smart 1993).

10. Cruz's situation resembles what Myerhoff discovered in her fieldwork in a southern California Jewish seniors' center (1979). Eli Kominsky was a motivated leader who worked hard for the center in an effort to enrich programs for senior citizens. He was also a social outsider, "not a leader generated from within the society, thrown into prominence because of his devotion to indige-

nous styles and norms. He was a prestigious link to the world outside" (Myer-hoff 1979: 120). In a sense, Cruz was an outsider like Kominsky. He did not follow local customs. He refused to drink with other villagers and promoted projects with no discussion. Furthermore, much of his status came from economic success that occurred outside the community. In Myerhoff's example, Kominsky's failures mounted until he removed himself from the group rather than change his approach. Cruz however, learned from his mistakes and began to change his approach to governing.

11. Touring the museum with villagers was often revealing. I often heard outlandish stories of local history, including claims that the stonework dating back to Monte Alban II (100 B.C.–A.D. 200) was carved by space aliens. There were also touching moments, such as watching an informant fill with pride as she explained the role of her grandfather in the Revolution, or a villager describing a special donation he had made to the collection.

12. During the celebration around the Día de los Muertos (Day of the Dead), most of the children in the community came to the cemetery for a dance. They performed in costumes from early evening to fairly late at night, while parents and friends looked on, celebrating with alcohol and fireworks. Watching the performance, I noticed that none of the children involved with the Casa del Pueblo were present. Walking home later that night, Maria and I found them practicing "folk" dances on the plaza. It struck me then that we were perhaps watching the homogenization of Mexican folk culture and the invention of a generic "native" tradition.

13. The Shan-Dany Museum has also attracted specialists to the community and assisted in the publication of *Como Hacemos Tapetes en Santa Ana del Valle* (How We Make Tapetes in Santa Ana del Valle) (Vásquez and Vásquez Dávila 1992).

14. In respect to weaving and technology, the Shan-Dany is also an important resource that documents and preserves "traditional" methods of weaving, spinning, dyeing, and dye sources (see Vásquez Dávila et al. 1992)

15. Weavers averaged fifty dollars in sales when one exhibit was sent to Tapachula, Chiapas, in 1993.

16. It was, in fact, during the renovation of the plaza to prepare for the construction of the basketball court that many of the artifacts and pre-Columbian burials now housed in the Shan-Dany Museum were found.

17. Looms typically measure 180 to 200 centimeters in width. The grant from FONART allowed weavers to purchase looms measuring 500 to 600 centimeters.

18. The reciprocal networks organized and used by Santañero migrants create village logic in transnational settings, and carry Santañero society to new situa-

tions (see Hirabayashi 1993; Kearney 1995; Smith 1992). I am currently carrying out research with Santañero migrants to better understand the transnational place of cooperation (see Conway and Cohen 1998).

Notes to Conclusions

1. Compare the functional, deterministic position of Putnam (1993) with the dynamic, reality-based model in Portes and Landolt (1996) and Granovetter (1985).

2. The experience of Don Pedro, a man in his eighties who returned to the village after nearly sixty years of absence, illustrates the costs and benefits that come from decisions not to cooperate. Don Pedro was recruited into the state's band as a clarinet player following the Mexican Revolution. He left Santa Ana, and with no family in the village, returned infrequently. He neither served in community offices nor contributed funds to cover his commitments. Nevertheless, in 1991, he returned to Santa Ana following the death of his wife (a woman who was not from the village).

   Don Pedro anticipated returning to Santa Ana, building a small house, and quietly living out his remaining years. He moved onto a small plot of land to the east of the plaza, a site where his family had once lived. The young unmarried daughter of a widow courted Don Pedro, in his words, to inherit his wealth and his land.

   The village authority had other ideas. The president and his supporters sanctioned Don Pedro for his failure to cooperate throughout his life and demanded a percentage of his wealth as well as the return of his land upon his death. Don Pedro confided in me his disgust for the system. He argued that he had returned to the village and had offered free music lessons in a number of different instruments to anyone in the village. No one took his offer; therefore, he was absolved of any communal debt. Through 1996, the argument continued. Don Pedro (near ninety years of age) gave up fighting with the village hierarchy. He did not marry the widow's daughter, ending a much-talked-about scandal. Finally, he began playing in the village band for free. He remains outside the local system of status and prestige. While he is respected for his success as a member of the state's band and as music instructor, he is disparaged for his lack of community support.

3. Nader's (1990) model of local practice as an alternative to the state is contradicted by Collier's (1987) frightening account of the state's penetration into local legal and political affairs in Chiapas (and see González 1989).

References Cited

Abrahams, Roger D.
1970   "A Performance-Centered Approach to Gossip." *Man* 5 (2): 290–301.

Acevedo, María Luisa, and I. Restrepo
1991   *Los valles centrales de Oaxaca.* Oaxaca: Centro de Ecodesarrollo,
            Gobierno de Oaxaca.

Acheson, James M.
1972   "Accounting Concepts and Economic Opportunities in a Tarascan
            Village: Emic and Etic Views." *Human Organization* 31 (1): 83–91.
1996   "Household Organization and Budget Structures in a Purepecha
            Pueblo." *American Ethnologist* 23 (2): 331–351.

AGEO
1580   *Relaciones de Teotlán del Valle.* Oaxaca: Archivo General del Estado de
            Oaxaca (AGEO).
1815   *Solícita licencia para sacar mezcal en el pueblo de Santa Ana del Valle.*
            Real Intendencia de Oaxaca. Oaxaca: Archivo General del Estado de
            Oaxaca.

Alarcón, Rafael
1992   "Norteñización: Self Perpetuating Migration from a Mexican Town."
            In *U.S.-Mexico Relations: Labour Market Interdependence,* edited by
            J. Bustamante, R. Hinojosa, and C. Reynolds. Pp. 302–318. Stanford:
            Stanford University Press.

Alexander, E.
1979   *Museums in Motion: An Introduction to the History and Functions of
            Museums.* Nashville: University of Tennessee Press.

Allison, M. T.
1981   "Competition and Cooperation: A Sociocultural Perspective." In *Play
            as Context,* edited by A. T. Cheska. Pp. 92–101. West Point, N.Y.:
            Leisure Press.

Alvarez, Robert R.
1994   "Changing Ideology in a Transnational Market: Chile and Chileros in
            Mexico and the U.S." *Human Organization* 53 (3): 255–262.

Alvarez, Robert R., and George A. Collier
1994   "The Long Haul in Mexican Trucking: Traversing the Borderlands of the North and South." *American Ethnologist* 21 (3): 606–627.

Amariglio, Jack L., S. A. Resnick, and R. D. Wolff
1988   "Class, Power, and Culture." In *Marxism and the Interpretation of Culture,* edited by C. Nelson and L. Grossberg. Pp. 487–501. Urbana: University of Illinois Press.

Appadurai, Arjun
1990   "Disjuncture and Difference in the Global Cultural Economy." *Public Culture* 2 (2): 1–24.

Arizpe, Lourdes
1981   "The Rural Exodus in Mexico and Mexican Migration to the United States." *International Migration Review* 15 (14): 626–649.

Attwood, Donald W.
1989   "Does Competition Help Co-operation?" *Journal of Development Studies* 26 (1): 5–27.

Axelrod, Robert
1984   *The Evolution of Cooperation.* New York: Basic Books.
1997   *The Complexity of Cooperation.* Princeton: Princeton University Press.

Bailón Corres, Moisés Jaime
1979   *Articulación de modes de producción: Producción mercantil simple y sistema comercial en los valles centrales de Oaxaca.* Universidad Autónoma Benito Juárez de Oaxaca. Oaxaca Instituto de Investigaciones Sociológicas.

Barabas, Alicia M.
1995   "El proceso de desidentificación etnica de los Chochos de Oaxaca." *Primer anuario de la dirección de etnología y antropología social del INAH.* Pp. 127–149. Mexico City: Instituto Nacional de Antropología e Historia.

Barkin, David
1990   *Distorted Development: Mexico in the World Economy.* Boulder, Colo.: Westview Press.

Barth, Fredrik
1969   "Introduction." In *Ethnic Groups and Boundaries: The Social Organization of Culture Difference,* edited by F. Barth. Pp. 9–38. London: George Allen & Unwin.
1992   "Towards Greater Naturalism in Conceptualizing Societies." In *Conceptualizing Society,* edited by A. Kuper. Pp. 17–33. New York: Routledge.

Basch, Linda G., N. G. Shiller, and C. S. Blanc

1994   *Nations Unbound: Transnational Projects, Postcolonial Predicaments, and Deterritorialized Nation-States.* Amsterdam: Gordon and Breach Science Publishers.

Beltran, Aguirre

1967   *Regiones de refugio: El desarrollo de la comunidad y el proceso dominical en Mestizo América.* Mexico City: Institutio Nacional Indigenista.

Bender, Thomas

1978   *Community and Social Change in America.* New Brunswick, N.J.: Rutgers University Press.

Bennett, Diane O.

1989   "Saints and Sweets: Class and Consumption Ritual in Rural Greece." In *The Social Economy of Consumption,* edited by H. J. Rutz and B. S. Orlove. Pp. 177–209. Monographs in Economic Anthropology, no. 6. Lanham, Md.: University Press of America.

Bernal, Victoria

1994   "Gender, Culture, and Capitalism: Women and the Remaking of Islamic 'Tradition' in a Sudanese Village." *Comparative Studies in Society and History* 36 (1): 36–67.

Berry, Sarah

1985   *Fathers Work for Their Sons: Accumulation, Mobility, and Class Formation in an Extended Yoruba Community.* Berkeley: University of California Press.

Black, Jan Knippers

1991   *Development in Theory and Practice: Bridging the Gap.* Boulder, Colo.: Westview Press.

Bloch, Maurice, and J. Parry

1989   "Introduction: Money and the Morality of Exchange." In *Money and the Morality of Exchange,* edited by J. Perry and M. Bloch. Pp. 1–32. Cambridge: Cambridge University Press.

Bourdieu, Pierre

1977   *Outline of a Theory of Practice.* Translated by R. Nice. Cambridge: Cambridge University Press.

1986   "The Forms of Capital." In *Handbook of Theory and Research for the Sociology of Education,* edited by J. G. Richardson. Pp. 242–258. New York: Greenwood Press.

1990   *In Other Words: Essays towards a Reflexive Sociology.* Translated by M. Adamson. Stanford: Stanford University Press.

Brandes, Stanley

1988   *Power and Persuasion: Fiesta and Social Control in Rural Mexico.* Philadelphia: University of Pennsylvania Press.

Brandomín, José María

1978   *Crónicas (de Oaxaca de hace cincuenta años)*. Oaxaca.

Bustamante, Don Carlos Maria de

1963   *Memoria estadística de Oaxaca y descripción del valle del mismo nombre estractada de la que grande trabajó el señor Don Jose Murguia y Galardi*. Originally published in 1821. Mexico City: La Secretaría del Patrimonio Nacional.

Campbell, Howard

1994   *Zapotec Renaissance: Ethnic Politics and Cultural Revival in Southern Mexico*. Albuquerque: University of New Mexico Press.

Campbell, Howard, et al.

1993   *Zapotec Struggles: Histories, Politics, and Representations from Juchitán, Oaxaca*. Washington: Smithsonian Institution Press.

Cancian, Frank

1965   *Economics and Prestige in a Maya Community: The Religious Cargo System in Zinacantán*. Stanford: Stanford University Press.

1990   "The Zinacantán Cargo Waiting Lists as a Reflection of Social, Political, and Economic Changes, 1952–1987." In *Class, Politics, and Popular Religion in Mexico and Central America,* edited by L. Stephen and J. Dow. Pp. 63–76. Society for Latin American Anthropology Publication Series, no. 10. Washington: Society for Latin American Anthropology.

1992   *The Decline of Community in Zinacantán: Economy, Public Life, and Social Stratification, 1960–1987*. Stanford: Stanford University Press.

Chance, John K.

1978   *Race and Class in Colonial Oaxaca*. Stanford: Stanford University Press.

1990   "Changes in Twentieth-Century Mesoamerican Cargo System." In *Class, Politics, and Popular Religion in Mexico and Central America,* edited by L. Stephen and J. Dow. Pp. 27–42. Society for Latin American Anthropology Publication Series, no. 10. Washington: Society for Latin American Anthropology.

Chiñas, Beverly L.

1983   *The Isthmus Zapotecs: Women's Roles in Cultural Context*. Prospect Heights, Ill.: Waveland Press.

Clements, Helen Peeler

1987   "Weaving in Two Oaxacan Communities: An Historical Perspective." Oaxaca, Mexico: Paper presented at 47th Annual Meeting of the Society for Applied Anthropology.

1996   "Hitting the Wall and Changing the Question: Studying Folk Art Production in Oaxaca." San Francisco: Presented at the 1996 American Anthropological Association Meeting.

CMSD
1992   *Foleto del Museo Shan-Dany.* Santa Ana del Valle, Tlacolula, Oaxaca: Comité del Museo Shan-Dany, Instituto Nacional de Antropología e Historia, y Gobierno Constitucional de Santa Ana del Valle, Tlacolula, Oaxaca.

Cockcroft, James D.
1983   *Mexico: Class Formation, Capital Accumulation, and the State.* New York: Monthly Press.

Cohen, Abner
1993   *Masquerade Politics: Explorations in the Structure of Urban Cultural Movements.* Berkeley: University of California Press.

Cohen, Jeffrey H.
1989   "Museo Shan-Dany: Packaging the Past to Promote the Future." *Folklore Forum* 22 (1/2): 15–26.
1990   "Markets, Museums and Modes of Production: Economic Strategies in Two Zapotec Weaving Communities of Oaxaca, Mexico." *Society For Economic Anthropology Newsletter,* 1990, pp. 12–29.
1993   "Danza de la Pluma: Symbols of Submission and Separation in a Mexican Fiesta." *Anthropological Quarterly* 66 (3): 149–158.
1994   "The Challenge of Grassroots Development: Society, Economy and Change in Southern Mexico." Occasional Paper #26. *A Monograph of the Indiana Center on Global Change and World Peace.* Bloomington: Indiana Center on Global Change and World Peace.
1997   "Popular Participation and Civil Society: The Shan-Dany Museum and the Construction of Community in Mexico." *Practicing Anthropology* 19 (3): 36–40.
1998   "Craft Production and the Challenge of the Global Market: An Artisans' Cooperative in Oaxaca, Mexico." *Human Organization* 57 (1): 74–82.
1999   "The Artisan's Society of Santa Ana del Valle, Oaxaca, Mexico: Household Competition and Cooperative Management." In *At the Interface: The Household and Beyond,* edited by D. B. Small and N. Tannenbaum, pp. 15–29. Lanham, Md.: University Press of America.
n.d.   "Transnationalism, Migration and Conversion: Negotiating Community and Identity in a Zapotec Village." Unpublished manuscript.

Coleman, James S.
1988   "Social Capital in the Creation of Human Capital." *American Journal of Sociology* 94 (supplement): s95–s120.

Collier, George A.
1987   "Peasant Politics and the Mexican State: Indigenous Compliance in Highland Chiapas." *Mexican Studies/Estudios Mexicanos* 3 (1): 71–98.

CONAPO

1987 *Indicadores sobre fecundidad, marginación y ruralidad a nivel municipal: Oaxaca.* Mexico City: CONAPO.

Conway, Dennis, and Jeffrey H. Cohen

1998 "Consequences of Return Migration and Remittances for Mexican Transnational Communities." *Economic Geography* 74 (1): 26–44.

Cook, Scott

1978 "Petty Commodity Production and Capitalist Development in the 'Central Valleys' Region of Oaxaca, Mexico." *Nova Americana* 1: 285–332.

1984 *Peasant Capitalist Industry: Piecework and Enterprise in Southern Mexican Brickyards.* Lanham, Md.: University Press of America.

1993 "Craft Commodity Production, Market Diversity, and Differential Rewards in Mexican Capitalism Today." In *Crafts in the World Market: The Impact of Global Exchange on Middle American Artisans,* edited by J. Nash. Pp. 59–83. Albany: State University of New York Press.

Cook, Scott, and Leigh Binford

1990 *Obliging Need: Rural Petty Industry in Mexican Capitalism.* Austin: University of Texas Press.

Cook, Scott, and M. Diskin

1976 *Markets in Oaxaca.* Austin: University of Texas Press.

Cook, Scott, and Jong-Taick Joo

1995 "Ethnicity and Economy in Rural Mexico: A Critique of the Indigenista Approach." *Latin American Research Review* 30 (2): 33–60.

Cornelius, Wayne A., and Jorge A. Bustamante

1989 "Mexican Migration to the United States: Origins, Consequences, and Policy Options." *Dimensions of United States-Mexican Relations,* #3. San Diego: Center for U.S.-Mexican Studies, University of California, San Diego.

Corrigan, Philip, and D. Sayer

1985 *The Great Arch: State Formation, Cultural Revolution.* Oxford: Basil Blackwell.

Crumrine, N. Ross

1969 *Ceremonial Exchange as a Mechanism in Tribal Integration among the Mayos of Northwest Mexico.* Tucson: University of Arizona Press.

CTV

1748 *Libro IV, que contiene las jurisdicciones del recinto del Obispado de Oaxaca, Capítulo XII: De la jurisdicción de Teotitlán y sus pueblos.* Oaxaca: Curato de Teotitlán de el Valle Su Patrona Titular.

Cuadros Sinópticos
1986 *Colección de "Cuadros Sinópticos" de los pueblos, haciendas y ranchos del estado libre y sobrerano de Oaxaca*, Tomo I, II Anexo #50, a la Memoria Administrativa. Originally published 1883. Oaxaca: H. Congreso del Estado.

de la Fuente, Julio
1949 *Yalálag: Una villa Zapoteca serrana*. Mexico City: Museo Nacional de Antropología.

Deere, Carmen Diana
1990 *Household and Class Relations: Peasants and Landlords in Northern Peru*. Berkeley: University of California Press.

Dennis, Philip A.
1987 *Intervillage Conflict in Oaxaca*. New Brunswick, N.J.: Rutgers University Press.

Dirlik, Arif
1990 "Culturalism as Hegemonic Ideology and Liberating Practice." In *The Nature and Context of Minority Discourse*, edited by A. R. JanMohamed and D. Lloyd. Pp. 394–431. Oxford: Oxford University Press.

Domínguez, Jorge I.
1982 *Mexico's Political Economy: Challenges at Home and Abroad*. Beverly Hills, Calif.: Russell Sage Foundation.

Donham, Donald L.
1990 *History, Power, Ideology: Central Issues in Marxism and Anthropology*. Cambridge: Cambridge University Press.
1994 "An Archaeology of Work among the Maale of Ethiopia." *Man* 25 (1): 147–159.

Dow, James
1977 "Religion in the Organization of a Mexican Peasant Economy." In *Peasant Livelihood: Studies in Economic Anthropology and Cultural Ecology*, edited by R. Halperin and J. Dow. Pp. 215–226. New York: St Martin's Press.

Durand, Jorge, W. Kandel, E. A. Parrado, and D. S. Massey
1996a "International Migration and Development in Mexican Communities." *Demography* 33 (2): 249–264.

Durand, Jorge, Emilio A. Parrado, and Douglas S. Massey
1996b "Migradollars and Development: A Reconsideration of the Mexican Case." *International Migration Review* 30 (2): 423–444.

Durkheim, Emile
1964 *The Rules of Sociological Method*. Translated by Sarah A. Solovay and John H. Mueller. London: The Free Press of Glencoe.

The Economist

1993   "A Survey of Mexico: Into the Spotlight." Special Supplement
            (February 13).

El-Guindi, Fadwa

1986   *The Myth of Ritual: A Native's Ethnography of Zapotec Life-Crisis
            Rituals.* Collaboration with and translated by A. Hernández Jiménez.
            Tucson: University of Arizona Press.

El-Guindi, Fadwa, and H. A. Selby

1976   "Dialectics in Zapotec Thinking." In *Meaning in Anthropology,* edited
            by K. H. Basso and H. A. Selby. Pp. 181–196. Albuquerque: Univer-
            sity of New Mexico Press.

Embriz, Arnulfo

1993   *Indicadores socioeconómicos de los pueblos indígenas de México, 1990.* Mex-
            ico City, D.F.: Dirección de Investigación y Promoción Cultural Sub-
            dirección de Investigación, Instituto Nacional Indigenista.

Eriksen, Thomas Hylland

1991   "The Cultural Contexts of Ethnic Differences." *Man* 26: 127–144.

Feierman, Steven

1991   *Peasant Intellectuals: Anthropology and History in Tanzania.* Madison:
            University of Wisconsin Press.

Feinman, Gary

1982   "Patterns in Ceramic Production and Distribution, Periods Early I
            through V." In *Monte Alban's Hinterland, Part I: The Prehispanic Settle-
            ment Patterns of the Central and Southern Parts of the Valley of Oaxaca,
            Mexico,* edited by R. E. Blanton, S. Kowalewski, G. Feinman, and
            J. Appel. Pp. 181–206. *Prehistory and Human Ecology of the Valley of
            Oaxaca,* vol. 7. Ann Arbor: Memoirs of the Museum of Anthropol-
            ogy, University of Michigan #15.

FONATUR

1992   *Bahias de Huatulco: Magproyectos fonatur.* Mexico City: Fondo Na-
            cional de Fomento al Turismo (FONATUR) and the Mexican Gov-
            ernment Tourism Office.

Foster, George M.

1961   "The Dyadic Contract: A Model for the Social Structure of a Mexican
            Peasant Village." *American Anthropologist* 63: 1173–1192.

1963   "The Dyadic Contract in Tzintzuntzan, II: Patron-Client Relation-
            ship." *American Anthropologist* 65: 1280–1294.

1979   *Tzintzuntzán: Mexican Peasants in a Changing World.* New York:
            Elsevier.

Freundheim, Betty

1988   "Wall Hangings from Oaxaca." *New York Times* (January 10), p. 6.

Frye, David
1996   *Indians into Mexicans: History and Identity in a Mexican Town.* Austin: University of Texas Press.

Fukuyama, Francis
1995   *Trust: The Social Virtues and the Creation of Prosperity.* New York: The Free Press.

Gaither, Edmund Barry
1992   "'Hey! That's Mine': Thoughts on Pluralism and American Museums." In *Museums and Communities: The Politics of Public Culture,* edited by I. Karp, C. M. Kreamer, and S. D. Lavine. Pp. 56–64. Washington: Smithsonian Institution Press.

García Canclini, Néstor
1993   *Transforming Modernity: Popular Culture in Mexico.* Translated by Lidia Lozano. Austin: University of Texas Press.

Garner, Paul
1990   "Oaxaca: The Rise and Fall of State Sovereignty." In *Provinces of the Revolution: Essays on Regional Mexican History, 1910–1929,* edited by T. Benjamin and M. Wasserman. Pp. 163–184. Albuquerque: University of New Mexico Press.

Gay, José Antonio
1986   *Historia de Oaxaca.* Mexico City: Editorial Porrúa, SA.

Giddens, Anthony
1984   *The Constitution of Society.* Berkeley: University of California Press.

Gilmore, David
1975   "Friendship in Fuenmayor: Patterns of Integration in an Atomistic Society." *Ethnology* 14 (4): 311–324.

Gledhill, John
1994   *Power and Its Disguises: Anthropological Perspective on Politics.* Boulder, Colo.: Pluto Press.

Gluckman, Max
1963   "Gossip and Scandal." *Current Anthropology* 4 (3): 307–316.

González, María del Refugio
1989   "La intervención del estado en la economía y en la sociedad en México: Sus orígenes y desarrollo, una propuesta de interpretación." *Mexican Studies/Estudios Mexicanos* 5 (1): 25–68.

Goody, Jack
1993   "East and West: Rationality in Review." *Ethos* 58 (1/2): 6–36.

Gramsci, Antonio
1988   *An Antonio Gramsci Reader: Selected Writings, 1916–1935.* New York: Shocken Books.

Granovetter, Mark

1985   "Economic Action and Social Structure." *American Journal of Sociology* 91 (3): 481–510.

1995   "The Economic Sociology of Firms and Entrepreneurs." In *The Economic Sociology of Migration: Essays on Networks, Ethnicity, and Entrepreneurship,* edited by A. Portes. Pp. 128–165. New York: Russell Sage Foundation.

Greenberg, James B.

1981   *Santiago's Sword: Chatino Peasant Economies and Rebellion.* Berkeley: University of California Press.

1989   *Blood Ties: Life and Violence in Rural Mexico.* Tucson: University of Arizona Press.

1995   "Capital, Ritual, and Boundaries of the Closed Corporate Community." In *Articulating Hidden Histories,* edited by R. Rapp and J. Schneider. Pp. 67–81. Berkeley: University of California Press.

Gudeman, Stephen, and A. Rivera

1990   *Conversations in Colombia: The Domestic Economy in Life and Text.* Cambridge: Cambridge University Press.

Hannerz, Ulf

1992   "The Global Ecumene as a Network of Networks." In *Conceptualizing Society,* edited by A. Kuper. Pp. 34–56. New York: Routledge.

1997   "Scenarios for Peripheral Cultures." In *Culture, Globalization, and the World-System: Contemporary Conditions for the Representation of Identity,* edited by A. D. King. Pp. 107–128. Minneapolis: University of Minnesota Press.

Hardin, Kris L.

1993   *The Aesthetics of Action: Continuity and Change in a West African Town.* Washington: Smithsonian Institution Press.

Harris, Marvin

1964   *Patterns of Race in the Americas.* New York: Walker.

Harris, Max

1996   "Moctezuma's Daughter: The Role of la Malinche in Mesoamerican Dance." *Journal of American Folklore* 109 (432): 149–179.

Harris, Neil

1990   *Cultural Excursions: Marketing Appetites and Cultural Tastes in Modern America.* Cambridge: Harvard University Press.

Hart, Keith

1982   "On Commoditization." In *From Craft to Industry: The Ethnography of Proto-industrial Cloth Production,* edited by E. N. Goody. Pp. 38–49. Cambridge: Cambridge University Press.

Haviland, John B

1977   *Gossip, Reputation and Knowledge in Zinacantan.* Chicago: University of Chicago Press.

Hendrickson, Carol

1995   *Weaving Identities: Construction of Dress and Self in a Highland Guatemala Town.* Austin: University of Texas Press.

Heyman, Josiah McC.

1990   "The Emergence of the Waged Life Course on the United States–Mexico Border." *American Ethnologist* 17 (2): 348–359.

Higgins, Michael J.

1974   *Somos gente humilde: Etnografía de una colonia urbana pobre de Oaxaca.* Mexico City: Instituto Nacional Indigenista.

Hill, Robert M.

1992   *Colonial Cakchiquels: Highland Maya Adaptation to Spanish Rule 1600–1700.* Fort Worth, Tex.: Harcourt, Brace, Jovanovich.

Hill, Robert M., and J. Monaghan

1987   *Continuities in Highland Maya Social Organization: Ethnohistory in Sacapulas, Guatemala.* Philadelphia: University of Pennsylvania Press.

Hirabayashi, Lane Ryo

1983   "On the Formation of Migrant Village Associations in Mexico: Mixtec and Mountain Zapotec in Mexico City." *Urban Anthropology* 12 (1): 29–44.

1993   *Cultural Capital: Mountain Zapotec Migrant Associations in Mexico City.* Tucson: University of Arizona Press.

1994   "Mountain Zapotec Migrants and Forms of Capital." *PoLAR* [Political and Legal Anthropology Review] 17 (2): 105–116.

Holmes, Douglas R.

1989   *Cultural Disenchantment: Workers in Northeast Italy.* Princeton: Princeton University Press.

Howell, Jayne

1993a   "Educating Maria: New Directions for Rural Oaxacan Women": Paper presented at American Anthropological Association, annual meeting 1993.

1993b   "Education, Employment, and Economic Growth: New Directions for Rural Oaxacan Women": Ph.D diss., State University of New York at Stonybrook.

Hulshof, Marje

1991   *Zapotec Moves: Networks and Remittances of U.S. Bound Migrants from Oaxaca, Mexico.* Amsterdam: University of Amsterdam.

Hunt, Eva, and J. Nash
1967   "Local and Territorial Units." In *Handbook of Middle American Indians,* edited by M. Nash. Vol. 6, pp. 253–282. Austin: University of Texas Press.

INEGI
1983   *X censo general de población y vivienda* (1980), tomo 20, numero I y II, Oaxaca. Aguascalientes: Instituto Nacional de Estadísticas, Geografía, y Informática (INEGI).
1992a   *Perfil sociodemográfico, XI censo general* (1990). Aguascalientes: Instituto Nacional de Estadísticas, Geografía, y Informática (INEGI).
1992b   *XI censo general de población y vivienda* (1990), estado de Oaxaca. Aguascalientes: Instituto Nacional de Estadísticas, Geografía, y Informática (INEGI).

Jenkins, Richard
1992   *Pierre Bourdieu.* New York: Routledge.

Jones, Pamela
1988   "'There Was a Weeping Woman': La Llorona in Oregon." *Western Folklore* 47: 195–211.

Jones, Richard C.
1995   *Ambivalent Journey: U.S. Migration and Economic Mobility in North-Central Mexico.* Tucson: University of Arizona Press.

Karp, Ivan
1992   "Museums and Communities." In *Museums and Communities: The Politics of Public Culture,* edited by I. Karp, C. M. Kreamer, and S. D. Lavine. Pp. 1–17. Washington: Smithsonian Institution Press.

Kearney, Michael
1986   *The Winds of Ixtepeji: Worldview and Society in a Zapotec Town.* Prospect Heights, Ill.: Waveland Press.
1994   "Desde el indigenismo a los derechos humanos: Etnicidad y política más allá de la mixteca." *Nueva Antropología* 14 (46): 49–67.
1995   "The Effects of Transnational Culture, Economy, and Migration on Mixtec Identity in Oaxacalifornia." In *The Bubbling Cauldron: Race, Ethnicity, and the Urban Crisis,* edited by M. P. Smith and J. R. Feagin. Pp. 226–243. Minneapolis: University of Minnesota Press.
1996   *Reconceptualizing the Peasantry: Anthropology in Global Perspective.* Boulder, Colo.: Westview Press.

Kemper, Robert Van
1977   *Migration and Adaptation: Tzintzuntzan Peasants in Mexico City.* Beverly Hills, Calif.: Sage Publications, Inc.

Kicza, John
1993   "Introduction." In *The Indian in Modern Latin America,* edited by J. Kicza. Scholarly Resources, Inc.

Kirby, Anne V. T.
1973   "The Use of Land and Water Resources in the Past and Present Valley of Oaxaca, vol. 1. Mexico." In *Prehistory and Human Ecology of the Valley of Oaxaca,* vol. 1. Ann Arbor: Memoirs of the Museum of Anthropology, University of Michigan #5.

Knight, Alan
1990   "Racism, Revolution, and Indigenismo: Mexico 1910–1940." In *The Idea of Race in Latin America, 1870–1940,* edited by R. Graham. Pp. 71–114. Austin: University of Texas Press.

Kowalewski, Stephen
1982   "Population and Agricultural Potential: Early I through V." In *Monte Alban's Hinterland, Part I: The Prehispanic Settlement Patterns of the Central and Southern Parts of the Valley of Oaxaca, Mexico,* edited by R. E. Blanton, S. Kowalewski, G. Feinman, and J. Appel. *Prehistory and Human Ecology of the Valley of Oaxaca,* vol. 7. Ann Arbor: Memoirs of the Museum of Anthropology, University of Michigan #15.

Kowalewski, Stephen A., and Jacqueline J. Saindon
1992   "The Spread of Literacy in a Latin American Peasant Society: Oaxaca, 1890–1980." *Comparative Studies in Society and History* 34 (1): 110–141.

Kroeber, Alfred L.
1952   *The Nature of Culture.* Chicago: The University of Chicago Press.

Kropotkin, Peter
1989   *Mutual Aid: A Factor of Evolution.* Montreal: Black Rose Books.

Kuper, Adam, ed.
1992   *Conceptualizing Society.* New York: Routledge.

Lambek, Michael
1990   "Exchange, Time and Person in Mayotte: The Structure and Destructuring of a Cultural System." *American Anthropologist* 92 (3): 647–671.

Lavenda, Robert H.
1992   "Festivals and the Creation of Public Culture: Whose Voice(s)?" In *Museums and Communities: The Politics of Public Culture.* Washington: Smithsonian Institution Press.

Lavine, Steven D.
1992   "Audience, Ownership, and Authority: Designing Relationships between Museums and Communities." In *Museums and Communities: The Politics of Public Culture,* edited by I. Karp, C. M. Kreamer, and S. D. Lavine. Pp. 137–157. Washington: Smithsonian Institution Press.

Lees, Susan H.
1973   "Sociopolitical Aspects of Canal Irrigation in the Valley of Oaxaca." In *Prehistory and Human Ecology of the Valley of Oaxaca,* vol. 5. Ann Arbor: Memoirs of the Museum of Anthropology, University of Michigan #6.

Leslie, Charles M.

1960   *Now We Are Civilized: A Study of the World View of the Zapotec Indians of Mitla, Oaxaca.* Detroit, Mich.: Wayne State University Press.

Littlefield, Alice

1978   "Exploitation and the Expansion of Capitalism: The Case of the Hammock Industry of Yucatan." *American Ethnologist* 5 (3): 495–508.

Lomnitz, Larrisa Adler

1977   *Networks and Marginality: Life in a Mexican Shantytown.* New York: Academic Press.

López-Cortés, Eliseo

1991   "Política informal y caciquismo en la Mazateca Baja." In *Etnia y sociedad en Oaxaca,* edited by A. Castellanos Guerrero and G. López y Rivas. Pp. 83–90. Mexico City: Universidad Autónoma Metropolitana.

MacLeod, Murdo J.

1973   *Spanish Central America, a Socioeconomic History, 1520–1720.* Berkeley: University of California Press.

Malinowski, Bronislaw

1984   *Argonauts of the Western Pacific: An Account of Native Enterprise and Adventure in the Archipelagoes of Melanesian New Guinea.* Prospect Heights, Ill.: Waveland Press.

Mallon, Florencia E.

1983   *The Defense of Community in Peru's Central Highland: Peasant Struggle and Capitalist Transitions, 1860–1940.* Princeton: Princeton University Press.

Mandle, Jay R., and J. D. Mandle

1990   "Amateur Basketball in Trinidad and Tobago." *Sociology and Social Research,* 74 (2): 95–103.

Marshall, T. H.

1973   *Class, Citizenship and Social Development.* Westport, Conn.: Greenwood Press.

Marx, Karl

1906   *Capital.* Volume I. New York: The New Library.

Massey, Douglas S., Luin Goldring, and Jorge Durand

1994   "Continuities in Transnational Migration: An Analysis of Nineteen Mexican Communities." *American Journal of Sociology* 99 (6): 1492–1533.

Mathews, Holly F.

1992   "The Directive Force of Morality Tales in a Mexican Community." In *Human Motives and Cultural Models,* edited by R. G. D'Andrade and C. Strauss. Pp. 127–164. Cambridge: Cambridge University Press.

Mauss, Marcel
1990   *The Gift: The Form and Reason for Exchange in Archaic Societies.* Trans-
            lated by W. D. Halls. New York: W. W. Norton.

McLellan, David, ed.
1977   *Karl Marx: Selected Writings.* Oxford: Oxford University Press.

Miller, William I.
1993   *Humiliation.* Ithaca, N.Y.: Cornell University Press.

Mintz, Sidney, and Eric Wolf
1950   "An Analysis of Ritual Co-Parenthood (Compadrazgo)." *Southwestern
            Journal of Anthropology* 6: 341–367.

Monaghan, John
1990   "Reciprocity, Redistribution and the Structure of the Mesoamerican
            Fiesta." *American Ethnologist* 17 (1): 148–64.
1995   *The Convenants with Earth and Rain: Exchange, Sacrifice, and Revela-
            tion in Mixtec Sociality.* Norman: University of Oklahoma Press.

Moore, Sally F.
1975   "Epilogue: Uncertainties in Situations, Indeterminacies in Culture."
            In *Symbols and Politics in Communal Ideology,* edited by S. F. Moore
            and B. Myerhoff. Pp. 210–239. Ithaca, N.Y.: Cornell University Press.

Morales Lersch, Teresa, and C. Camarena Ocampo
1987   "La experiencia de constitución de Museo 'Shan-Dany,' de Santa Ana
            del Valle, Tlacolula, Oaxaca." *Antropología, Boletín Oficial de Instituto
            Nacional de Antropología e Historia* (14): 9–11.

Mousse, Chantal
1988   "Hegemony and New Political Subjects: Toward a New Concept of
            Democracy." In *Marxism and the Interpretation of Culture,* edited by
            C. Nelson and L. Grossberg. Pp. 89–101. Urbana: University of Illi-
            nois Press.

Murphy, Arthur D., and A. Stepick
1991   *Social Inequality in Oaxaca: A History of Resistance and Change.* Phila-
            delphia: Temple University Press.

Myerhoff, Barbara
1979   *Number Our Days.* New York: E. P. Dutton.

Nader, Laura
1969   "The Zapotec of Oaxaca." In *Handbook of Middle American Indians,*
            edited by R. Wauchope. Pp. 329–359. Austin: University of Texas
            Press.
1990   *Harmony Ideology: Justice and Control in a Zapotec Mountain Village.*
            Stanford: Stanford University Press.

Nangengast, Carole, and M. Kearney

1990   "Mixtec Ethnicity: Social Identity, Political Consciousness, and Political Activism." *Latin American Research Review* 25 (1): 61–91.

Nash, June

1994   "La producción artesanal y el desarrollo de la industria: Cambios en la transmisión cultural por medio de las mercancías." In *Semillas de industria: Transformaciones de la tecnología indígena en las Américas,* edited by M. Humberto Ruz. Pp. 99–122. Mexico City and Washington: Centro de Investigaciones y Estudios Superiores and the Smithsonian Institution.

1996   "The Reassertion of Indigenous Identity: Mayan Responses to State Intervention in Chiapas." *Latin American Research Review* 30 (3): 7–41.

Netting, Robert McC., Richard Wilk, and Eric Arnould, eds.

1984   *Households: Comparative and Historical Studies of the Domestic Group.* Berkeley: University of California Press.

Nicholas, Linda, et al.

1986   "Prehispanic Colonization of the Valley of Oaxaca, Mexico." *Human Ecology* 14 (2): 131–162.

Nutini, Hugo

1984   *Ritual Kinship: Ideological and Structural Integration of the Compadrazgo System in Rural Tlaxcala.* Volume II. Princeton: Princeton University Press.

Nutini, Hugo, and B. Bell

1980   *Ritual Kinship: The Structure and Historical Development of the Compadrazgo System in Rural Tlaxcala.* Volume I. Princeton: Princeton University Press.

Oglesby, Catherine

1940   "Weaving for Use and for Sale." *Mexican Life.* Pp. 18–22, 54–56.

Ortner, Sherry

1973   "On Key Symbols." *American Anthropologist* 75 (5): 1338–1346.

Parnell, Philip C.

1988   *Escalating Disputes: Social Participation and Change in the Oaxacan Highlands.* Tucson: University of Arizona Press.

Parsons, Elsie Clews

1936   *Mitla: Town of the Souls.* Chicago: University of Chicago Press.

Peñafiel, A. (coordinador)

1904   "Censo general de la República Mexicana," tomo II (1900) *Dirección general de estadísticas.* Mexico City: Oficina Tipográfic de la Secretaría de Fomento.

Peterson, Nicolas
1993   "Demand Sharing: Reciprocity and the Pressure for Generosity
            among Foragers." *American Anthropologist* 95 (4): 860–874.

Piot, Charles D.
1991   "Of Persons and Things: Some Reflections on African Spheres of
            Exchange." *Man* 26 (3): 405–424.

Plattner, Stuart
1965   *The Economic Structure of Santa Ana del Valle*. Stanford: Stanford Uni-
            versity Field School, Oaxaca Archive.

Polanyi, Karl
1968   "Our Obsolete Market Mentality." In *Primitive, Archaic and Modern
            Economies,* edited by G. Dalton. Pp. 59–77. New York: Anchor Books.

Portes, Alejandro, and P. Landolt
1996   "The Downside of Social Capital." *The American Prospect* (May–
            June 1996): 18–21, 94.

Putnam, Robert D.
1993   "The Prosperous Community." *The American Prospect* (Spring): 35–42.

Ramírez Gómez, Alfredo
1991   "Protestantismo y conflicto en una comunidad indígena." In *Etnia y
            sociedad en Oaxaca,* edited by A. Castellanos Guerrero and G. López y
            Rivas. Pp. 91–98. Mexico City: Universidad Autónoma Metropolitana.

Redfield, Robert
1928   "The Calpolli-Barrio in a Present-day Mexican Pueblo." *American
            Anthropology* 30 (2): 282–294.
1950   *A Village That Chose Progress: Chan Kom Revisited*. Chicago: Univer-
            sity of Chicago Press.
1960   *Peasant Society and Culture and the Little Community*. Chicago: Uni-
            versity of Chicago Press.

Redmond, Elsa M.
1983   *A Fuego y Sangre: Early Zapotec Imperialism in the Cuicatalán Cañada,
            Oaxaca*. Ann Arbor: Memoirs of the Museum of Anthropology,
            University of Michigan, #16.

Reichert, Joshua
1982   "A Town Divided: Economic Stratification and Social Relations in a
            Mexican Migrant Community." *Social Problems* 29 (4): 411–423.

Robben, Antonius C.G.M.
1989   *Sons of the Sea Goddess*. New York: Columbia University Press.

Roger, Barbara
1980   *The Domestication of Women*. London: Tavestock.

Roseberry, William

1989 *Anthropologies and Histories: Essays in Culture, History, and Political Economy.* New Brunswick, N.J.: Rutgers University Press.

1996 "Hegemony, Power, and Languages of Contention." In *The Politics of Difference: Ethnic Premises in a World of Power,* edited by E. N. Wilmsen and P. McAllister. Pp. 71–84. Chicago: University of Chicago Press.

Rostow, Walt W.

1960 *The Stages of Economic Growth.* Cambridge: Cambridge University Press.

Rothman, D. J.

1978 "Introduction." In *Doing Good: The Limits of Benevolence,* edited by W. Gaylin, I. Glasser, S. Marcus, and D. J. Rothman. Pp. ix–xv. New York: Pantheon Books.

Rouse, Roger

1991 "Mexican Migration and the Social Space of Postmodernism." *Diaspora* 1 (1): 8–23.

1992 "Making Sense of Settlement: Class Transformation, Cultural Struggle, and Transnationalism among Mexican Migrants in the United States." In *Toward a Transnational Perspective in Migration: Race, Class, Ethnicity, and Nationalism Reconsidered,* edited by N. G. Schiller, L. Basch, and C. Blanc-Szanton. Vol. 645, pp. 25–52. New York: Annals of the New York Academy of Science.

Royce, Anya P.

1975 *Prestigio y afiliación en una comunidada urbana: Juchitán, Oaxaca.* Mexico City: Instituto Nacional Indigenista.

1981 "Isthmus Zapotec Households: Economic Responses to Scarcity and Abundance." *Urban Anthropology* 10 (3): 269–286.

1993 "Ethnicity, Nationalism, and the Role of the Intellectual." In *Ethnicity, and the State,* edited by J. Toland. *Political and Legal Anthropology Series* 9: 103–122. New Brunswick, N.J.: Transaction Publishers.

Rubel, Arthur J.

1984 *Susto: A Folk Illness.* Berkeley: University of California Press.

Rubin, Jeffrey W.

1987 "State Policies, Leftist Oppositions, and Municipal Elections: The Case of the COCEI of Juchitán." In *Electoral Patterns and Perspectives in Mexico,* edited by A. Alvarado. Pp. 127–160. Center for U.S.-Mexican Studies, Monograph #22. San Diego: University of California, San Diego.

Sahlins, Marshall D.

1963 "Poor Man, Rich Man, Big-Man, Chief: Political Types in Melanesia and Polynesia." *Comparative Studies in Society and History* 5: 285–303.

Sault, Nicole L.

1985   "Baptismal Sponsorship as a Source of Power for Zapotec Women in Oaxaca, Mexico." In *Journal of Latin American Lore* 11 (2): 225–243.

Schulz, Donald E., and E. J. Williams, eds.

1995   *Mexico Faces the 21st Century*. Westport, Conn.: Greenwood Publishing Group.

Scott, James C.

1976   *The Moral Economy of the Peasant*. New Haven: Yale University Press.

1986   "Everyday Forms of Resistance." *Journal of Peasant Studies* 13 (2): 5–35.

1989   "Prestige as the Public Discourse of Domination." *Cultural Critique*, issue 12: 145–166.

SEN

1934   *Quinto censo de población, 1930*. Mexico City: Secretaría de la Economía Nacional (SEN).

Sheridan, Thomas E.

1988   *Where the Dove Calls: The Political Ecology of a Peasant Corporate Community in Northwestern Mexico*. Tucson: University of Arizona Press.

Shipton, Parker

1989   *Bitter Money: Cultural Economy and Some African Meanings of Forbidden Commodities*. Washington: American Ethnological Society.

SIC

1971   *Noveno censo de población, 1970*. Vol. 21. Mexico City: Secretaría de Industria y Comercio (SIC).

Smart, Alan

1993   "Gifts, Bribes, and Guanxi: A Reconsideration of Bourdieu's Social Capital." *Cultural Anthropology* 8 (3): 388–408.

Smith, Carol A.

1984   "Does a Commodity Economy Enrich the Few While Ruining the Masses? Differentiation among Petty Commodity Producers in Guatemala." *Journal of Peasant Studies* 11 (3): 60–95.

Smith, Gavin

1989   *Livelihood and Resistance: Peasants and the Politics of Land in Peru*. Berkeley: University of California Press.

Smith, Robert

1992   "Mixteca in New York; New York in Mixteca." *NACLA, Report on the Americas* 26 (1): 39–41.

Stark, Oded

1992   "Nonmarket Transfers and Altruism." In *Understanding Economic Process,* edited by S. Ortiz and S. Lees. Pp. 9–20. *Monographs in Economic Anthropology* #10. Lanham, Md.: University Press of America.

Stephen, Lynn

1987a   "Weaving Changes: Economic Development and Gender Roles in Zapotec Ritual and Production." Ann Arbor, Mich.: UMI Dissertation
Information Service.

1987b   "Zapotec Weavers of Oaxaca: Development and Community Control." *Cultural Survival Quarterly* 11 (1): 46–48.

1990   "The Politics of Ritual: The Mexican State and Zapotec Autonomy,
1926–1989." In *Class, Politics, and Popular Religion in Mexico and Central America*, edited by L. Stephen and J. Dow. Pp. 43–60. Society for
Latin American Anthropology Publication Series, # 10. Washington:
Society for Latin American Anthropology.

1991a   "Export Markets and Their Effects on Indigenous Craft Production:
The Case of the Weavers of Teotitlán del Valle, Mexico." In *Textile
Traditions of Mesoamerica and the Andes: An Anthology,* edited by
M. Scheville, J. C. Berko, and E. B. Dwyer. Pp. 381–402. New York:
Garland.

1991b   *Zapotec Women.* Austin: University of Texas Press.

1992   "Women in Mexico's Popular Movements: Survival Strategies against
Ecological and Economic Impoverishment." *Latin American Perspectives,* issue 72, 19 (1): 73–96.

Stocking, George W., Jr.

1985   "Essays on Museums and Material Culture." In *Objects and Others:
Essays on Museums and Material Culture,* edited by G. W. Stocking, Jr.
Pp. 3–14. Madison: University of Wisconsin Press.

Sullivan, Robert

1990   "Marxism and the 'Subject' of Anthropology." In *Modernist Anthropology: From Fieldwork to Text,* edited by M. Manganaro. Pp. 243–328.
Princeton: Princeton University Press.

Tambiah, Stanley J.

1990   *Magic, Science, Religion, and the Scope of Rationality.* Cambridge: Cambridge University Press.

Taussig, Michael

1980   *The Devil and Commodity Fetishism in South America.* Chapel Hill:
University of North Carolina Press.

Taylor, William B.

1972   *Landlord and Peasant in Colonial Oaxaca.* Stanford: Stanford University Press.

1976   "Town and Country in the Valley of Oaxaca, 1750–1812." In *Provinces
of Early Mexico: Variants of Spanish American Regional Evolution,* edited
by I. Altman and J. Lockhart. Pp. 63–95. Philadelphia: University of
Pennsylvania Press.

1979   *Drinking, Homicide, and Rebellion in Colonial Mexican Villages*. Stanford: Stanford University Press.

Tendler, Judith
1983   *What To Think about Cooperatives: A Guide from Bolivia*. Washington: Inter-American Foundation.

Tester, Keith
1992   *Civil Society*. New York: Routledge.

Thorner, D., B. Kerblay, and R.E.F. Smith, eds.
1966   *A. V. Chayanov on the Theory of Peasant Economy*. Homewood, Ill.: Pichard D. Irwin for the American Economic Association.

Tice, Karin E.
1995   *Kuna Crafts, Gender, and the Global Economy*. Austin: University of Texas Press.

Turner, Stephen
1994   *The Social Theory of Practice: Tradition, Tacit Knowledge and Presuppositions*. Chicago: University of Chicago Press.

Vásquez, Marcus, and L. Vásquez Dávila
1992   *Como hacemos tapetes en Santa Ana del Valle*. Oaxaca: Casa de la Cultura Oaxaqueña, Instituto Technológico Agropecuario de Oaxaca.

Vásquez Dávila, Luz Elena, M. A. Vásquez, and M. B. Solís
1992   "Fitoquímica tradicional: Las plantas tintóreas de Santa Ana del Valle, Oaxaca." In *Etnias, desarrollo, recursos y tecnologías en Oaxaca*, edited by Á. González and M. A. Vásquez. Pp. 205–236. Oaxaca: CIESAS y Gobierno del Estado de Oaxaca.

Vázquez Rojas, Gonzalo
1991   "Definición y metodología en los museos communitarios de Oaxaca." In *Etnia y sociedad en Oaxaca*, edited by A. Castellanos Guerrero and G. López y Rivas. Pp. 177–180. Mexico City: Instituto Nacional de Antropología e Historia, y la Universidad Autónoma Metropolitana.

Vélez-Ibañez, Carlos G.
1983   *Rituals of Marginality: Politics, Process, and Culture Change in Central Urban Mexico, 1969–1974*. Berkeley: University of California Press.

Verduzco Igartúa, Gustavo
1995   "La migración Mexicana a Estados Unidos: Recuento de un proceso histórico." *Estudios Sociologicos* 13 (39): 573–594.

Wacquant, Loïc J. D.
1987   "Symbolic Violence and the Making of the French Agriculturalist: An Enquiry into Pierre Bourdieu's Sociology." *Australian and New Zealand Journal of Sociology* 23 (1): 65–88.

Wasserstrom, Robert

1983 *Class and Society in Central Chiapas.* Berkeley: University of California Press.

Watanabe, John M.

1992 *Maya Saints and Souls in a Changing World.* Austin: University of Texas Press.

1995 "Unimagining the Maya: Anthropologists, Others, and the Inescapable Hubris of Authorship." *Bulletin of Latin American Research* 14 (1): 25–45.

Weber, Max

1946 *From Max Weber: Essays in Sociology.* New York: Oxford University Press.

Wellman, Barry

1979 "The Community Question: The Intimate Networks of East Yorkers." *American Journal of Sociology* 84 (5): 1201–1231.

White, Jenny B.

1994 *Money Makes Us Relatives: Women's Labor in Urban Turkey.* Austin: University of Texas Press.

Whitecotton, Joseph W.

1977 *The Zapotecs: Princes, Priests and Peasants.* Norman: University of Oklahoma Press.

Wilk, Richard R.

1989 "Decision Making and Resource Flows within the Household: Beyond the Black Box." In *The Household Economy,* edited by R. R. Wilk. Pp. 23–52. Boulder, Colo.: Westview Press.

1991 *Household Ecology: Economic Change and Domestic Life among the Kekchi Maya in Belize.* Tucson: University of Arizona Press.

1993 "Altruism and Self-Interest: Towards an Anthropological Theory of Decision Making." *Research in Economic Anthropology* 14: 191–212. New York: JAI Press.

1996 *Economies and Cultures: Foundations of Economic Anthropology.* Boulder, Colo.: Westview Press.

Wilson, Richard

1993 "Anchored Communities: Identity and History of the Maya-Q'eqchi'." *Man* 28: 121–138.

1995 *Maya Resurgence in Guatemala: Q'eqchi' Experiences.* Norman: University of Oklahoma Press.

Wolf, Eric

1957 "Closed Corporate Communities in Mesoamerica and Java." *Southwestern Journal of Anthropology* 13 (1): 1–18.

1986 "The Vicissitudes of the Closed Corporate Peasant Community." In *Directions in the Anthropological Study of Latin America: A Reassessment,* edited by J. Rollwagen. Pp. 211–219. Monographs of the Society for Latin American Anthropology, #8.

Womack, John, Jr.

1969 *Zapata and the Mexican Revolution.* New York: Vintage Books.

Wood, William W.

1995 "Zapotec Artisans: The Genealogy of an 'Other'." American Anthropological Association, Annual Meeting, Washington, D.C.

1996 "Teotitlán del Valle: A Maquiladora in Oaxaca, Mexico." American Anthropological Society Annual Meeting. San Francisco, Calif.

Zimmerman, Carle C., and M. E. Frampton

1935 *Family and Society: A Study of the Sociology of Reconstruction.* New York: D. Van Nostrand.

Index

Mintz, Sidney, 94
Mitla, 20, 50
Mixe, 101, 170 n.9
mozos, 29, 58

Nader, Laura, 21, 89
New Spain, 25
nombramientos, 120
norteñización, 43

Oaxaca, 17, 25, 26, 34, 44, 55; climate of,
    20, 21; demography of, 172 n.15; ge-
    ography of, 17, 21
Oaxaca City, 25, 37, 50, 51, 52, 53
Ocotlán, 20

padrinos del bautismo, 94. *See also com-
    padrazgo,* and kinship
paisanazgo, 94, 168 n.4
Pan-American Highway, 18, 34,
    169 n.4
Parsons, Elsie Clews, 67, 93
pasajes, 51
patrona, 23
peones, 29, 88
Plattner, Stuart, 15
plias, 44
promesas, 60, 64–65, 102–105

rebozos, 44
reciprocity. *See* cooperation
religion, 31, 32; *congregaciónes,* 23, 25,
    26; Dominicans, 15, 17, 23, 25, 26,
    44; and social ties, 93
repartamiento, 25
Roseberry, William, 167 n.3

San Miguel, 18, 20, 54
Santa Ana, 18–23, 35, 37; conquest and
    colonial history of, 25–27; ethnicity
    of, 21–22, 170; and Mexican Revolu-
    tion, 28, 29–31; mining in, 28–29;
    and *municipio,* 19, 27; and politics,
    135–146; population of, 38–39; *Porfi-
    riato* in, 27–29; post-Revolutionary
    history of, 31–34; pre-Columbian

history of, 23–25; and village divi-
    sions, 110–111
secciones, 112–113, 170 n.12
Selby, H. A., 88
Serranos, 29, 30, 31
servicio, 110, 120, 123, 129
Shan-Dany Museum, 31, 73, 126; exhib-
    its at, 150–152; programs and pro-
    jects of, 148–150; purpose, 146–147;
    social response to, 147–148; and
    Union of Oaxacan Community
    Museums, 178 n.7
Sheridan, Thomas E., 41
Sierra, 29, 31
Sierra Madres, 30, 31, 50
Solidaridad, 176 n.8
status, 32, 41, 89; and *cargo* participa-
    tion, 120–121, 124–132; and *compa-
    drazgo,* 96–98
Stephen, Lynn, 43, 175 n.3

Tapachula, 61
tapetes, 15, 37, 54, 171 n.9
Tehuantepec, Isthmus of, 18, 34
Tenochtitlán, 26
Teotitlán, 24–27, 43, 53–54
Teotitlán del Valle. *See* Teotitlán
tequio, 62, 110, 123, 176 n.7; participation
    in, 114–116; types of projects, 114,
    116–117
textile production. *See* weaving
Tlacochahuaya, 21, 26
Tlacolula, 32, 38, 39, 50, 54
Todos Santos. *See* celebrations,
    religious
transnationalism, 16, 17, 35, 169; in pre-
    history, 24

union libres, 71, 172 n.16
United States, 34, 38, 55–57

Wasserstrom, Robert, 122
Watanabe, John M., 68, 167 n.2
weaving, 26, 34, 179 n.15; and appren-
    ticeship, 69–70; contract, 47–52,
    70–71, 73; cooperatives, 53, 148, 153–

157; and exhibition of textiles, 150–151; and gender, 45; and independent production, 47–48, 51; and local buyers, 52–53; markets for, 37, 38, 44, 53–54, 58; materials for, 46–47; motifs of, 50, 51, 54, 69, 151; patrons of, 48, 50–51; and seasonal production, 40, 45; and social class, 98; specialization in, 51–52; technology of, 44

Wellman, Barry, 65
Welte Institute, 23
Wilk, Richard R., 66
Wolf, Eric, 59, 94, 122, 177 n.11

Zaachila, 26, 35
zacate, 74
Zapotecs, 21, 22, 24, 26, 35; and social organization, 88–89; Taleans, 89

Printed in the United States
152357LV00001B/61/P